Praise for

the Leader Launchpad

"The world is moving fast. People are overwhelmed. It's never been more critical to make sure your organization is learning fast enough to keep up with the frenetic pace. Howard Shore elegantly illustrates a methodology to ensure your company not only survives but thrives in this new, rapidly evolving landscape. Nimble organizations now have a competitive advantage over their slower counterparts."

—John Ratliff,
CEO, Scaling Up Coaches

"Howard Shore has yet again written a must-read business leadership book for anyone in the growth phase. Read this and learn from one of the best."

—Guy Kurlandski,
co-founder, Premonition

"A must-read if you want to scale up and accelerate your growth...loaded with practical advice that you can implement right away."

—Ron Antevy,
CEO, E-Builder

"Howard has distilled his vast experience, identified the key levers for acceleration, and conveyed them through real-life stories that are interesting and illuminating."

—Brad Smart,
author; pesident and CEO, Topgrading™ Inc.

"I am astounded by how much I've learned from this book. The principles I learned from Howard Shore in even a short discussion allowed my company to move past a hurdle I'd thought was impossible. I recommend this book to everyone leading a business today."

—Cheryl Snapp Conner,
author; columnist; speaker; founder and CEO, SnappConner PR

"*The Leader Launchpad*—it's a winner! Howard Shore does a fantastic job pointing out the hard-to-deal-with areas that prevent many business leaders from achieving extraordinary results. If sustained profitable growth is your objective, use the five-step process in this book."

—R. Victor Giorgini,
president and CEO, Equiflor LLC

"Hypothetical scenarios are worthless; our lives are not fictional, they're very tangible. I watch hundreds of clients stay in a zone of complacency, completely waste valuable resources, and watch with regret as others pass them by. Howard Shore has developed a strategy to propel you to new heights!"

—Aaron Walker,
bestselling author of *View from the Top*

"This is a must-read book. Take action, apply the five succinct steps, and get ready to experience the rapid business growth you always planned for. Have fun and enjoy the outcome!"

—Shannon Byrne Susko,
author of *The Metronome Effect* and *3HAG Way;* CEO, Metronome United

"As a startup founder who on multiple occasions has led scaleup efforts with expectations of triple-digit growth results, I know firsthand that the sales and marketing engine inside a company consists of a highly delicate set of people, actions, and culture that needs to be constantly calibrated. Howard is a pro, and the framework outlined in his book is the bible for growth leaders who truly want to win!"

—Albert Santalo,
CEO, 8base; serial entrepreneur

"Unlike the crowd of authors who write from either ivory towers or armchairs, Howard works daily in the business trenches, coaching leaders and getting results. From establishing a clear and compelling purpose to identifying your target market to committing to an audacious goal, *The Leader Launchpad* covers it all.

If you need to speed up your company's growth, then you need this book! Howard Shore lays out a simple plan that will lead to phenomenal results."

—Richard Outram,
CFO, Cross Country Home Services

"This book describes step-by-step exactly what to do if you want to expand your business and continue on a path of success. Even experienced managers need to be reminded of the steps Howard lays out in a simple plan. It's worth every bit of energy you put into it. Read *The Leader Launchpad*, invest just a little, and watch the growth that comes from it."

—Andre L. Teixeira,
CFO, Graham Companies

"Howard Shore has done it again. His first book, *Your Business is a Leaky Bucket*, described the sources of leaks that cause underachievement and explained how to plug those leaks. His second book shows how these types of issues prevent companies from achieving rapid growth. His advice for accelerating growth is direct, practical, and forces the reader to think. He also provides downloadable tools to help put his advice into practice. I don't know of a company that would not benefit from applying Howard's advice."

—Arthur Levine,
CFO, Sensus Healthcare

"In *The Leader Launchpad,* Howard provides you the roadmap to ignite your rocket ship. It provides CEOs with a logical and step-by-step process to work on your business!"

—Salomon Sredini,
managing director, Ocean Azul Partners

"Howard Shore continues to put out high-quality content material that helps so many people achieve success! I give this book a phenomenal endorsement, due to the enormous amount of content that can help entrepreneurs achieve success and break down barriers that may be holding them back in their businesses!"

—Marques Ogden,
former NFL athlete, keynote speaker, and author of *The Success Cycle*

"Howard Shore is a trusted advisor and thought leader, his content is phenomenal, and he and his team deliver results!"

—Andrew Langsam,
CEO, Dynamic Advertising Solutions, Inc.

the
Leader
Launchpad

Five Steps to Fuel Your Business and Lift Your Profits

Howard M. Shore

Business Growth Expert and Author of
Your Business is a Leaky Bucket

www.amplifypublishing.com

For more information, please contact:
Amplify Publishing
620 Herndon Parkway #320
Herndon, VA 20170
info@amplifypublishing.com

Library of Congress Control Number: 2020904407

CPSIA Code: PRFRE0520A
ISBN-13: 978-1-64543-481-8

Printed in Canada

To Sylvia, thank you for choosing to share your life with me. You have always inspired me to become a better husband, father, son, family member, and human being.

To Michael and Gabriel, may you always act with a character that will lead to eternal happiness.

CONTENTS

PART I

INTRODUCTION

"The will to win, the desire to succeed, the urge to reach your full potential... these are the keys that will unlock the door to personal excellence."

— Confucius[1]

CHAPTER 1

LAUNCHING YOUR
ROCKET

I magine an entrepreneur's nirvana: Three years have passed; your team has accomplished all its established goals and more. You have a stronger leadership team, a higher percentage of fully engaged employees, and your competitors want to learn how you built such an influential culture.

That is what happened for one company that mastered the principles in this book.

This company was doing well even before they hired us. They had achieved good growth in the last three years. Their net profit margins were well above industry norms. But the CEO realized that the benefits they'd gained by working with one external advisor had reached a plateau. He wanted to have a more significant industry impact and create employment for many more workers. It had taken almost 20 years to grow to $7 million in revenue. He knew that he and his team of 32 employees had so much more potential. It was time for a fresh approach.

We introduced our Business Acceleration System™ to leadership, established their Audacious Goal, and developed a strategy to create a profitable market position. We developed a three-year plan to grow the company to $14 million in revenue, increase profit margins, and strengthen their employer brand in the marketplace. During those three years, I am proud to say they far exceeded their goals by applying the concepts in this book!

Being Successful in Business Has Not Changed

While people have been impacted by globalization, technology, and other circumstances, how you achieve success in business has not changed. Over time, you will need to discuss changing conditions, and have a robust operating system maneuvering these issues. But I have concluded that while most entrepreneurs pride themselves on their speed in getting things done, I see them running in circles. More creative entrepreneurs may make lots of rapid right turns instead of circles, but they find themselves in the same place and with the same problems as the people running in circles, never achieving acceleration.

In math, when we add direction to speed, we have velocity. Good companies apply some of the concepts in this book and achieve *velocity*. The difference between the good and the great companies is having the discipline and perseverance to use all the ideas in the book and stick to their plans. The great companies, like the one in my opening story, achieve *acceleration*. I wrote this book and created my firm, Activate Group, Inc., because I wanted to teach more leaders how to accelerate.

Once you have read this book and realize how many opportunities there are to easily improve your business, you might wonder why a company allows millions of dollars in lost revenue and profit to occur at all. It takes discipline to work *on* the business rather than *in* it. It takes perseverance to stick to your plans and to focus on a limited number of objectives while saying "no" to others.

In *Your Business is a Leaky Bucket,* I identified 15 leaks present in every business.[1] The bigger the business, the bigger the leaks. Those leaks are the drags on acceleration. There are three primary reasons why those leaks continue to recur throughout the life of your business:

1. **Mediocrity**—You know your organization and people are capable of more, but you allow *average* to become the standard for your business. Sometimes, this happens because you attempted but failed to raise the bar in the past. There is also a tendency to compare your business to industry norms and become comfortable if it's doing better than the industry average—even if that industry average is a massive bottleneck in your business. Accepting the lower standard may be common in your industry, so you accept it, too. For example, high turnover has become the accepted norm in certain positions in some industries. But excessive turnover is a significant drag on a company's ability to grow and scale. Ask yourself, how often have you taken too long to replace someone you know is not capable of doing his or her job? These are examples of accepting mediocrity!

2. **Mastery**—It takes discipline and perseverance to continually improve and address the issues that cause slower growth, lower profitability, and cause leaders to be tied to their work. Let's be honest; when you started your career, were you thinking, "I am going to be a master craftsman at stewardship, strategy, accountability, planning, and human capital management?" Each of those areas requires skills and knowledge, continuous learning, and continuously increasing your level of mastery. However, as your business grows, so do the challenges in these areas. The typical leader would prefer to focus on industry knowledge, serving customers, and making better products and services rather than think about, discuss, and address those other, less tangible issues. In reality, stewardship, strategy, accountability, planning, and human capital management form the business operating systems that you use to run your business.

3. **Invisibility**—Financial statements do not capture the substantial costs of the weaknesses in your business operating system. Generally accepted accounting principles are only designed to capture actual transactions, assets, and liabilities. There is not a place in

accounting principles to capture the cost of mediocrity and lack of mastery. Like most leaders, you do not go out of your way to quantify these costs. This allows the slowdown in growth, and costs that lower profitability, to hide in plain sight. Here are some examples of mediocrity that should be monitored:

- The cost of keeping underperformers
- The cost of lost sales because of mistakes in the sales process
- The cost of customers who left because of their disappointment with your quality and bad processes
- The cost of a bad strategy leading to higher customer turnover or slower customer growth

There are no financial statement line items for these costs, yet they exist in every business. Such losses are much more significant than you want to face, so you don't! You are complacent with being good enough, especially if you are growing rapidly and profitably.

To succeed in business, leaders must have a business operating system and toolkit that help them work *on* the business in a way that allows their team members to make clear decisions and act regardless of the noise. Success is the result of your commitment to that system and how well you use the tools that support it. For the past 100 years and into the next 100, you will find that business challenges are the consequence of how effectively leaders handle these five areas:

1. Stewardship
2. Human Capital Management
3. Strategy
4. Planning
5. Accountability

Stewardship. Are the people commanding your ship impeding its forward progress? If you have people problems in the middle or at the bottom of your ship, the nexus of the issue resides at the top. Everything starts at the top and rolls downhill. Often, we find that the leadership team who took the organization to where it is may not be the right one to get it to its Audacious Goal. If you have the right people at the helm, human capital management, planning, and accountability function effectively. In many cases, you have the right leadership team, but it is not functioning well or working in sync. That dysfunction can disrupt the effectiveness of other employees.

Leaders who practice stewardship clearly define the purpose of the organization and shape its culture. *Purpose* serves as the foundation for your company and represents *why* the company exists. *Culture* defines the environment in which everyone works, the rules by which everyone makes decisions, and how people behave and act in a given situation. This culture is essential to building a great company and will be a key influencer on whether people want to come to work and stay working for your company. In today's competitive labor market, candidates are evaluating you as much as you are evaluating them. You can no longer depend solely on a corporate brand. You must develop and manage your employer brand to attract the right people.

Human Capital Management (HCM). As Jim Collins stated in his book, *Good to Great*, "First who, then what."[2] Are you still relying on a traditional human resources mentality to grow and manage the people within your organization? If so, it's likely keeping you from acquiring and retaining top talent.

Effective human resources departments have embraced a new paradigm, "human capital management" (HCM). This ideology recognizes that employees are assets managed through a system of activities. It is essential to understand the difference between a *resource* and an *asset*. *We use resources, but we grow assets.* It is vital that leadership refine all elements of their system to extend the life of those assets and achieve a maximum return on investment in them. Such a system considers acquiring, growing, keeping, and optimizing your workforce.

Understand that "the right people" are only those people who live all your core values and can consistently achieve reasonably high performance standards. Your organizational structure must support its strategy, and the right people should be in the proper roles and asked to do the right things. The CEO is accountable to ensure there is a robust process for hiring the right people, having the right structure, filling positions quickly, rewarding the right people, and removing the others. This is where stewardship and HCM intersect. If your business needs different results in the area of HCM, learn how the tone set from the top is causing wrong outcomes. Your problems never start at the bottom of your organization.

Strategy. Consider strategy from three perspectives. The first, *external* perspective, addresses growth. In all industries, there is more supply than demand. You cannot approach business without considering all the others who want to attract the same customers. So, you must carefully consider why and how customers choose your products and services over others. You must have a soundly constructed approach to acquire them. The external dimension is insufficient if you are not growing at least three times faster than the rate of the market.

The second perspective is your *internal strategy*. You are creating a business model that will turn your revenue into a sizeable profit and produce enough cash. If you generate revenue that cannot provide adequate cash, you will go bankrupt or give away too much equity! You know you have a great business model if you have an abundance of cash and your net profit margin is two to three times the industry average.

The third perspective is your *ability to sustain growth*. Too often, leaders believe that by continuing to do the same things that are successful today, they can expect their current growth rates to stay the same forever. Understanding your share of the market, changes in market conditions, and customer behaviors are critical. Many companies have found that they need to reinvent themselves and develop new products and services to continue to grow, and in some cases, not become obsolete in the marketplace. You must be proactive in this regard.

Planning. Simply put, *planning* is about clarifying what is important. It is about prioritization. It is a process of understanding the long-term goals and objectives for your organization and its stakeholders. You must connect the longer-term goals and objectives to the present tense. Make sure that what you are doing today will lead you to where you want to emerge tomorrow. You must help your team focus and clarify the goals, strategies, and initiatives required over the next three years, one year, and a single quarter to achieve the longer-term objectives. The planning process balances survival, profit, and growth objectives in the short term while building capabilities to ensure reaching your three-year goals. When done well, it accelerates growth and profits by minimizing the effort it takes to achieve long-term aspirations. Your team considers both internal and external considerations in order to mitigate risks that might negatively impact the business. Your team takes pride both in achieving objectives and in determining what *not* to do.

Accountability. Accountability is active when you consistently achieve annual and quarterly priorities while also consistently delivering monthly budgeted results. Great accountability systems help each member of your team take responsibility for the right actions. You must use the right metrics and data to motivate everyone properly. Doing so enables each employee to understand whether it was a good or bad day. Your indicators should sufficiently lead the team to make decisions.

What Does Unlocking True Potential Look Like?

When people ask what my company does, I tell them we help leaders launch rockets and create freedom! The leaders who work with me and my colleagues are CEOs who want to impact society, change their industries, and achieve other Audacious Goals. Being anything less than the best is deplorable to them. Most companies have a lot more impact, growth, and profit potential; we help them achieve that in full.

Before I go further, it is important to share some views on success and freedom. For many leaders I work with, financial results are only a byproduct of what they would define as *success*.

The best way to approach the concept of success is to share a conversation with my then 16-year-old son, Gabriel, whose world view is in some ways very mature. We were discussing his future. I wanted to make sure he understood what it was going to take to have a great life and achieve great things. I started the conversation and asked what success looked like to him. In front of him was a piece of paper with two columns, one labeled "1 year" and the other "5 years." I asked him to write down what he wanted to accomplish in each period. He looked me in the eye and said, "I don't like the word *success*." He asked if he could change it to "happiness." What a great shift! He saw clearly what many of my clients had yet to learn. When people say they want to be *successful*, they are indicating they want to achieve *happiness*. Most people find that earning a lot of money has a short-term impact on happiness and is only part of the equation.

Let's discuss freedom. Many people earn a great living and are never fulfilled, truly happy, or enjoying freedom. Like happiness, *freedom* has a different meaning for different people. Let me share with you what it means to one of my clients. He is living his definition of freedom at age 39. When we met, he had been working in his industry for about 14 years and running his own company for about 10. The company did well financially, and like most founders, he was very hands-on, which in many ways, was a bottleneck. No decisions were made without him; his leadership team was not fully developed, and he did not have much time for a personal life.

Fast-forward five years. By working through our system and with one of our coaches, we had helped this client achieve his vision of freedom. He is no longer a member of his company's leadership team. He handed over the day-to-day leadership responsibilities to a colleague who he promoted to president. He has a fully formed leadership team that helped triple the size of his company in the last three years. He is currently on a two-month sabbatical. Upon completion of the sabbatical, he will become an advisor to the leadership team as a board member. He wants to spend no more than one-third of his time on matters related to his business and other ventures, one-third of his time as an activist in his community, and the rest pursuing other endeavors that include traveling the world.

Most leaders struggle for years before finding their success formula. They go from one wild guess to another, using trial and error to find the magic equation that leads to remarkable growth. Until then, they have little-to-no profit, 100-hour workweeks, and anemic growth.

Apple Inc. is one such example. People forget what happened before Apple became the most valuable and one of the most admired companies in the world. Before 2003, the company averaged only 3 percent growth, had removed its founder, and was considered a mess. After solving its early-stage issues, the company has consistently averaged 40 percent growth. Many companies take 10 to 20 years to find their formula for success. Most never see it.

Whether you are just starting your business, want to improve it, or are ready to scale it, the concepts in this book can provide you with the processes and tools to help your organization accelerate its progress. The growth opportunities covered in this book will not be found in financial statements. *Accelerate* is **not** about cash management. While I want you to quantify the benefits whenever possible, our subjects are *business acceleration* and *freedom*.

Business Acceleration System™

Running a business is a never-ending process of balancing (5) major categories:

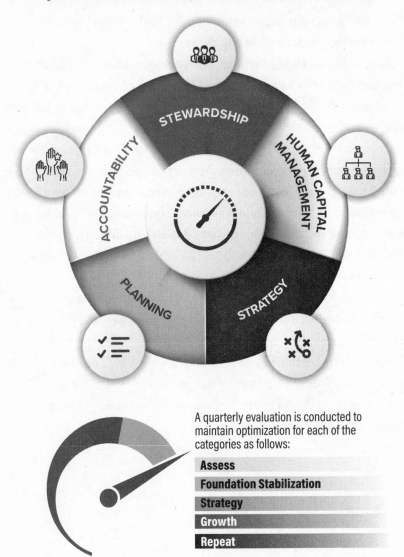

A quarterly evaluation is conducted to maintain optimization for each of the categories as follows:

Assess

Foundation Stabilization

Strategy

Growth

Repeat

You can improve mastery in each category. I want to challenge you to consider the impact that mastery will have on your growth, profits, and freedom. As you apply the concepts and see the differences they make, please email me at howard@howardmshore.com to let me know what you did and how it worked. I wrote this book to have an impact. It will make my day to see that I have done so.

Measuring the impact of these ideas is not easy. Where appropriate, I will provide you with tools to do so. As you read and think about growing your business, imagine you are launching a rocket toward freedom. The more areas you address and continue to master with your leadership team, the straighter your rocket will launch, moving farther and faster into orbit. The launch will experience less friction. The slower you are to address these items, or if you ignore them completely, the less likely you are to break out of the atmosphere. Consider each chapter topic as a drag on the acceleration of your growth, profitability, and freedom. The graphic depicts our proprietary *Business Acceleration System*™.

Find out how much the drags on your growth and profits cost your business with the *Business Acceleration Calculator*™. You can download it for free by going to www.howardmshore.com/tools. I developed this tool to help leaders quantify and prioritize their business issues and opportunities. Throughout the book, I will offer tips on how to complete this tool to provide a sense of what deserves your attention. I have yet to have a CEO fill this tool out honestly and *not* conclude that they can accelerate the business by at least $2 million. Each year, we help our clients continually find additional millions using these practical concepts.

My goal is to help leaders clarify and achieve Audacious Goals and free them from being slaves to their businesses. Our team has worked hard to create the *Business Acceleration System*™ to help businesses grow from start-up to billions. To do this, you need to consider how to work through all the obstacles along the way.

You will notice that I reference some great books and use their concepts. However, those books were incomplete systems. They are usually strong in some areas, but not all five. My fellow coaches and I have worked to make up for these weaknesses. You deserve one complete system to follow. Our system is rooted in the five aspects you will need.

I divided the book into five sections: Stewardship, Human Capital Management, Strategy, Planning, and Accountability. While businesses are always spinning all five of these plates at the same time, I have put the sections in this order for a reason. *Stewardship* is the foundation of your rocket. If you have a broken foundation, you may grow, but it will take some heavy lifting to keep the rocket intact. Eventually, it may burn up. When it comes to *strategy,* too many leaders have none or a bad one, as proven by their numbers. They try to fix their numbers by moving personnel around, the equivalent of rearranging deck chairs on the *Titanic.* If you have the wrong people, it won't matter what you want them to do—what you need to get done won't happen. Then there are the companies that have not thought through their *plan* and aligned everyone to achieve their well-thought-out strategy and goals, so they zigzag all over the place. Or they have a plan but do not hold anyone *accountable* for following it.

You will find this book worth reading if you hate complacency, love being the best at everything you do, want to find practical ways to accelerate the growth of your business, find more profit and cash while growing your business, and would like to have more fun and personal time while doing it.

In my last book, I described a company that extended more than $200 million in quotations the previous year but had only generated $16 million in revenue. The good news was that they had captured the full value of the business they had quoted during the year, which is not required by generally accepted accounting principles. The bad news: They had to admit that they lost many of their bids. When I asked how many of these bids were lost because of pricing mistakes, broken relationships, and other issues that could be addressed by the company, they couldn't provide an answer. Recently, I learned that the company was forced to sell by its ownership group after the CEO failed to develop a profitable growth strategy after several years at the helm.

In that example, the CEO was a proven leader who was confident in his abilities. The board hired him because they believed in him. But he failed because he did not apply the principles in this book. Sometimes, the most obvious business principles get in our way. He was more focused on working *in* his business than working *on* it, and he eventually failed.

Most cases are not as severe, which makes them more significant. They are like slow leaks of air from a tire—almost undetectable. Cars with tires that are not full get lower fuel economy and do not run smoothly. If the tire gets too flat, it can lead to much bigger problems. It is crucial to detect leaks—so you can run your business as smoothly as possible with maximum fuel economy at top speeds.

The principles in this book are most helpful once you've acknowledged that your business can accelerate faster and be more profitable, and once you've put your ego aside. It will be a book that you will highlight and revisit regularly. Colin Powell once said, "There are no secrets to success. It is the result of preparation, hard work, and learning from failure."[3]

The remainder of this book will help you build the necessary game plan to locate opportunities to accelerate the growth of your business. I have designed the book so you can work on one growth accelerator at a time or use our complete *Business Acceleration System*™ and *Business Acceleration Tools*®.

I look forward to helping you find and capture at least $1 million in the next 12 months. Reading this book may be the most profitable investment you have ever made in your business. Again, please tell me how this book has helped you by emailing howard@howardmshore.com.

LAUNCHING YOUR ROCKET

- It takes discipline to work *on* the business rather than *in* it.
- It takes perseverance to stick to your plans and focus on a limited number of objectives while saying "no" to others.
- In *Your Business is a Leaky Bucket*, I identified 15 business leaks that are present in every business. The bigger the business, the bigger the leaks. Those leaks are the drags on acceleration.
- Your financial statements do not capture the substantial costs of the weaknesses in your business operating system. Generally accepted accounting principles are only designed to capture actual transactions, assets, and liabilities.
- To succeed in business, leaders must have a business operating system and toolkit that help them work *on* the business in a way that allows team members to make clear decisions and act regardless of the noise.
- If you have the right people at the helm, then human capital management, planning, and accountability function effectively.
- In many cases, you have the right leadership team, but it is not functioning well and working in sync. That dysfunction can also disrupt the effectiveness of all the other employees.
- As stewards, leadership must clearly define the purpose of the organization and shape its culture.
- To attract the right people in this competitive labor market, you must develop and manage your employer brand.
- "Human capital management" (HCM) ideology recognizes that employees are assets managed through a system of activities.
- Your organizational structure must support its strategy. The right people must be in the proper roles and asked to do the right things.

- The CEO is accountable to ensure there is a robust process for hiring the right people, having the proper structure, filling positions quickly, growing the right people, rewarding them, and removing the wrong people.
- You must consider strategy from three perspectives:
  » Growth – You must carefully consider why and how customers choose your products and services over other choices.
  » Internal – A business model that will turn your revenue into a sizeable profit and produce enough cash.
  » Endurance – Ability to sustain growth.

- Simply put, planning is about clarifying what is important. It is about prioritization.
- Planning balances survival, profit, and growth objectives in the short term while building your capabilities to ensure reaching your three-year goals.
- Great accountability systems help each member of your team to take responsibility for the right actions.
- You have a problem with accountability when your organization is more reactive than proactive.
- When people say they want to be successful, they are indicating they want to achieve happiness.
- Like happiness, freedom has a different meaning for different people.
- The growth opportunities covered in this book will not be found in financial statements. *Accelerate* is not about cash management. While I want you to quantify the benefits whenever possible, our subjects are business acceleration and freedom.
- Find out how much the drags on your growth and profits cost your business with the *Business Acceleration Calculator*™. Download it for free by going to www.howardmshore.com/tools.

I developed this tool to help leaders quantify and prioritize their business issues and opportunities.

- As a leader or business owner, you have five essential responsibilities:

  1. Stewardship – Create a highly functioning leadership team and culture to serve a definite purpose.
  2. Human Capital Management – Ensure your organization has implemented the very best practices for talent acquisition, management, and optimization.
  3. Strategy – Deliver a unique mix of value to your clients through a business model that produces extraordinary profits.
  4. Planning – Establish planning protocols to make sure the initiatives and goals for the long-term and short-term are clear and that everyone in your organization is aligned.
  5. Accountability – Establish accountability systems so those long- and short-term goals happen.

CHAPTER 2

LEADERSHIP
MINDSETS FOR
ROCKET LAUNCHERS

Are you worried that while your business may appear to be doing well, there may be trouble looming somewhere? You are not alone. This is a concern for all business owners. When a business operating system is not fully functioning, you can assume your business is losing potential growth and profit and may be quickly losing its competitive advantage. This is a scary proposition, but one that you do not need to accept.

To find and address the issues that slow the acceleration of your business growth and profitability, there is no better place to start than by looking at the top tier of your company. Leadership is essential to the success of any business. Show me a great leader, and I will bet that a strong team, operation, and business are following close behind.

If you are in a leadership position, it is crucial to have a basic understanding of the lens you are looking through when making decisions. Your mindset and its corresponding actions will often dictate just how organized and successful your business can be. We start our head-to-toe evaluation of your business with the man or woman upfront.

What Type of CEO Are You?

An important question you need to ask is: "What kind of CEO/leader am I?" The next question you must ponder is: "How balanced is my strategic decision making?" The answers to these questions will help you determine which of the four most common lenses drive your organization's strategies:

- Growth
- Product/Service
- Waste
- Reactive

The most effective leader uses all four lenses. Each one is important. Unfortunately, most leaders lack balance and overemphasize one lens. Usually, a leader is either very product/service-oriented or growth-oriented, but not both. Being overweight in one lens leads to tremendous waste. Rather than fixing the one, overweight area, the single-lens leader unconsciously damages the others. For example, if you are a product- or service-oriented leader, your sales and marketing function is probably not producing sufficiently. In these cases, it is common to find under-investment or cost-cutting in sales and marketing while continuing to invest heavily in improving products and services. This is a justified move because your existing customers love you! But the problem is that extra love does not result in enough growth. In many cases, the additional cost of delivering added services and product features results in waste because the market will not accept the pricing needed to justify the added features and benefits. Customers will be happy to take what you are offering for free but are not willing to pay for it. Some leaders learn about waste in these areas but lack the discipline to address it. I'll explain this further as I describe the different leadership styles.

Are You a Growth-Oriented Leader?

Growth-oriented leaders focus most of their organization's energy on sales and marketing activities. In these organizations, it is common to hear, "More sales will make all your problems go away." This is true—to a degree. Let's face it; sales fund everything. Without sales, you burn cash, and the more sales you generate, the more money you can spend.

Such leaders are important. They find it unacceptable not to grow rapidly. They expect operations to solve whatever it needs to in order to support extraordinary growth. They do not believe in waiting to grow. Growth is their mandate. They see opportunities, seize them, and force operations to catch up. Keeping up with growth-oriented leaders is like trying to catch lightning bolts. It is incredible to look at different companies within the same industry and recognize these people at work. Their companies grow so much faster than the competition.

People who are not growing their companies will justify that lack by claiming to have better products and services—implying that those fast-growing companies are somehow tainted. Amazon's Jeff Bezos is a clear example of a growth-oriented leader. Founded in 1994, his company is one of the world's largest, generating $233 billion in revenue, a 31 percent increase over the prior year.[1] Think of how many smaller companies (tiny in comparison) will develop excuses as to why they cannot even grow 10 percent.

The identity of your business may be sales-oriented, the founder and CEO may have grown up in sales. Some say that your company can sell ice to Eskimos. That is not enough to be successful in business. In Bezos's case, being able to build sales volume was only one of the ingredients to his success. It's true; having an aggressive growth orientation has made him one of the world's wealthiest people and Amazon one of the world's most valuable companies. However, most CEOs' growth strategies are not as well thought out. That aggressive growth orientation was essential to his business model. His strategy required investing in a very expensive technology—a sales and distribution platform. He realized that this would be his core differentiator. Once it was built, he would have a competitive advantage. Winning would require sales volume in the hundreds of billions. He and his investors took on what appeared to be a significant risk and it paid off. Without rapidly building sales volume, Amazon's model would have failed.

Many leaders have similar aspirations to Bezos but fail. They have a growth plan, but no differentiated business model. Twitter is one such company. At Twitter, there is a heavy emphasis on increasing user volume, but they failed to think through how their differentiated business model could produce both cash and value to owners. In most industries, the game Bezos played is dangerous and foolish. You need more balance in the equation; you need to genuinely understand your business model, and you need to consider focus.

Even though it appears Bezos took a lot of risks, he did focus quite a bit more than people realize and kept his model simple from a macro perspective. First, he built his business model around the book segment. He perfected increasing visitors interested in buying books, attracting third-party sellers wanting to sell books, and expanded and improved distribution. As there were more sellers, this lowered prices, which increased customer visits, and that attracted more third-party sellers. After Bezos completed his platform and distribution model around one product line, he began to extend product offerings, which again increased customer visits. This attracted more third-party sellers, and he continued to build out distribution capabilities.

Today, we can purchase, and Amazon can deliver, almost anything the same day. In the end, this model grew company revenues at an almost exponential rate with seemingly minimal effort. As the revenue momentum grew, those expensive platform and distribution costs were no longer growing at high rates and now were being spread over a much larger revenue base. A key to Amazon's success is to reduce fixed costs as a percentage of revenue. With revenue in the hundreds of billions, Amazon is profitable and the leader in the market.

However, growth-oriented leaders often fail to consider the following factors:

- Cost of acquiring clients;
- Importance of segmenting marketing;
- Impact of expanding the product line;
- Quality of existing and prospective clients;
- Profitability of current and potential clients;
- Impact the revenue habit is having on operations; or
- Ability to service customers properly.

Many growth-oriented CEOs are prone to sell anything and everything. This causes a nightmare for their service operations and makes it difficult for marketing to delineate what makes them different from their competitors. It is difficult for a growth-oriented leader to understand the concept of "bad revenue." They think catering to each additional need is "simple," that the customer is always right, and they are always wired to say yes. Making promises that your organization cannot deliver will result in a client revolving door—old clients going out as fast as new ones are coming in.

Are You a Product- or Service-Oriented Leader?

Product- or service-oriented leaders are masters of their craft, always focused on perfecting their deliverables. They are excellent at what they do. They can demonstrate tons of metrics proving why they are better than everyone else, but they do not have the revenue to show for it. They spend all their time perfecting processes and creating perfect products and services.

In these organizations, we must watch for three common problems: 1) undercharging for products and services relative to their cost; 2) giving away features and benefits that can be charged for; and 3) focusing on product features that are not important to customers. Product- or service-oriented leaders feel their actions are justified because their customers stay with them forever.

The real challenge is to have high growth *and* excellent products and services. You can look at any industry. If you are in business services, you can look at KPMG, Omnicom, Baker McKenzie, and Booz Allen Hamilton. In other areas, consider Trader Joe's, Chick-fil-A, Costco, and Samsung. These are companies that have snowballed *and* have a quality product and service.

I recently spoke with the CEO of a talented public relations firm, possibly one of the best in the country. This person suffered from a perennial problem for this type of leader. The mantra is to "grow smartly." The firm is always concerned with whether it can service and support new clients. It looks at the other firms and questions the quality and value of campaigns and work product they produce for their clients. But their firm never breaks $5 million in revenue. This is the typical ceiling for most such firms. When I asked if there was enough work for their company to do $100 million, the answer was yes. I also wondered if there were enough people in the industry to deliver the products and services needed The answer to that question was also yes. The problem was the company and its leadership orientation. There was a fear of growth. In the minds of the leaders in this organization was the belief that they can't grow quickly and still deliver a quality product or service. If they scrapped that erroneous belief and determined that doing both was essential, they would figure out how to do it. This is what great companies do!

Are You a Waste-Oriented Leader?

Waste-oriented leaders have a balanced set of key performance indicators, goals, and targets for *everything*. You can also call them *aggressive growth leaders with a profit-centered mindset*. They want to multiply and have a net profit margin knowing this will drive their business valuation. They understand their business models and live for continuous improvement. Rather than thinking like accountants, they consider how much revenue they want to make and at what net profit margin. They then figure out how much expense is left over to generate that revenue and net profit margin. For example, if I want a 20 percent net profit margin and have a $10 million revenue target, then total expenses cannot exceed $8 million. The profit-centered leader forces the team to achieve the $10 million revenue target without spending more than $8 million.

Waste-oriented leaders are more balanced in decision-making and seek to understand what needs to happen to increase the growth and profitability of their companies. They look through the sales and product/service lenses and determine how both lenses are operating as they relate to their purpose and the needs of the core customer(s). They are continually asking the following questions:

- How efficient are we at aggressively acquiring clients? How can we gain more clients faster?
- Which clients are the most profitable, and which ones are less profitable—and why?
- Which clients are more trouble than they are worth?
- How efficient are we at making our products and delivering our services?
- Are we achieving high standards of quality for our products and services to meet the critical needs of our core customers?
- Are we then making the tough decisions, in areas that are not important to our customers, to reduce our costs?
- How do we scale the client acquisition function?

- Are costs optimized to acquire each new customer?
- Are we doing the right things to preserve our relationships with existing customers, to minimize lost customers, and to get all customers to spend more with us?
- Are we elevating our employee relationships to increase our employee engagement and retention and to attract top talent?

As you reflect on waste-oriented leadership, you will notice that it takes input from more than one leader. The never-ending *constructive* conflict that naturally exists between sales- and operations-oriented leadership is ideal! In great organizations, they often bang up against one another. If you do not find conflict like this occurring in your company, beware. You need extreme leadership from both sides to keep pushing the boundaries. The conflict and mediation bring you to proper balance. If you do not experience this type of discussion in your meetings, you are probably losing growth, profit, or both.

Amazon's leadership added waste-oriented decision making to its toolkit. The company needed to focus only on books at the start. It was a carefully chosen product segment. By perfecting their capabilities in that one segment, they created and built the foundation for the company's success today. Offering too much too soon would have been unwise. Amazon has always been—and still is—a growth-oriented company, but Jeff Bezos's team has proven its ability to implement waste-oriented thinking as well.

Later in its evolution, Amazon better understood their business model and made a new growth move to become a profitable company. They are now one of the most extensive managed services and cloud services providers in the world. They understood that Amazon is not a retailer; it is a technology company. One of the highest costs in its infrastructure is the technology platform that powers its retail and distribution platform. To offer such a great platform, Amazon had to build the world's most reliable cloud services platform. Once they created a comprehensive and stable platform, it sold the use of that platform as a service to others through Amazon Web Services (AWS). Today, AWS represents 11 percent of Amazon's total revenue or approximately $26 billion in revenue. This move is the primary driver of profitability, with Amazon.com earning $5 billion in profit from retail and $7 billion in profit from AWS.[2]

The Reactive CEO: "Fire, Ready, Aim"

Reactive CEOs try to run their businesses based on day-to-day conditions instead of following the strategic plans they've agreed to support. Too many lack the discipline to stick to the agreed-upon method to lead their organizations. I would describe this leadership style as "fire, ready, aim." This is the most common type of leader in entrepreneurial companies.

Before you read this and feel beaten, face it: S#@t happens! We cannot be so stubborn in our positions and plans that we ignore what is going on around us. I have seen people stick to their plans and processes when they need to pause and reconsider. If the boat is sinking, you don't ignore it. If a significant client (one that represents 20 percent or more of your revenue) is at risk, don't ignore it. There might also be positive changing conditions to consider.

One of my clients recently (and flawlessly) responded to a $9 million job. To give you perspective, this was a $7 million company three years ago. They completed the huge job in 60 days as if they had done projects like it regularly—which they had not. You can distinguish organizations that react well from those that "fire, ready, and aim." They act like a seasoned emergency room team rather than starving animals fighting for a piece of meat. Have you ever noticed how organized and calm it is in an emergency room? Alarms are sounding everywhere, yet these team members were relaxed and laughing together, having fun, smiling, and no one was stressed. Everything moved as it was supposed to.

The typical, reactive, "fire, ready, aim" CEO makes key decisions without including other leaders and members of the organization. Others are left to deal with the consequences of those decisions—usually resulting in a lot more work for everyone else. Such leaders feel justified in how they handled things, oblivious to the adverse effects of their actions.

Ask this kind of leader: "Why do you make decisions without others' input, buy-in, and commitment?" Brace yourself. The answers you hear will be: the company needed faster decisions, others were not capable, "I knew what was best," and similar nonsense. These answers are rarely accurate. Even if they were, when a leader makes decisions this way and shoves them down everyone's throats, it limits the potential of their company. Also, if the decision is wrong, the leader will get resistance, lose everyone's trust, lose time in implementation, demotivate others, and lose the respect of colleagues.

Some reasons that leaders do not take the time to include input from others are that they have poor emotional intelligence, have trouble working in teams, lack humility, lack patience, disrespect everyone, lack integrity, and so on. If this is how teammates see a leader, the consequences are enormous. An organization cannot mature and thrive if its leader continues to behave in such a manner.

Growth without exercising discipline and making strategic choices creates a lot of waste and burns cash. To make significant decisions, it is essential that you include the other members of your team and people in the front lines. In every organization my company works with, we conduct the "Gallup Survey" to measure employee engagement, and we have found that organizations whose leaders are "fire, ready, aim" have the following characteristics:

- The lowest employee engagement scores
- The hardest time recruiting employees
- The highest turnover
- Declines in labor efficiency
- Higher numbers of employee sick days
- Lower growth rates in revenue

A real-life example is a CEO, whom we will call Greg, who runs an international manufacturing, distribution, and retail operation that is stuck at approximately $10 million in revenue. Many outsiders believe this company has the potential to become a $1 billion entity. This is unlikely to happen unless Greg changes his leadership style or steps out of his company.

Greg is your typical visionary CEO but he lacks discipline. He claims he does not want to be involved in the day-to-day operations of his business. He hired a president to run his company and agreed to stick to one strategy, a business plan, and abdicate all operating decisions to this new person. Despite this agreement, he sends daily emails to individual employees about his displeasures. He walks around the building changing processes and plans set by the president. He recently hired a chief technology officer (CTO) and chief marketing officer (CMO) without involving the president. He continues to wreak so much daily havoc that the president cannot focus on the planned activities to carry out the agreed-upon strategy.

The president is not only sure to fail in this scenario, but the CEO sees nothing wrong with his actions. When asked about his behavior, he responded that he is CEO and should be able to make decisions. He believes he knows better than everyone else what the company needs. Not surprisingly, his president no longer trusts him. The entire company fears for their jobs because they do not know what to expect next. They are no longer committed to the new plan because the CEO has not shown his commitment to it. Unsurprisingly, the leadership team is not embracing people the CEO hired without their participation. They believe the former CTO was stronger than the new one, and the new CMO is not qualified for what they need. Both people are now set up for failure.

Right or wrong, had the CEO gone about making those decisions differently, he would have affected his organization more productively. It will take far more work—and a lot of discipline—to recover from the damage he caused.

How you make decisions, whether you include others in those decisions, and how you demonstrate character in decision making has a tremendous influence on employee engagement!

Are You Playing to Win or Not to Lose?

Understanding behavioral styles is essential to building a well-rounded and functioning leadership team. It is a critical component in our coaching programs to help leaders see when they are building a team with too many people like themselves, undervaluing key people, or compromising the effectiveness of others because they are the leader's opposites.

Merrick Rosenberg and Daniel Silvert's book, *Taking Flight!: Master the DISC Styles to Transform Your Career, Your Relationships...Your Life,*[3] is recommended for its simplicity on the subject. We suggest you read it and let us know if you want to understand how your behavioral style may be affecting your leadership orientation. Armed with an understanding of behavioral styles and how they affect teamwork and communication, you can learn how to work better together with your team.

Let's address a common mindset of many leaders—and possibly some of yours. Have you ever been on a team, in school, sports, or business, where everyone was playing to win? How did you know? What did it feel like? I have been there. It gets tense at times—tempers can sometimes flare when people care. When someone is giving his or her all, you can see it on their face and feel it in the air. Team members hold each other accountable. The bar set for outcomes is exceptionally high. Anything less than first place, getting an "A," or landing the big deal is unacceptable. You have left it all on the court—or in the office. No matter what the outcome, everyone knows they did their best, could not give any more, and is ready to do it again.

Have you ever been on a team where everyone is *not* playing to win? A team where people are complacent? A team where people have more to give and are not giving it? How do you know? What did it feel like? What did it look like? Unfortunately, I see this latter situation more often than the former when I meet with leaders. The environment is relaxed. There is little if any accountability, especially at senior levels. These companies should be renamed "Excuseville Limited." I find minimal conflict, and when I do, it involves nonsense. Somebody ate someone else's lunch, or someone forgot to say good morning. These are the most critical issues the leaders want to worry about. Don't get me wrong. I like a harmonious culture, but one that cares about winning and is accountable, not an assembly of bobbleheads.

While most such entrepreneurs like the idea of being successful, they are not playing to win! They are holding back, not taking the necessary risks that others are willing to take in the same industry. They're playing it safe. They may have been playing to win at one time, but they've stopped. Good became the enemy of great. Once they started making money, they shifted to protection mode. They stopped being willing to make risky moves.

I have let clients go for this reason. I remember one CEO complaining that when she hired me, she did not realize that meant she was going to have to work harder, invest money in her business, and take risks. She did not like the fact that her business was not growing but was unwilling to face the fact that she was the problem. She was no longer doing things that, in the early days had caused her business to grow. She was playing it safe, and it cost her. Instead of building her business, she was taking her money out of it and investing it in real estate. She was more determined to be successful in real estate than to be successful in her manufacturing and distribution business. She was sure to continue struggling.

The successful are obsessive. They give massive effort and do things that others find crazy. Are you doing things others are not willing to do? Are you ready to sacrifice everything to achieve your ultimate vision of success? Are you playing to win—taking risks, developing winning moves, focusing continuously on exceptional growth—or are you playing not to lose, having already achieved a measure of success? Will aversion to risk and the comfort of winning today become the complacency that leads to losing tomorrow?

Ponder those questions as you continue reading. To become great, you must be *playing to win!* Many fast-growing and profitable companies dream about doing so again. They dream about being great but are just average at best.

Become obsessed with success and challenge your employees to do the same. Our most impactful and successful clients believe that average is unacceptable. No one on their teams wants to be average. Leaders should model wanting to be great and create environments where everyone thinks that average is terrible.

If you are not playing to win, you cannot accelerate like a rocket!

LEADERSHIP MINDSETS FOR ROCKET LAUNCHERS

- An important question you need to ask is: "What kind of CEO/ leader am I?" The next question you must ponder is: "How balanced is my strategic decision making?" Why do you need to ask these questions? The answers will help you determine which of the four most common lenses drive your organization's strategies:

  1. Growth
  2. Product/Service
  3. Waste
  4. Reactive

- Growth-oriented leaders focus most of their organization's energy on sales and marketing activities.
- The people who are not growing their companies will justify their lack of growth by claiming they have better products and services and that those other growth companies are somehow tainted. Amazon, led by Jeff Bezos, is a clear example of a growth-oriented leader.
- Many leaders have Bezos-like aspirations but fail. They have a growth plan but no differentiated business model.
- Growth-oriented leaders often fail to consider the:

  » Cost of acquiring clients;
  » Importance of segmenting marketing;
  » Impact of expanding the product line;
  » Quality of existing and prospective clients;
  » Profitability of current and potential clients;

- » Impact the revenue habit is having on operations; or
- » Ability to service customers properly.

- Growth-oriented CEOs are prone to sell anything and everything, causing a nightmare for their service operations and making it difficult for marketing to delineate what makes them different from their competitors. It is difficult for a growth-oriented leader to understand the concept of "bad revenue."
- Product or service-oriented leaders must watch for three common problems:

  - » Undercharging for products and services relative to what they cost;
  - » Giving away features and benefits that can be charged for; and
  - » Focusing on product features that are not important to their customers.

- In product- or service-oriented leaders there is a fear of growing too fast. In their minds, they can't grow quickly and deliver quality products and services for their clients.
- The real challenge is to have high growth and excellent products and services.
- Waste-oriented leaders have a balanced set of key performance indicators, goals, and targets for everything. You can also call them aggressive growth leaders with a profit-centered mindset.
- You need extreme leadership from both sales and operations-oriented leaders to keep pushing the boundaries, and the conflict and mediation bring you to proper balance. If you do not experience this type of discussion in your meetings, you are likely losing growth, profit, or both.
- Reactive CEOs try to run their business based on day-to-day conditions instead of following the strategic plans they've already agreed to support.

- You can distinguish the organizations that react well from those that "fire, ready, and aim." You react well when you operate like an emergency room team rather than a pack of starving animals fighting for a piece of meat.
- Growth without exercising discipline and making strategic choices creates a lot of waste and burns cash.
- Understanding behavioral styles is essential to building a well-rounded and functioning leadership team.
- One book you may want to read because of its simplicity on the subject of understanding behavior styles is *Taking Flight!: Master the DISC Styles to Transform Your Career, Your Relationships... Your Life*, by Merrick Rosenberg and Daniel Silvert.
- While most entrepreneurs like the idea of being successful, they are not playing to win.
- If you are not playing to win, you cannot accelerate like a rocket!

CHAPTER 3

MODERN-DAY GROWTH
ACCELERATORS

I n the previous chapter, we placed a mirror in front of your company to determine if you had the leadership mindsets to become a rocket launcher. Too often, the changes I discuss in this book never happen because the person running the company lacks those mindsets but pretends to be determined to want to launch a rocket. They are not willing to do what it takes, which is what this book teaches you to do. Those of you still reading may be ready to make it to the next level, and I want to help!

To launch a rocket, you must plot a course and increase speed. You must have high velocity and have enough discipline to increase acceleration or scale your current level of acceleration to take your company into orbit. This book is designed to help make that happen. It will help you analyze what is working well in your business and what is not, and then to discuss the next best steps with your team. It spells out actual, modern-day growth accelerators that work for any organization or industry—if its leadership is committed to following them.

As stated in Chapter 1, most modern-day growth accelerators occur in five distinct areas of your business:

1. Stewardship
2. Human Capital Management (HCM)
3. Strategy
4. Planning
5. Accountability

Opportunities to increase growth in revenue, profits, and cash can occur throughout a business, but I have found that it is best to have a framework. This one has worked best for me in my business and those of our clients. Now, let's look at the list of growth accelerators that address issues likely to be plaguing your company. These include:

Stewardship Accelerators

Stewardship accelerators address the drags on growth, profits, and cash that occur because of leadership deficiencies and failure to establish a meaningful ideological foundation. These ideologies define *why* the company exists and shape the environment in which everyone works.

Growth Accelerator #1: Replace Poor Managers

When you make allowances for a poor manager, you are deciding that a substandard manager has more to offer than everyone else put together—a fool's bet. Your ineffective manager causes everyone else to perform at lower levels. You lose access to a lot of great ideas. People are less apt to work for your organization, let alone willingly give extra effort.

At a recent trade show, I met Mary, a manager who was complaining about how lazy her millennial workers were. Mary was a long-term employee, considered an expert in her functional area. After hearing her story, I tactfully suggested that she was likely to be the root of the problem. She was befuddled at first, and then I asked her a crucial question. "Was there ever a time when you were highly productive in a company, but then they changed your manager and your productivity changed?" She sheepishly grinned and said, "Yes!" At the current company, she had been a star performer until her original manager quit. The owner gave the vacant position to his daughter, who had no subject matter expertise, no management experience, and failed to earn the trust of her team. As a reaction to the owner's bad decision, Mary purposely stopped working as hard as she previously had. She admitted her production dropped to at least half of what it had been previously. Fast forward to this trade show. Mary is now the manager of her department and getting poor performance from those reporting to her. After looking in the mirror, Mary had to face the fact that her team was following her footsteps, and she was the problem!

Growth Accelerator #2: Address Team Dysfunction

You may have leaders who are great functional experts with substantial institutional and industry knowledge, but that does not make them great team members. You must function effectively as a team so that the sum becomes greater than the parts. Failure to address dysfunction in the leadership team has a multiplying effect on the rest of the organization's ability to accelerate.

Have you ever been on a great team, whether in sports, work, or any other environment? It does not take great players to produce great results. I once coached a basketball team of 14- to 16-year-old boys. We had a mediocre group of players. Looking at the roster, you would expect us to be competent, but not competing for any championships. From the start, my strategy was to work hard on building trust among the players, on developing their ability to address each other's unproductive behaviors, and on their learning to communicate effectively. Everyone knew each other's strengths and weaknesses and focused on strengths. We started the season with one of the worst records in the league, but we knew by the end of the season that we could beat anyone in that league. In the end, because we built a great *team*, we made it to the finals and earned the respect of everyone in the league.

Growth Accelerator #3: Establish a Clear and Compelling Purpose

The day you start your business, you must place "purpose" at the forefront. Purpose is a critical issue that fails to get enough attention. Many business owners who are asked, "What is the purpose of your business?" will answer "to make money" (or something similar). You may be thinking, "Isn't that the purpose of any for-profit business?" I can confidently say no.

Purpose is a direction, not a destination. It is a place we never quite reach because it is an ideological objective. It is the big, central idea that we want everyone to think about every moment they are playing their role in our company. It is a centralizing idea that should be so compelling that it inspires and motivates people to give extra effort, develop creative solutions, break down barriers, and better serve clients. At Activate Group, Inc., our central idea is to "propel leaders toward their true potential, so they achieve Audacious Goals and freedom." We know that our work has a tremendous impact on job creation, the economy, industry innovation, and lives. All our team members come to work inspired by the central idea of "unlocking true potential" and pushing towards "Audacious Goals and freedom" as the reasons for doing our work rather than the methodology we use to get there or the financial rewards we may achieve.

Human Capital Management (HCM) Accelerators

Effective Human Resources departments have been transformed into a new paradigm: Human Capital Management or HCM. This ideology addresses a company's key people processes. It recognizes that employees are assets managed through a system of activities. Leadership must refine all elements of the system to extend the life of those assets and achieve a maximum return on its investment in them. This system considers acquiring, growing, keeping, and optimizing your workforce.

Growth Accelerator # 4: Develop a Strong Culture

Show me a high-performing organization that employees love and clients rave about; where growth is high and there is exceptional profitability. That is an example of an organization that has a remarkable culture. *Culture* begins with core values, but its reach is so much wider. *Culture* refers to how everyone in the company conducts themselves and the environment that everyone operates in.

Culture is created, shaped, and nurtured in particular ways. It starts with clearly defined core values that are consistently demonstrated by all leaders and expected from every employee. *Culture* also encompasses how leaders, managers, and coworkers treat each other and their clients. It represents the working conditions in general, which includes available tools, resources, and physical workspace.

Growth Accelerator #5: Optimize Your Return on Human Assets

Leaders have three different roles to play when it comes to people: Acquire great people, help them reach their highest potential, and get the highest return on investment in them. The chapter on this Growth Accelerator will help you discover how to optimize return on your people assets. It's a balancing act. The needs of all the stakeholders and the objectives of maximizing stewardship, human capital management, strategy, planning, and accountability sometimes compete with one another. That is what makes managing people so tricky and takes excellent management and leadership skills.

Many organizations use the wrong measures for determining how to manage human assets. Labor rates, turnover, and other commonly-used measures are not the right ones. In this area, we will teach you how to measure and improve your Labor Efficiency Ratio™ to determine how well your company is managing its human assets.

Growth Accelerator #6: Increase the Percentage of Performing Talent

Increasing the percentage of performing talent is critical to acceleration. Productivity, morale, and profits deteriorate when your internal processes do not correctly identify "nonperforming" talent—or take too long to act when someone is a nonperformer. These are people that fail to consistently demonstrate *all* your core values and achieve the reasonably high performance standards established for their position. Additionally, you may be classifying people as "performing" for the wrong reasons, while the real performers quit, get fired, or become less engaged in their positions.

We often find employees retained and considered "performing" because they have a lot of domain or historical company knowledge. While such knowledge is valuable to the company, these people are often disruptive and underperforming in other ways, drawbacks that cannot be overlooked. The cost of these decisions always outweighs the benefits of keeping people. Management teams constantly fail to properly calculate the cost and overestimate the value of keeping such people. We have yet to see one of our clients suffer consequentially when one of these people quits. On the contrary, our clients always remark that they should have acted sooner.

Growth Accelerator #7: Address Vacant Positions

Many challenges result from how much emphasis is placed on limiting the time that positions remain vacant. Other problems occur because of the failure to create necessary new jobs. Another pitfall is filling open positions with inadequate talent because of the substandard compensation level offered for that job. Organizations are so concerned about what a new hire will cost that they lose significant opportunities to acquire people who can bring in revenue and operational efficiency that far exceeds their earnings package. Meanwhile, existing employees get burned out trying to make up for empty seats. Strategic efforts are poorly executed because people are spread too thin.

Recently a client realized that they were not filling open positions fast enough, and it cost them business. When we investigated the reason, they concluded that no one person was accountable for recruiting or had the time to focus on it. They had underestimated the time and effort needed to generate and screen enough good candidates to fill the number of positions that were vacant every month. As soon as they created a new position dedicated to recruiting, they found they had more and better job applicants for every position. Now they no longer need to turn down new business, and recruiting employees requires less management time. They estimate that the annual cost of the dedicated recruiting position they created was paid for in the first 45 days.

Growth Accelerator #8: Increase Hiring Success

How do you measure hiring success? Hiring success means you hired someone that fits your culture and performs at the reasonably high standards set for them, given their tenure and experience. Too many times, companies are making the mistake of measuring hiring success just by using turnover as a yardstick. Cultivating the right or wrong environment and onboarding process for those you hire can have profound effects on whether people stay or leave. The turnover measure does not tell you how well you hired. You must measure culture fit first, and then go deeper to determine how well your hiring processes are working. You must capture good data and then dig deep to understand that data.

One of our clients was using an excellent recruiting system but had high turnover, lackluster performance among existing employees, and trouble getting candidates to apply for open positions. The CEO was putting a lot of pressure on the director of human resources to change the recruitment and hiring process. After examining the HR data, we were able to validate through reference-checking that many of the people whose performance was in question had strong track records of success before joining the company. Upon closer examination, we saw that these new hires had started strong but their performance fell off later. In the end, the culprits were identified as the company culture and the managers that new employees were reporting to, not the recruitment and hiring process.

Strategy Accelerators

Strategy is primarily about how well you have designed your business model. Consider whether your company is growing at an acceptably high level, whether this growth rate is predictable, and whether you believe it will continue for the next several years. Does your business model create enough cash flow? Our philosophy of the importance of cash flow is: *Revenue is vanity, profit is sanity, and cash is king!* Lastly, evaluate the sustainability of your growth rate. At what point do you need to consider new products and services because your existing ones have limited potential going forward? Our four strategy accelerators in this section help you address these considerations.

Growth Accelerator #9: Design a Profitable and Scalable Business Model

A *scalable business model* can maintain or improve profit margins while sales volume increases. The most innovative leaders examine their industries and are determined to grow faster and with less effort than their competitors and to demand extraordinary profit margins. Their less-ambitious competitors do the opposite. Whenever there are challenges in their businesses, mediocre leaders throw people and money at the problems. They accept issues as norms and allow those problems to make lives difficult, increase their cost structure, slow their delivery times, increase complexity, and create waste. When excellent leaders get the business model right, their growth rate is at least three times their industry's average, and they have three times the net profit margin. If your company is not at those levels, you need to improve your business model.

Growth Accelerator #10: Narrow Your Target Market

In order to grow your revenue portfolio, you must identify the ideal clients you need to acquire and keep. If analyzed today, your customer database is likely to have too many "wrong" clients. These pay poorly, are less profitable, complain a lot, are hard to service, and do not give referrals. You are probably in this situation because companies find it easier to get bad clients, particularly when they first open and need income to survive.

Another reason that companies keep the wrong clients is that many leaders mistakenly think that all revenue is created equal. Not so. In practice, a lack of focus on a target market segment of clients drains organizational energy and profits. Furthermore, building a base of bad clients creates a wrong brand image and handcuffs your company.

A good market segmentation example is Ikea USA. It focused on a segment of people looking for products with simple designs, basic quality, a few inexpensive options, and not made to last. This singular focus allowed them to become one of the largest and most profitable furniture manufacturers in the world in a relatively short time.

Growth Accelerator #11: Differentiate Properly

Does your business strategy encompass a clear value proposition—one that would be considered an unusual offering critical to your target client's buying decision? Are you delivering on the promises embedded in that offering? The answers to these questions may be the primary reasons your sales force hasn't achieved its quotas, your market share hasn't increased, and you've found it increasingly difficult to grow your business.

Imagine you want to purchase a car. People choose their cars for many different reasons, including safety, quality, comfort, style, speed, serviceability, and sustainability. Volvo worked hard to own "safety" as its strong point. BMW wants to be known as the "ultimate driving machine." These companies drew lines in the sand and wanted to make a distinction between what they offer and what their competitors do. It is now up to their organizations to deliver on the brand promises, to stand out and lead in those categories to draw in the buyers that find those factors the most desirable.

Growth Accelerator #12: Lay the Foundation for Continuous Growth

A common mistake is to believe that if you continue to operate well, you will continue to grow at your current rate forever. Smart leaders watch trends in technology, competition, and buying behavior. They adjust their strategies when appropriate. They enter new markets and expand to new customer segments to harvest an existing strategy as much as possible. Unfortunately, as Toys"R"Us and the retail industry, in general, have learned, one must innovate and change to prevent growth from slowing or declining. Companies like Apple have continued to innovate into new product and service categories to gain additional share of the consumer wallet while retaining their relationship with the clients they worked so hard to earn.

Planning Accelerators

Planning is about clarifying what is essential. It is about prioritization. It is a process of understanding the long-term goals and objectives of your organization and its stakeholders. You must bring the longer-term focus to the present tense—and make sure that what you are doing today will lead you to where you want to emerge. You must help your team focus and clarify the goals, strategies, and initiatives required over the next three years, the next year, and the next quarter, to achieve longer-term objectives.

Growth Accelerator #13: Commit to an Audacious Goal

Is your team working toward a truly Audacious Goal? Our business coaches often go into good organizations, but not great ones. The CEOs acknowledge that their teams are capable of more, but they are not sure how to motivate everyone to deliver more. The secret lies in setting the company's *Audacious Goal*. This is the essential number that signifies progress toward your company's purpose and is your "Mount Everest." When used correctly, it galvanizes everyone in a way that banishes complacency, drives change, and causes everyone to think bigger and achieve more.

Jim Collins's book, *Built to Last,* described The Audacious Goal. It is a goal designed to engage your people in a significantly transformative way. It is tangible, energizing, highly focused. When you "get it right," it will help you do something great. An example of the results of such a goal was Boeing in the 1970s, when it made the decision to put a primary focus on the commercial jet aircraft space and bet a quarter of its net worth on the creation of the 707. This bet led to Boeing leading the industry for years. Another Audacious Goal cited in the book was Henry Ford's proclamation, "to build a motor car for the great multitude... It will be so low in price that no man making a good salary will be unable to own one."[1]

Growth Accelerator #14: Establish a Long-Term Plan

A key to being able to set annual priorities is knowing what you want to accomplish three years from now. We found that by setting aggressive three-year goals, we can break a team from short-term and incremental thinking habits. By understanding that your existing capabilities cannot carry the weight of such aggressive growth, your team will understand it needs to start driving changes in systems, processes *now*—without procrastinating.

Growth Accelerator #15: Establish a One-Year Plan

One of the most significant gifts to any leadership team is knowing what they should say *no* to. This becomes difficult, if not impossible, without a solid annual plan. All that is clear is that the company wants to be bigger, better, faster, and more profitable than last year. Without clarifying the minimum and best moves needed to make that happen, you have to say *yes* to everything. For many businesses, current year goals are often determined the previous year. Your annual planning process helps prioritize what must get done in the current year to achieve current year goals and sets the company up for the next year's success. So you are making the big moves for future years; you must get them right.

Growth Accelerator #16: Establish a Quarterly Plan

For most companies, establishing the quarterly plan is where the rubber meets the road. As discussed earlier, *our job as leaders is to paint a vision of where we are headed in the long term and to bring that focus down to the short term.* We then break that short-term goal down into 13-week "sprints." These sprints need to consider that you have likely staffed your company in a lean way. In other words, your people, particularly leaders, are not sitting around with a lot of idle time on their hands. Quarterly plans help focus leaders' and departments' discretionary, strategic time on what is most critical to raising the company to the next level.

Accountability Accelerators

Finally, *accountability accelerators* are processes and systems that help focus and align everyone in the company, increasing the likelihood of maximum success. These are tools that help a company use time and resources efficiently and effectively.

Growth Accelerator #17: Create a Culture of Accountability

Why do so many annual plans fail? Does your organization fail to achieve its key plan priorities? You are not alone! Most leaders will admit that when they analyze their results. They are often unwilling to reveal exactly how they did it. Failing to create a culture of accountability allows team members to be unfocused, use time in unwise ways, accomplish the wrong outcomes, and slow acceleration.

Growth Accelerator #18: Everybody Knows Their Numbers

Numbers matter. Almost every business recognizes that. However, business leaders often focus their attention on the wrong numbers. As with issues like purpose, many companies do not pay enough attention to goal setting. What's more, many organizations set goals and fail to reach them.

Focusing on the right numbers will help you increase acceleration. It will help you answer questions like, what is the critical weakness in my business model? What is the most significant gap in my operations? What is causing us not to gain customers? What is causing us to lose customers? What is causing our cost structure to be out of line with our competition's cost structure?

Growth Accelerator #19: Strengthen Communications

In my experience, the number-one complaint of employees everywhere is a lack of communication. I want to address the communication issues that I see inside companies that are affecting your ability to implement the other growth accelerators. I will discuss how complexity plays a role in holding your company down. We will cover how communication conditions change performance and the factors that are critical to creating optimal communication conditions.

Do You Want Your Business to Run at Peak Performance?

After reading all this, you may feel overwhelmed. You may even say there is no way your organization can handle it all. Don't sweat it! With a bit of practice, our clients have found that what I have described can be implemented with less effort than what you do today. Some of our clients doubled in size and worked half as much. They just had to change some mindsets and rethink how they ran their companies. My chapter on "meeting rhythms" in *Your Business is a Leaky Bucket* is a secret sauce to making that happen.

The first step toward increasing your business success is: Accurately identify the growth accelerators that need the most attention. Prioritize the five sections, and work on the area that you think has the biggest drag on revenue and profits. When we bring the Business Acceleration System™ to a client, we are careful to make the concepts digestible. Trying to do everything at once is not prudent and will fail. It usually takes at least three years to move toward fully grasping all the concepts in this book. Anyone who tries to short-circuit the process underperforms and lacks the discipline to launch the rocket.

A Strong Business Acceleration System™ Includes the Following Aspects:

1. Regular, strategic discussions throughout the year.
2. A purposeful organization with a strong culture.
3. A healthy, aligned leadership team that understands each other's differences and priorities.
4. Alignment of the entire organization to three-year, one-year, and quarterly plans designed to make significant progress toward your Audacious Goal.
5. An established communication rhythm, where information moves through your organization accurately and quickly.
6. Clear accountability for every role, process, and financial statement line item, ensuring that goals are achieved.
7. A system for collecting and using employee input that generates regular use and is causing meaningful changes to your business.
8. A system for collecting and using customer feedback and data to improve existing operations and for developing new products and services is functioning well.
9. A human capital management system for acquiring, onboarding, growing, developing, retaining, and optimizing your human assets.
10. An innovation process that ensures your business will keep growing long into the future.[2]

You may think this list is extreme. As a business and executive coach, I have found that many of the processes I bring to clients are perceived as obstacles to getting things done rather than the means of achieving the desired results. If implemented in the wrong way, they can be.

For example, do you consider strategic planning, business planning, and meetings a waste of your time? Are you the one in the room trying to rush your meetings to get to what you believe should be the point? If so, you have probably never experienced good meetings and effective planning. If you had, they would be permanent business rituals!

As we delve deeper into the most common growth accelerators, I should mention that there are many companies that have won "Best Place to Work" awards or are on "Fastest-Growing Company" lists or have won numerous other awards that have *not* implemented these growth accelerators. My point: Just because you have not fully implemented an accelerator does not make your company a bad company. It just means you are leaving significant opportunity on the table—and probably causing others in your organization to work harder than is necessary.

MODERN-DAY GROWTH ACCELERATORS

- Stewardship accelerators address the drags on growth, profits, and cash that occur because of leadership deficiencies and failure to establish a meaningful ideological foundation.
- Human Capital Management addresses a company's key people processes.
- Employees are assets managed through a system of activities. Leadership must refine all elements of the system to extend the life of those assets and achieve a maximum return on investment in them.
- Strategy is primarily about how well you have designed your business model.
- Consider whether your company is growing at an acceptably high level, whether this growth rate is predictable, and whether you believe it will continue for the next several years.
- Revenue is vanity, profit is sanity, and cash is king!
- Determine the point at which you will need to consider new products and services because your existing ones have limited potential going forward.
- Planning is about clarifying what is essential. It is about prioritization.
- Planning is a process of understanding what your long-term goals and objectives are for your organization and its stakeholders.
- You must bring the longer-term focus to the present tense and make sure that what you are doing today will lead you to where you want to emerge.

- Accountability accelerators are processes and systems that help focus and align everyone in the company, increasing the likelihood of maximum success. These are the tools that help a company use time and resources efficiently and effectively.

PART II
STEWARDSHIP

**LEADERSHIP
TEAM HEALTH**

**PURPOSE
(WHY)**

**CULTURE
(HOW)**

"Someone is sitting in the shade today because someone planted a tree a long time ago."

— Warren Buffett [1]

CHAPTER 4

Growth Accelerator #1:

REPLACE POOR
MANAGERS

The CEO of a manufacturing company recently approached a coach because he was frustrated by his organization's performance. He knew it was underperforming, failing to achieve his objectives, and had never had positive cash flow. But he could not put his finger on why all this was happening. He thought that implementing our Business Acceleration System™ would make all his problems go away. Little did he know that poor management was the cause, and everything else was effect!

The coach facilitated a three-day retreat with the executive team that made clear why this company was having trouble. The company needed our Business Acceleration System™ to help guide them to make better and faster decisions, create winning strategies, limit the focus on a few key priorities, align everyone, and hold people accountable. However, it faced a bigger problem. The main issue was dysfunction among the leadership team itself. Not surprisingly, the CEO could not see that his behavior was the center of it. He loved to argue every point, hated to lose more than he loved to win, belittled others at every turn, and had to put his stamp on everything.

After several working sessions with the coach, the team came clean and told the CEO how they felt. Rather than taking this as an opportunity to grow and shift, the CEO's ego took hold. He told everyone in the room that he did not believe he needed to change. If they could not stand the heat, they should find another place to work! As his coach tried to show how his people had become "yes" people—the opposite of what he said he wanted—he became even more adamant that maybe they were just the wrong people. We call someone like this, "not coachable." While the coach could help implement the Business Acceleration System™, the effectiveness of the system was severely compromised by the inadequacy of the CEO, leaving an enormous amount of profit and growth potential on the table.

Clearly, poor management creates unbelievably poor results, but this still comes as a surprise to some business leaders. Earlier, we discussed the different mindsets many leaders possess and how those can hold them back. Before I continue further, I must clarify that leadership is a role, not a title. No one is just a leader. Many of us play the roles of leader, manager, or doer. This chapter addresses the role of managers. When a person's primary role in an organization is manager, you must measure how well they perform as a manager. A manager's mindset significantly impacts the general direction and attitude of the entire company.

One mindset is not necessarily better than another, but each manager's style and philosophy come with their own sets of strengths and weaknesses. Team members who look to their managers to lead the charge may be left feeling confused or unsatisfied. These feelings will affect their work production and result in a substantial impact on their engagement and that of others. Steve Jobs said, "Be a yardstick of quality. Some people aren't used to an environment where excellence is expected."[1] The truth is that great managers not only expect success but also create a culture that demands it. To expect anything less is just asking for mediocrity. How you communicate and conduct yourself as a manager can create mediocrity or excellence.

There is empirical data to support our book's assertions. Gallup, Inc., well-known and highly regarded for its ability to conduct research, published an important study, titled *State of the American Workplace*. Its findings and best practices speak to employees' evolving wants and needs. It gives leaders a clear understanding of what it takes to have an exceptional workplace. Gallup developed the study using data collected from more than 195,600 US employers via the Gallup Panel and Gallup Daily tracking in 2015 and 2016, and more than 31 million respondents through Gallup's Q12 Client Database. First launched in 2010, the report is now in its third iteration. This study inspired the work of our organization and our ability to help our clients improve the number of engaged employees! Using this data, we have been able to work with companies and managers, helping them improve in areas essential to igniting mastery of human capital management.[2]

The latest results showed that there were improvements from the last study, but they are not ones to be proud of. Only 33 percent of all workers in the United States are *"engaged employees"*—those who work with passion and feel a profound connection to their companies. Such employees are enthusiastic about their jobs and make their organizations better every day.

While this latest number is the highest in Gallup's 15-plus years of tracking employee engagement, it's not a cause for celebration. Most employees are not engaged and haven't been for some time. With all the money spent on improving the workplace, leadership development, and training, it is clear that the leadership operating systems and philosophies used in most workplaces do not work. Leaders continue to replicate the same broken models and share the same philosophies with each other.[3]

Only 33 Percent of Employees Are Engaged

According to Gallup, a staggering 67 percent of today's workforce in the United States are being paid to be either "*not engaged*" (51 percent) or "*actively disengaged*" (16 percent). To be "not engaged" means they may give you extra effort at times, but could do so more consistently and have a lot more to offer you and your customers. In other words, they are putting time rather than energy or passion into their work. To quote Jim Clifton, Chairman and CEO at Gallup, "they are just there!" The remaining "actively disengaged" employees aren't just miserable at work; they're busy acting out their unhappiness. Every day, these workers undermine what their engaged coworkers accomplish.[4]

What exactly is causing such a significant disconnect? What I learned from this study I wished I had learned much earlier in my career. First, one of the most critical decisions you will make as a leader is who you name as "manager." Second, you need to equip the ones you choose with the right leadership operating systems—to help them become great managers. Gallup's research concluded that employees who are supervised by highly engaged managers are 59 percent more likely to be engaged than those supervised by actively disengaged managers.[5]

We also found that the principles in our book are essential to success. There were many references in the Gallup findings pointing to our framework as solutions to improving employee engagement. The operating system management uses to create a motivational environment for its employees is crucial. For example, the research found that most employees have little belief in their company's leadership:

- Only 22 percent of employees strongly agree the leadership of their organization has a clear direction for the organization.
- Only 15 percent of employees strongly agree the leadership of their organization makes them enthusiastic about the future.

- Only 13 percent of employees strongly agree the leadership of their organization communicates effectively with the rest of the organization.

By implementing the Business Acceleration System™ in your company, we help you instill confidence in everyone, thereby causing more engagement.[6]

When I talk to any business leader and ask them to identify their top obstacles to growth, acquiring new talent is always among their top three issues. With today's historically low levels of unemployment, employee engagement gives you a competitive advantage. Conversely, the more disconnected employees feel, the greater their readiness to job hop. While 37 percent of engaged employees are looking for jobs or watching for opportunities, higher numbers of not-engaged and actively disengaged employees are doing the same (56 percent and 73 percent, respectively). Actively disengaged employees are almost twice as likely as engaged employees to seek new jobs. We have seen that our clients with more highly engaged employees are finding it easier to recruit new employees. They can fill positions faster and have more qualified applicants for each open position when engagement scores are high compared to the competition.[7]

Some leaders and managers believe the ultimate goal of employee engagement is to achieve higher levels of worker happiness and satisfaction. Happier workers certainly benefit an organization, but the real goal of employee engagement is improved business outcomes. Engaged employees contribute to the economic health of their company in ways that other employees do not. Gallup estimates that actively disengaged employees cost the United States $483 billion to $605 billion in lost productivity each year. Business or work units that score in the top quartile in their organization in employee engagement have nearly double the odds of success. Highly engaged business units experience:

- 41 percent reduction in absenteeism and a 17 percent increase in productivity.
- 28 percent reduction in shrinkage (the dollar amount of unaccounted-for lost merchandise) and a 40 percent reduction in quality defects.
- 70 percent decrease in employee safety incidents and a 58 percent decrease in patient safety incidents.
- 10 percent increase in customer metrics.
- 20 percent increase in sales.
- 21 percent greater profitability.[8]

Engaging employees takes work and commitment, but it's not impossible. One-third of the overall US workforce is engaged, but many companies have much lower percentages. The average engagement level among our first-year clients is below 20 percent. As we help them shift their approach, these organizations begin to realize improvements in performance. The average engagement scores among all our highest performing clients have engagement scores above 50 percent. This compares with a national average of 10 percent employee engagement. I mention this so you won't be discouraged by the data. By applying the concepts in this book, you can become an exception to the data. Recognizing a lack of engagement and committing to action to improve the percentage of engaged employees are essential steps forward.[9]

How Do You Measure Manager Performance?

Do any of your managers act in a way that might cause otherwise engaged employees to become not engaged or actively disengaged? You must ask some fundamental questions: Do you have any poor managers? How do you currently measure manager performance? In what ways might you be causing the problems you see and blaming them on your subordinates, like the CEO in the example at the beginning of the chapter?

I find it baffling that while managers receive the largest salaries, they are the people who are measured and held accountable the least! Ask yourself whether you've set two or three key performance indicators that each manager is responsible for improving. When they don't take those crucial steps, do you fire them? Do you focus on the goals or methods used to achieve them? You probably do not. It is easy to hire people we perceive to be great managers and then shift our attention elsewhere. We assume they will just get the job done, but there is no justification for that belief.

My opening example may not convince you of the point of this chapter, so let me give you a little more information.

For a brief period, the coach in that example—me—had some very uncomfortable discussions with the CEO, although I was able to help his company become cash-flow positive. The CEO fired me anyway. He explained that if he'd realized he was going to be asked to change, he would never have hired me. After we parted ways, the company promptly ran into cash-flow problems, continued to struggle for 18 months after I left, and is still struggling today.

Another example of what happens when you don't replace a poor manager comes from a discussion I had with the CEO of a midmarket company about his chief financial officer. He said the CFO was a great performer. He went on to say that he liked the CFO because he worked hard, cared about the company, and was intellectually smart. The CFO said the right things, came from a great background, had all the appropriate certifications, and provided sound financial counsel. Of course, those attributes are the basic requirements and expectations for any CFO. This CFO did not excel in any area. He maintained the status quo and got the job done, but only barely.

The CEO ignored the fact that his CFO was only performing in one aspect of his job! He demonstrated strong financial acumen and had shown he could be a good financial advisor to the CEO. The CEO did not pay attention to the numerous attributes the CFO lacked as a manager, including:

- For an entire year, the CFO had failed to deliver any of the department priorities identified as crucial to the company rising to the next level.
- It took 45 days from month's end to close the books. In other words, the management team was always relying on outdated financial data to make its decisions.
- The entire team reporting to the CFO had been identified as poor performers who did not live the core values of the company. The CFO had done nothing to replace any of them, even after acknowledging that they were not performing and having to compensate for their lack of performance by hiring other workers.
- On more than one occasion, the CEO had been forced to create analytics on his own because he could not depend on the CFO or the accounting department to get it done.
- The CFO was consistently condescending to the rest of the management team, which they did not appreciate.
- The CFO struggled with understanding things from other people's points of view. Worse, he saw no need to do so.
- When others made valuable contributions in meetings, he would demean the importance of their comments.
- His team members did not care for him and only tolerated him because they had to. As a result, they would try to avoid him when making critical decisions rather than seek him out for his financial acumen.

By allowing such a weak leader to continue, a CEO communicated to his team that the inept person designated to lead has more to offer than everyone else put together—always a poor implication. The number-one priority as a manager must be to get, keep, and grow a team of people who perform at levels that exceed the competition. It is a best practice to measure your managers' performances on the basis of their recruiting, coaching, developing, motivating, and nurturing people! If you use the wrong standards, you shouldn't then expect the right behaviors.

Alignment is key to the overall accomplishment of business goals. To help with this, ensure that each individual manager reports their group's objectives to the CEO. This approach will support the notion that the entire team is moving in the same and right direction.

Inept managers cause everyone around them to perform at lower levels, and you then lose access to a lot of great ideas. People are less apt to willingly give extra effort when they feel it either won't be noticed or doesn't matter in the first place. If you have a manager on your team who is not able to get top performances from his or her team, stop harassing the frontline people and address your real issue: management.

A Person's Character Is the Foundation of Great Leaders

Consider all the leaders you have encountered in government, schools, jobs, and organizations. How many of them have you thought of as excellent or even above average? Recently, I have been pondering why there are so few contemporary leaders I admire and perceive as great. What surprises me is that while they may be hardworking, determined, wealthy, smart, and considered successful in many ways, I still do not see them as great leaders.

With so many books written and courses offered on leadership and leadership training, we still lack great leadership everywhere. The books have great content, and the training was valuable, yet something is missing! What's become evident is that we may be focusing on the wrong attributes. Furthermore, there is no single, recognized standard as to what it means to be a great leader! You can go through the motions and activities of leadership and still fail as a leader.

Some people believe leadership is a title. But we do not need a title to lead, and we can have a title and not be an effective leader. This was well illustrated by the high school students from Parkland, Florida, after the horrific mass shooting that occurred in 2018. Many students took leadership into their own hands and had a significant impact on our nation. The fact is that one can lead every day of their life.

Some people believe great leadership is about achieving outcomes. However, the focus on results has caused many leaders to go to great lengths to produce them at any cost. Notable examples in recent times are the Wells Fargo fake accounts, Bernie Madoff's Ponzi scheme, and Cambridge Analytica's use of our records on Facebook. These are extreme cases, but to what extent do outcomes outweigh someone's impact on others and society? Where does personal conduct come to present itself? Think about Bill Cosby and Harvey Weinstein. We need to place weight on how leaders affect the trust and confidence of others along the way as we measure their accomplishments. While results are essential, we must place equal or greater importance on how one obtained the results, how that leader has impacted others, and how they have conducted themselves—both publicly and privately.

After evaluating hundreds of leaders, I identified the critical attribute of some great ones: Abraham Lincoln, Nelson Mandela, Margaret Thatcher, and Warren Buffett. We are far more fascinated by them as people than by their accomplishments and the impact they have had on society. Our interest has more to do with how they conducted themselves over a lifetime. We call this *character*! They are not perfect, and each has had missteps and done things people disagree with, but these are people of tremendous character.

Let me share the five character traits I look for in leaders to define them as great. I think you will agree that Lincoln, Mandela, Thatcher, and Buffett demonstrate these.

The first trait is *integrity*. Do the right thing always. Integrity is being able to put your self-interests aside and take the right action. Too many people choose their own interests without hesitation and then act surprised by the suggestion that anyone else would consider another choice. I tell my team members not to do anything they would be embarrassed to read about on the front page of a newspaper or on social media.

The second character trait for great leaders is *humility*. **Be humble and curious; it is essential.** People who lack humility think that only an elite few, if any, have contributed to their success. Great leaders realize that their success is a consequence of efforts by many others, if not all, the people in their lives. When you are humble, you continually examine others' ideas and methods because you know you can always get better. To me, this is quite possibly the most potent character trait.

The third character trait for great leaders is *expressing care*. **Show everyone that they are special.** You must care for others; everyone deserves it. Too many leaders believe they are entitled to be cared for, but when it comes to giving care, they dole it out as if there is a class system, and then are surprised by the repercussions. Great leaders have the extraordinary ability to put themselves in the place of another, to empathize with what others are feeling, and to understand others' motives and desires. Weak leaders are oblivious to other points of view— nor do they care about them.

The fourth character trait is *consistency*. **Be reliable and predictable.** When you have someone in your life you find unreliable and unpredict- able, someone who has been known to demonstrate erratic behavior, how does that make you feel? Dealing with someone whose response is inconsistent causes stress and disharmony. Imagine spending every day consumed with worry about what the leader is going to do. So much time is wasted discussing what these people have done or might do next; it is unproductive. But when someone gives and keeps his or her word, is reliable and predictable, it allows you to feel free to operate at full capacity, be creative and confident, and reach your full potential.

The fifth character trait is *influence*. **Have a positive impact on others.** This last trait is important because it demonstrates that a leader is there to serve others, not themself. Poor leaders believe that others are there to help *them*. They try to figure out how to use people to their advantage.

Influence is the ultimate superpower. Great leaders go big or go home. Their influence is not just on a small team. They impact their communities and perhaps the world.

A person's character is the only way to measure great leadership. Earlier in the chapter, I mentioned that we all fulfill multiple roles. Every employee may have to act as a leader at a given time. Therefore, we all must demonstrate good character. The beautiful thing is that we can choose whether we want to have integrity, be respectful, have humility, be consistent, be influential—or not. In every interaction, we have a choice. Lincoln, Mandela, Thatcher, and Buffett spent lifetimes choosing to demonstrate these traits; there is no reason you cannot make the same choices. Managers must set an example for their subordinates!

Can Actions Be Taken?

Managers are responsible for people, functional roles, and processes. You need to set your managers up for success. Accomplish this by clarifying the following for every manager in the organization:

1. The essential character traits needed to excel as a manager;
2. Where the company is headed;
3. Long- and short-term goals to be achieved;
4. How they contribute—their key accountabilities and the key performance indicators measuring successful outcomes; why do they get paid?
5. Key people and processes for which they are accountable.

Who you name as manager may be one of the most important decisions you ever make. Getting these decisions right is crucial to the engagement of many others in your organization. It is important to know when a team is floundering under a manager and take swift action regarding that manager. The action may be some form of developmental coaching, demotion, or removal from your organization. Taking no action will be very costly to your company.

Key Points for Chapter 4, Growth Accelerator #1

REPLACE POOR MANAGERS

- Only 33 percent of all workers in the United States are "engaged employees."
- Engaged employees work with passion and feel a profound connection to their companies. These employees are enthusiastic about and committed to their work and workplace.
- 67 percent of today's workforce in the United States are being paid to be "not engaged" or "actively disengaged."
- A staggering 51 percent of employees are "not engaged," meaning they may give you extra effort at times, but they could do that more consistently and have a lot more to offer you and your customers.
- The remaining 16 percent are "actively disengaged." These employees aren't just miserable at work; they're busy acting out their unhappiness. Every day, these workers undermine what their engaged coworkers accomplish.
- Employees who are supervised by highly engaged managers are 59 percent more likely to be engaged than those supervised by actively disengaged managers.
- The operating system that management uses to create a motivational environment for your employees is crucial. Gallup's research found that employees have little belief in their company's leadership.
- The more disconnected employees feel, the greater their readiness to job hop. While 37 percent of engaged employees are looking for jobs or watching for opportunities, higher numbers of not-engaged and actively disengaged employees are doing the same (56 percent and 73 percent).

- The real goal of employee engagement is to improve business outcomes.
- If you measure managers by the wrong attributes, you shouldn't expect the right behaviors.
- Every manager must have two or three key performance indicators that measure how effective he or she is as a manager.
- Inept managers cause everyone around them to perform at lower levels, and you then lose access to a lot of great ideas.
- Being smart, knowing an industry, working hard, having excellent communication skills, and being able to get things done all make for a good team member, but many times do not produce a great manager.
- A person's character is the only way to measure great leadership, which is the role each manager plays.
- The five character traits of great leaders are integrity, humility, expressing care, consistency, and influence.
- The primary responsibility of a manager is to coach, mentor, and nurture an environment where employees can stay motivated and do their best work.

BUSINESS ACCELERATION CALCULATOR™

Now it's time to pause and determine what failure to Replace Poor Managers costs your company. Go to www.howardmshore.com/tools and request our *Business Acceleration Tools*® to gain access to the *Business Acceleration Calculator*™ in both Excel and printable formats. I prefer the Excel version for this tool because it does all the calculations for you. This tool will help you keep track of all the leaks you find in your business as you continue to read this book.

Leadership is a very costly issue, and the more senior leadership, the more expensive it is. Smart & Associates claims to have done more studies on the costs of "mis-hiring" than any other organization. Based on their studies, they have determined the cost of a mis-hire to be as follows:[10]

LEVEL	COST VS. BASE SALARY
Supervisor	4 x base salary
Middle Manager	8 x base salary
Vice President	15 x base salary
Executive	27 x base salary

With this as a reference point, it is time to fill out the *Business Acceleration Calculator*™. Go to the tool, fill in the row, and follow the instructions for Leaders Not Performing. We are conservative and recommend you use a multiple of five in the *Calculator*.

Contact Me

As you apply the concepts and see the differences they make, please email me at howard@howardmshore.com to let me know what you did and how it worked. I wrote this book to have an impact, and it will make my day to see that I have done so.

CHAPTER 5
Growth Accelerator #2:
ADDRESS TEAM
DYSFUNCTION

Having identified how important selecting the right leaders is to grow your company, and having described a CEO whose ego caused him to be "not coachable," I now want to address team dysfunction and leadership issues that are counterproductive to teamwork. A dysfunctional team will have the most significant effect on your ability to maximize success and will compromise your ability to implement all the other principles in this book. These issues can be addressed with coaching—*if* the "students" are willing participants.

Your Company Is Made Up of Teams

Once you go past being a solopreneur, everything your organization does depends on teamwork. Every process, whether it is sales, production, manufacturing, administration, or service involves multiple people. Whether those people recognize it or not, they are a team. Most if not all the people in your company are involved in multiple teams. Effective teamwork determines how fast your company will grow and how profitable it can be.

While there are many factors that affect your teamwork, the primary hurdles I find compromising teams and their ability to implement our Business Acceleration principles are trust, ego, and one's ability to interact with others.

Trust Is Foundational

Imagine you are playing basketball. You are in the fourth quarter with 30 seconds left on the clock, and your team is down by one point. To win, it's critical to count on all the other team members to deliver a 100 percent effort. Visualize being part of a team where you can rely on any player's ability to make that final shot versus being on a team where you don't know if all the players can and will step up. When you need to stop the opponent from scoring before you get the chance to take that final shot, you must be able to depend on your team to play tough defense and get the ball back. How would you perform if you felt like someone on the team was not pulling his or her weight?

Every day distrust occurs in the workplace. If you do not work on building trust, you cannot maximize the performance of your organization. Trust starts with the premise that one's peers' intentions are good, and that there is no reason to "be careful" around group members. Once trust is violated, it is hard to re-establish; the violation is difficult to overcome.

In most teams, too much time and energy—and too many good ideas—are wasted trying to protect reputations by managing behaviors, comments, and interactions caused by a lack of trust created in previous communications. People are reluctant to ask for help and to help others, causing lower morale and unwanted turnover.

Distrusting others also causes people to create poor work behaviors. They choose to do things themselves instead of delegating. Or they take work away from others who don't act the way they like or seemingly aren't delivering on their promises. Worse, they may even set lower goals for themselves so they know they can be achieved without the assistance of others. All these behaviors could be avoided by addressing the trust issues head-on.

To address a lack of trust on a team, leaders must demonstrate vulnerability first, make sure they are authentic, and use proper timing when doing so. They must encourage open dialogue in meetings, look for behavior that demonstrates distrust, and bring trust issues into the open. They need to have everyone openly discuss the strength each team member brings to the team. They also need to describe behaviors that lead them to be distrustful and get them to address those behaviors. No one, including the CEO, is immune from this exercise. One bad apple will spoil the barrel.

Do you have absolute trust among your ownership and leadership teams? Do not answer too quickly. Every organization tells me they have trust; most do not. I've not seen published research about how much money organizations lose every year through lack of trust, but my experience shows that you can increase your revenue and profits substantially by facing and solving this issue. Cracks in trust undermine the foundation of teamwork and make it impossible to achieve peak performance in any organization.

Ironically, many owners tell me there is trust among the leadership team, but it breaks down below that level. In my experience, they are fooling themselves. This self-deception is why they have such a problem with the rest of their organization. I am working on this exact situation now with a client company. Each of the owners has confided in me the concerns they have about the others, and all have told me that I could not bring the issues out in the open.

In his book, *Five Dysfunctions of a Team*, Pat Lencioni points out that trust is the foundation of a strong team. He lists the five dysfunctions in a pyramid in the following order: 1) trust, 2) fear of conflict, 3) lack of commitment, 4) avoidance of accountability, and 5) inattention to results. One way to analyze whether your group has a problem with trust and teamwork is to watch your meetings and ask yourself these questions:

- Does everyone on the team look forward to these meetings?
- Is everyone actively engaged in the meetings?
- Is there a healthy debate on the issues brought up, or are people just being told what to do?
- Are people committed to decisions made at the meetings, or do they have to be asked repeatedly to follow through?
- Are team members holding each other accountable?
- Is there a clear plan of action and scorecard created to hold each other accountable?

- How much attention is given to individual needs (ego, recognition, etc.) as opposed to the goals of the team?

Getting back to George and John, I spent six hours with both, discussing significant issues I'd found in their business. John, the VP of Sales, barely spoke. George, the CEO, disagreed with most of my findings, deciding in advance that none of the suggested remedies would work in his business or his industry. These are common answers from people who do not trust and always need to be right. However, when a recommendation was consistent with something he had already concluded, he agreed with me. Again, while all this was going on, John rarely spoke. That confirmed to me that there is a significant trust issue between the partners.

Whenever George wanted to disagree with me, he would hammer me. If arguing from a weak position, he would turn to John and say, "Don't you agree with me?" With weak conviction and eyes averted, John would say yes. That showed me they were not willing to be vulnerable in front of each other. The clincher came at the end of the meeting. George called me aside to ask for some additional information, which I agreed to deliver the following week. Before leaving, I went to John's office to see if he could be available for next week's meeting. John asked, "What could he possibly want to do with that information?" When I pointed out that this was the list of accountabilities that George was going to agree and commit to assigning to him, John murmured under his breath "that will never happen. He is a control freak and will never give anything up." He then confided how he despised George, hated to come to work, and felt trapped.

According to Pat Lencioni, you know you have a good team when:

1. Everyone says they "unequivocally trust one another."
2. They engage in unfiltered, healthy conflict around ideas.

3. They commit to decisions and plans of action.
4. They hold one another accountable for those actions and plans.
5. They focus on the achievement of collective results.[1]

Ego Will Crush Teamwork

In Chapter 4, the CEO's ego caused our entire process to break down. He was the central cause of leadership dysfunction. After more than 35 years in the workforce, I determined the number-one hindrance to peak performance is ego. While you undoubtedly agree with me (and are probably thinking, "duh"), ego problems are the least-dealt-with issue in most organizations, and are the most severe the higher up we go. This is significant because top-tier leaders have more impact on their organizations than do their subordinates. When you have a senior leader with an overinflated ego, business life is a train wreck! It is an issue at all levels of an organization.

In keeping with the core values at my firm, we keep an eye out for anyone we deem to have an overinflated ego. We also look for clients with balanced levels of ego because we find we can achieve a much higher level of success for them (which is also a much higher level of success for us).

If you have not already read it, *The Ideal Team Player* by Pat Lencioni should be at the top of your must-read list. He recounts a story about leaders who discover the three virtues that are necessary to avoid having a**holes working for them. (Apologies for the language, but that was the storyline.) He correctly identifies that you are not an ideal team player if you do not possess three virtues: humility, hunger, and common sense about how to interpersonally deal with people. The leaders in Lencioni's book describe people who lack humility and interpersonal skills as "bulldozers." Imagine their effects on employee engagement, turnover, and productivity. There is no way any organization could operate near its peak performance under a leader with these characteristics. Worse, it would be hard for you to recruit top talent or talent in general. Who wants to work for a "bulldozer?"[2]

Are You Even Aware that Your Ego Is Causing a Problem?

Many people do not recognize when their egos are clouding their judgment, swaying decision making, causing favoritism, inciting organizational strife, stifling teamwork, and causing high turnover rates. They refuse to consider the ideas of others and, in many cases, do nothing because they are afraid to be wrong. Ego is a blinder and a form of self-sabotage. It stops people from accurately processing information and seeing the world as it is. In some cases, leaders are so self-absorbed and blinded by the beauty of their names in lights that they fail to realize it is not all about them. They fail to see that others contributed to their results, that others are not there to extol the leader's greatness, and that their job as a leader is to bring out the best in others.

My company asks these questions of each member of the leadership team when we assess a client company's issues:

- Do you easily compliment or praise teammates without hesitation?
- Do you readily admit mistakes?
- Do you easily take on lower-level work for the good of the team?
- How easily do you defer credit to the team for accomplishments?
- Do you readily acknowledge and seek help for your weaknesses?
- Do you offer and accept apologies graciously?

If your colleagues do not indicate that you "usually" act in that manner for each of these questions, you are the one with an ego problem.[3]

I recently heard a speech by Jeff Hoffman, co-founder of Priceline.com. He related a story about a time when a new employee joined the company. Jeff came into the office, approached the new employee, who did not know who he was, and watched the employee do his work. He was impressed by the entry-level employee's work and was proud of the hire that his leaders had made. He asked the person his name and if there was anything he could do for him to help him be more productive for the day. The employee whipped out a dry-cleaning ticket and told Hoffman that he could pick up his dry cleaning. Jeff took the ticket and went out the door. His leaders scurried after him, apologizing and explaining that the new employee had no idea who he was, and asking Jeff if he was leaving because he was super-angry. Jeff said no; he was leaving because the new hire was doing fantastic work and they needed to keep him doing that crucial work, so he was going to get the dry cleaning. Jeff believed that he was there to serve his employees, not the other way around.

Two Types of Ego Issues

There are two primary ways in which the ego manifests itself. The first is when people think too highly of themselves. These people spend a lot of their time making sure everyone knows how great they are, that they are front and center. You get to hear their incredible opinions, listen to them take credit for every success, see them post pictures every two minutes on Facebook and Instagram to show you everywhere they are, who they're with, and their latest recognized accomplishment. Pat Lencioni refers to this as "false pride."[4]

Conversely, the second ego issue is fear or self-doubt, which is when people think less of themselves than they should and are consumed with their shortcomings. In many cases, these people can be more damaging than the false-pride folks because they significantly erode their effectiveness or the effectiveness of their departments. A common occurrence here is a leader that is extremely slow or fails to make tough decisions. Ego is the common root cause.

One of the most difficult challenges for leaders is to remain grounded in the face of success. When everyone defers to you, it must be tempting to start believing your press releases. It is easy to think, I am smarter, more charismatic, and more powerful than everyone else. When leaders reach the point where they believe their opinion matters more than anyone else's, they stop listening to everyone else. That means they stop learning. Leaders dominated by false pride are often called *controllers*. Even when they don't know what they are doing, they have a high need for power and control.[5]

As an executive coach, I've encountered many CEOs who believe their people cannot possibly decide on anything without them. They become bottlenecks in their organizations because everything must flow through them. They honestly think they're right every time; that every change they've made to a document was crucial to its success; that they are the best at selecting new employees; and that they are experts at every function in the company. This is buffoonery, of course, but they cannot see it. They can see everyone else's mistakes but not their own. The organization spends its days cleaning up their leader's messes, doing double and triple the work, and keeping their ideas to themselves because no one else's views count.

At the other end of the spectrum are the fear-driven managers, often characterized as *do-nothing bosses*. They are often described as never around, always avoiding conflict, and not very helpful. They usually leave their team members alone, even when these individuals are insecure and need help. Do-nothing bosses don't believe in themselves or trust their judgment. They value others' thoughts more than their own, especially views from those they report to. Thus, they rarely speak out and support their team members.[6]

Leaders with low ego strength are more common than you think! Our coaches work closely with these leaders to understand why they don't decide to act. For example,

> *Last year, one of our coaches had a client that knew he needed to address the compensation of three of his primary leaders. The CEO identified he had made a mistake in structuring their current compensation, and was far overpaying them for the value they brought to the company. He knew their compensation had to be adjusted, was not quite sure how to restructure it, and came to his coach as he processed the problem. After reviewing the issue with his coach on numerous occasions, he developed a clear action plan, and had no doubt it was the right plan. But this particular CEO had a strong need for approval from his team. While he had great business sense, his need to be liked by his team was more important to him than making the correct business decision. One year after identifying this issue, he has still failed to take appropriate action.*

Solutions to the Ego Barrier

The great thing about the "ego" trap is that it's a coachable issue. Of course, people are only coachable if they are open to input and willing to change. If your "problem child" is not, then you need to fire him or her; such a person is what I call "not coachable." The more senior in role, the more damage this person can cause. I have witnessed many CEOs and senior leaders act like lids to organizations that have amazing potential because their egos are the size of Alaska.

In *The Ideal Team Player*, Lencioni suggests we make the three virtues—humility, hunger, and common sense—mandatory in our organizations. If someone is not willing to be coached and does not address his or her humility problem, I would advise removing that individual from the organization. In the long run, such people will cost far more than they are worth. They make everyone else less effective, and no one person is worth more than the many. If you happen to be subordinate to a person like this, and there is no chance they will be replaced (because the individual is the owner or CEO), then you should probably leave the organization. You will never receive the appreciation you deserve. Ego-driven leaders take credit when things go well and blame everyone else when they don't. As a result, you can expect constant turnover because no one will ever be good enough. The ego-driven leader will always cause unnecessary drama for you and other teammates, and there are always more pleasant places to work. Life is too short, and you deserve better!

If you want to address the ego barriers, here are some practical suggestions:

- **If you suffer fear or self-doubt, it is essential to identify the causes of your insecurity.** Work backward in time to discover when it started and how it manifested. Whatever the origins, it is often helpful to share your issue(s) with your teammates and manager and ask them for help to overcome them. While this seems counterintuitive, it is often liberating when you share it with others. You will usually receive a lot of empathy and support, and it makes it easier for others to coach you through it once they realize you are aware of your issues and want help.

- **Practice giving credit to others.** Giving credit to others helps break your habit of taking credit for everything. A great exercise every leader should practice is to find a least one genuine compliment you can give to at least one employee daily. Keep track and see how many times you give praise versus criticism daily; it is instructive. Leaders who lack humility struggle with this one at first. I remember a client with over 60 employees who refused to do this exercise—even after company culture survey results indicated that employees felt they rarely, if ever, received praise from managers. In this person's mind, it was the equivalent of giving everyone a trophy just for showing up to work. The CEO felt that it was not appropriate to compliment someone for doing their job. You will not be surprised to learn that this organization receives very low employee engagement scores every year and has a severe problem recruiting new employees.

- **Be vulnerable.** People cannot relate to superheroes. Recognize and acknowledge your weaker points. On a piece of paper, identify the skills you need to improve. Identify the behaviors that get in your way. Next, draw four squares on a piece of paper. In Square 1, list activities in the company that you are great at and love to do. In Square 2, list the activities you do that you are great at but don't like to do. In Square 3, make a list of the activities you are *not* good at but like to do. In Square 4, list the activities you do that you are not good at and don't like to do. If you do not have a fair number of items in Squares 2, 3, and 4, you either were not brutally honest or lack awareness. Next, sit down with your team and share with them what you have learned. Show your humility by immediately delegating everything in Squares 3 and 4 to others who can do those items substantially faster and better than you. Stop meddling. Ask your teammates if they agree with you regarding your strengths in Squares 1 and 2 and be willing to hear them out. Delegate anything that is transferred to Squares 3 or 4 as a result of that conversation. Then figure out what's still in Square 2 that can be given to someone else.

- **Seek mentorship.** Find at least three people you trust to serve as mentors. Choose mentors you can trust to tell you the truth even when it hurts. Commit to listening to their opinions with an open mind. I participate in two peer groups that have immensely helped me to grow. Sometimes I don't like what they have to say, but I need the kick in the rump.

Strength in Dealing with People

The second most crucial issue I see holding back organizations is how leaders treat their people. In Lencioni's *The Ideal Team Player*, the essential virtue of common sense about people, which he calls "smart," includes how to be interpersonally appropriate and aware in individual and group situations.[7]

I agree with Lencioni that this is an essential component in teamwork and being a leader. I believe there is another dimension to address, namely the leader's biases when they view subordinates and colleagues in general.

First, let's address the leader's common sense about people. Much has been written about *emotional intelligence*, but not enough has been done to apply it. Let's examine how most leaders have been selected in your organization (and countless others). Often, people who get the most attention are those who appear to be the hardest workers, those with the most industry knowledge or highest technical acumen, people you may feel comfortable with, and those who have been with the company the longest. "Soft skill" qualities like common sense or emotional intelligence are nominally identified as necessary but are often considered secondary.

Now consider how often you have seen leaders who are horrible communicators, cause tons of drama, and directly create the most turnover. They survive year after year because they deliver acceptable results or are coveted for the reasons described above. They are considered irreplaceable because of their customer relationships, contacts, or institutional knowledge. In the end, that individual's horrible interpersonal skills severely constrain your company. When top management decides that this one person is more valuable than the many being adversely affected, the many become demoralized, less productive, and less engaged.

By tolerating one person's mistreatment of others, the top tier communicates that being a jerk is okay. It indicates that treating people with dignity, respect, and character does not affect results. It validates a toxic culture, suggesting we should not care about the feelings of others. Just focus on results, because that is all we care about. If you deliver results, you are untouchable. Terrible. Is this the way you want your employees to view your corporate culture?

The Key Is Assertive Communication

Assertive communication is the ability to express positive and negative ideas and feelings in an open, honest and direct way. We are communicating our position while respecting that of others. It allows us to take responsibility for ourselves and our actions without judging or blaming other people.

I am sure if I audited your company, I would find at least one leader who has poor emotional intelligence, and you are tolerating it. Many times, it is the CEO who feels entitled to misbehave and does not understand, care, or face how much it costs the company. In our experience, allowing someone to torment their coworkers emotionally will cost you at least 2.5 times the salary of the tormentor. In other words, if you are paying a jerk $100,000, it costs you at least $250,000 in repercussions. It is a costly issue if you have many people like this.

As an executive and business coach, I witness this issue daily in every client organization. What I find frustrating is that leaders allow this dysfunction to continue. However, improving your decision making, leadership team chemistry, and organizational effectiveness can be achieved by merely helping that emotionally ignorant leader understand how to use the right communication style. An *assertive communication style* rarely results in the negative issues described above.

The degree of assertiveness you use in dealing with people provokes predictable reactions in others, which in turn helps determine how effective you are as a leader. *Assertive communication* is characterized by honesty. It enforces rules, requires results, and is a direct approach that shows concern for yourself and others. It communicates the message that "you are both okay."

This communication style involves treating all the individuals involved as equal, each deserving of respect, with one no more entitled than another to have things done their way. You feel connected to others when you are speaking to them and signify that you are trying to help them take control of their lives. You address issues and problems as they arise and create environments where others can grow.

The reason assertive communication is so effective is that it combines the positive dimensions of both aggressive and passive communicators. The assertive communicator is goal-oriented and direct and is also a good listener, considerate, and thoughtful. Thus, the assertive leader bridges the most positive aspects of the two other styles of behavior—aggressive and passive communication styles—while at the same time avoiding the negative issues of those two styles. The assertive style is both an excellent human relations style and effective team-building style for any organization. The assertive leader is viewed as someone strong, energetic, and both able and willing to fight for the resources needed by the department. Moreover, the assertive leader does not appear to play favorites, since they do not bend the rules or fail to enforce the rules to be liked by others. Team members and other employees most admire this leadership style, which is the best one for the health of your business.

In conclusion, let's consider the following: In too many cases, when we are deciding whether or not a person is a "performer," we look at that person only through the lens of individual performance and forget to look at them through a team context lens. Once we use both lenses in our evaluation, a substantial number of individuals will need to be moved from "performer" to "not performing." Not recognizing the team context is very costly.

ADDRESS TEAM DYSFUNCTION

- Effective teamwork determines how fast your company will grow and how profitable it can be.
- Business Acceleration principles address trust, ego, and one's ability to interact with others.
- "Trust" starts with the premise that one's peers' intentions are good, and there is no reason to be careful around group members.
- Distrust occurs in the workplace every day. If you do not work on building trust, you cannot maximize the performance of your organization.
- To address this lack of trust on a team, leaders must demonstrate vulnerability first and make sure they are authentic and use good timing when doing so.
- Cracks in trust undermine the foundation of teamwork and make it impossible to achieve peak performance in your organization.
- Read *Five Dysfunctions of a Team* by Pat Lencioni.
- One way to find out if your group has a problem with trust and teamwork is to observe behavior at your meetings.
- The number-one hindrance to peak performance is ego.
- Read *The Ideal Team Player* by Pat Lencioni.
- People who lack humility and interpersonal skills are often called "bulldozers."
- Ego is a blinder and a form of self-sabotage.
- You have an ego problem if your colleagues would not "strongly agree" with the following statements:

  » You easily compliment or praise teammates without hesitation.
  » You easily admit mistakes.
  » You easily accept lower-level work for the good of the team.

- » You easily defer credit to the team for accomplishments.
- » You easily acknowledge and seek help for your weaknesses.
- » You offer and accept apologies graciously.

- Two primary ways in which ego manifests itself:
  - » When people think too highly of themselves; false pride. They are often called "controllers."
  - » Fear or self-doubt—when you think less of yourself than you should and are consumed with your shortcomings; fear-driven managers, often characterized as "do-nothing bosses."

- Ego traps are coachable only when the student is a willing participant.
- In *The Ideal Team Player*, Lencioni suggests we make the three virtues (humble, hungry, and common sense, or "smart") mandatory in our organizations.
- If you are sincerely interested in addressing your ego barrier, here are some practical suggestions for enhancing your humility:
  - » If you suffer fear or self-doubt, it is essential to identify the cause of your insecurity.
  - » Practice giving credit to others.
  - » Be vulnerable.
  - » Seek mentorship.

- The second most crucial issue I see holding back organizations is how leaders treat their subordinates.
- In our experience, allowing someone to torment coworkers emotionally costs you at least 2.5 times the salary of the tormentor.
- The assertive communicator is goal-oriented and direct but, at the same time, is a good listener, considerate, and thoughtful.

CHAPTER 6
Growth Accelerator #3:
ESTABLISH A CLEAR AND COMPELLING PURPOSE

To this point, we have discussed the importance of having the right leaders and having a well-functioning team to help accelerate your organization. Another element to master in your role as a company steward is to establish a clear and compelling purpose. I recommend that you identify your purpose from the day you start your business and place that purpose at its forefront. As you develop and grow, be sure to maintain that vision and mission through thick and thin. Leaders who are determined to achieve their purpose fly higher and farther than those who worry about how much money they want to make.[1]

Why Purpose Matters

Purpose is like a lantern in a dark cave, guiding you through the unknown and helping you reach your destination safely. Many business owners mistakenly believe their purpose is to make money or create a financial gain. Maybe you're thinking, *isn't that the purpose of being in a for-profit business?* That may be one of your goals, but I can confidently say that making money is not aligned with a proper and meaningful purpose. By serving a purpose well and doing it profitably, you *will* make money. Remember, the more critical your overall purpose, and the better it can serve your community at large, the more money you can ultimately make by striving to fulfill it.[2]

If I met you at a party and asked you to tell me about your business, where would you start? Most people default to discussing their role, title, and function, or the product or service they offer. For example, one person might tell me they are the managing partner in an accounting firm, or a tax accountant, or an auditor. A CEO might say to me she owns a company that manufactures retail skin-care products. However, no matter how hard they sell it, those are merely titles and roles, not the purpose of their business.[3]

There is an oversupply of just about every conceivable product and service. Think about it. When was the last time you thought, "There isn't a tax accountant, lawyer, or banker to be found anywhere?" You never hear someone say, "I wish I had more choices of toothpaste, chips, hair gel, coffee, or skin-care products. There are just not enough of them." There is an overabundance of products and services. They are available everywhere you go, as well as online and over the phone, and can be delivered 24 hours a day, seven days a week.[4]

Now imagine that the people I spoke to at the party had a different view of their business purpose. As an example, let's look at an accounting firm focused on *increasing the wealth of its clients*. This firm builds a set of practice areas in tax, audit, technology, wealth management, and so on. To do so, they create a team for each client that uses the strengths of each team member to devise the best annual strategy to help maximize that client's wealth. While every sizeable firm may have the same practice areas, this firm's view of what they are doing and why they exist is the difference-maker for their business. It causes them to forge a nontraditional client relationship structure. To achieve their purpose, they must build specialized toolkits, focus on unique resources, and treat their clients with defined intentions. Not every accounting firm is creating the kind of relationship with their clients that would produce such positive outcomes, thereby leaving valuable opportunity on the table.[5]

Establishing your purpose allows you to address the essential questions:

1. What is the primary difference you want your organization to make for your community of clients?
2. How is that community being served, and what would be lost without your organization?
3. What will your client relationships and experience need to look like?
4. What boundaries and rules must you learn to break?
5. Why will the best employees want to work for you rather than your competition?[6]

The answers to these questions will unlock doors that would otherwise remain closed. They will reveal a great opportunity. By defining these answers, you can begin to recognize great results never thought possible.[7]

What Does It Mean to Act with Purpose?

When you act with purpose, you respond with more energy and enthusiasm. You are probably willing to give more effort to something that matters to you! Compare that kind of drive and persistence to the effort you'd be willing to give to accomplish something that may be important but does not pull at your heartstrings. Consider what your commitment would be to an endeavor that has not captured your mind or heart. You would go through the motions. Repeatedly, I find that when employees are not engaged, it is because they lack this crucial impetus. It would be safe to say their leaders have failed to instill purpose.[8]

When your work is not just about the revenue or the profit, it is much more satisfying. The purpose does not change the work, but it does inspire it. When the purpose is compelling enough, it gets people to work around obstacles. They expect difficulties but relish conquering the challenges they present. When the purpose is essential to someone, they are inspired to volunteer for extra work. They volunteer to take on challenges and to solve problems.[9]

Uell Stanley Andersen said, "The great men of this world accomplish in an hour what other mortals accomplish in a year. They are not more active. Their activity is guided, powerful, sure, because they are directed to their objectives by the unlimited resources and power of the Universal Subconscious Mind."[10] Anyone can hire employees and get minimum performance out of them—but getting purposeful action is monumental. Great success is achievable when you create an army of employees who believe in your goals and aspire to do whatever it takes to reach them.[11]

How Do You Find Your Purpose?

Average leaders perceive their businesses as boxes that revolve around products and services. They do not consider the problems and challenges of the people they want to serve. By defining and understanding your purpose, you can move with the changing needs of your customers and evolve your products and services. Time after time, business leaders try to force the external world to buy what they want to sell. They fail to consider whether what they want to sell is a real need and whether there is already too much supply that meets that need. If the need is already well-served or overserved, pumping more supply into the market will inevitably result in a painful journey for you and your colleagues.

Purpose is about identifying and addressing the underserved or unserved needs and desires of others.[12]

Understanding how to discover purpose is an integral piece of any organization. To aid you in that discovery, I offer you four categories of purposeful movement for your business. Purposeful companies usually focus on one or more of these areas. Great companies must *accomplish*, at a minimum, one of them.

1. **Disrupting Your Industry.** Airbnb changed the lodging industry forever. They created a very cost-effective and easy way for anyone to list their space and book unique accommodations anywhere in the world. By doing so, they made traveling more affordable and accessible to many people. Likewise, Uber's technology platform redefined the vehicle-for-hire industry. While neither of these companies has been without mishaps and blemishes, both not only changed the customer experience but also increased the size of the industry, altered the structure of asset ownership, provided a whole new way for people to make money, and caused a need to reevaluate the rules that have governed commerce related to these industries.

2. **Uncommon Services.** A company does not have to excel in all areas of service. It merely has to be better than its competitors in the right aspects of service. What could your company do that would redefine the customer experience in your industry? (I *wish* someone would do something in the airline industry.) Traditional companies that come to mind for providing uncommon service are Ritz-Carlton and Nordstrom. However, a company everyone is learning from is Amazon, where you can purchase almost anything at any time. They offer products at prices that are usually below manufacturers' suggested retail price and, in many cases, can deliver them directly to you on the same day. They are also using artificial intelligence to help do this with a few keystrokes. At the

rate Amazon is going, they'll be sending us stuff before we order it, and we'll be glad they did.

3. **Change the World.** Maybe you want to leave your imprint by helping the planet, society, or your community in some extraordinary way. Working on the probability that we will eventually exhaust Earth's fossil fuels, companies are racing to help address that eventuality by making sure we have power in the future. For almost two decades, First Solar has grown into the world's largest manufacturer of "thin-film" solar panels. Its factories churn out panels at a rate of roughly one per second, and to date, it has sold enough—13.5 gigawatts worth—to power more than two million American homes. Thanks to the company's R&D efforts, First Solar's large-scale farms can deliver energy to utilities at record-low prices—low enough to beat out power from dirty fossil fuels. That's a crucial milestone for those who hope to see the world transition to cleaner energy.[13]

4. **Excellence.** You can always find ways to change the features of products by increasing their speed, beauty, functionality, and other qualities. No company is going to get it right with every product, but Apple, Samsung, Ikea, Dyson, Google, and 3M have produced products that have stood out from their competitors in specific categories and are considered excellent.[14]

Look at purpose through these four lenses to determine which of the four ignites your passion. Then ask, "What purpose can my company serve within that category?" to ensure you choose a purpose that is not being served to the level you believe it could or should be. The key is to think big! Consider your purpose to be a pursuit rather than a destination. It will be a mantra for you and your organization for many years.[15]

To stimulate discussion among your leaders, request our Business Acceleration Tools at www.howardmshore.com/tools and request our

Business Acceleration Tools®, and you can gain access to the "Purpose Worksheet."

Four Ways to Bring Purpose to Life Within Your Organization

What actions can you and your business take to emphasize the importance of your highest purpose? Start with these:

1. Define your purpose clearly and simply.
2. Regularly reinforce your purpose in everything you do, and make sure your company decisions are tied to your purpose.
3. Develop measures to make sure that everyone in your company knows what actions it will take to move continually closer to your purpose.
4. At your annual planning session, ask questions like, "How can we better serve our purpose?" "Is our purpose inspiring our employees to serve at consistently high levels?" "Does our purpose set us apart from our competition?"[16]

ESTABLISH A CLEAR AND COMPELLING PURPOSE

- The more critical your overall purpose, the better you can serve your community at large, and the more money you can ultimately make by striving to fulfill it.
- Purpose is never about revenue and profit. It is about how to solve the problems and challenges of the people you want to serve.
- Having your employees act with purpose will inspire change.
- When you act with purpose, you respond with more energy and enthusiasm.
- When the purpose is important to people, they are inspired to volunteer for extra work. They volunteer to take on challenges and to solve problems.
- Establishing your purpose allows you to address the following essential questions:
  - » What is the primary difference you want your organization to make for your community of clients?
  - » How is that community being served, and what would be lost without your organization?
  - » What will your client relationships and experiences look like?
  - » What boundaries and rules must you learn to break?
  - » Why will the best employees want to work for you rather than your competition?

- Purpose usually drives your organization to accomplish one of the following: disrupt your industry, provide uncommon services, change the world, or embody excellence.
- To stimulate discussion among your leaders, go to www.howardmshore.com/tools and request our *Business Acceleration Tools*®, and you can gain access to the "Purpose Worksheet."
- By understanding your business's purpose, you can move with the changing needs of your customers and evolve your products and services.
- We identified four ways to bring purpose to life within your organization.[17]

BUSINESS ACCELERATION CALCULATOR™

It is time to pause and determine what the practices discussed in "Establish a Clear and Compelling Purpose" cost your company. Go to www. howardmshore.com/tools and request our *Business Acceleration Tools*® to gain access to the *Business Acceleration Calculator*™. This will help you keep track of all the revenue-saving opportunities you need to learn about in this book.

Let's assume you have a well-defined purpose. If any of your managers are failing to "act with purpose," or lead their team toward purpose, they are likely underperforming! Consider this when evaluating managers in Chapter 4.

CHAPTER 7
Growth Accelerator #4:
DEVELOP A STRONG
CULTURE

In the last chapter, we focused on "why" your company exists. In this chapter, we want to clarify "how" everyone conducts themselves and the environment that everyone operates in. When you encounter a high-performing organization, you are sure to discover a strong culture. *Culture* starts with clearly defined core values that are consistently demonstrated by every leader and expected from every employee. However, it is much more than that. *Culture* encompasses how leaders, managers, and coworkers treat everyone; working conditions in general; available tools and resources; and the physical workspace.

To Improve Outcomes, Start with Culture

Cindy Kirschner Goodman's *Miami Herald* article, "Culture Change: Just Do It," cited two examples of successful cultural transformations in progress. The article was about how Barbara Simmons, CEO of Plantation

General Hospital, had rallied her employees' customer service and job satisfaction, and the efforts of Kim Cripe, CEO of Children's Hospital of Orange County, to increase her institution's quality of service. These are two common examples of what must happen if you want to drive different organizational results—you must change the behavior.[1]

In both cases, the CEOs realized the need to make changes to their corporate culture to improve outcomes. Most companies claim they want to change results but are not committed and determined to do what it takes. They usually announce changes to some policies and procedures and throw in a training course. While those steps are valid parts of the journey, the real issues are generally cultural, beginning at the top and cascading down. They are flawed leadership and management philosophies and are hidden weaknesses that prevent organizations from moving forward. Another key factor I have seen (corroborated in the article) is that there will be no sustainable improvements in the rest of the organization until the CEO takes responsibility and makes personnel changes.

Goodman's article pointed to three critical factors for success in driving successful *cultural transformation*. First, for cultural transformation to take hold, an organization must be ready to make a two-to-three-year commitment to implementing it. Employees will likely push back, anticipating yet another "program of the month" that will fade shortly after being announced. Because change is never comfortable, they will try to make things stay the same. Second, it is essential to create a purpose for everyone to rally around and to clarify the non-negotiable core values that are expected from everyone. You then must train *everyone* on what behaviors demonstrate those values and institutionalize them. Lastly, and most importantly, the CEO and top leaders must put themselves out there as the catalysts for change. They must be the exemplars for behaviors they want to see in their company. You cannot outsource or delegate this to a consultant, trainer, coach, or subordinate.[2]

Core Values Are Critical to Your Success as a Leader

Several clients indicated that the single most important lesson they learned from working with our firm was how we helped them discover, reinforce, and build their organizations around core values. *Core values* are the rules that, when practiced daily by all employees, shape and define how people behave in your culture. When implemented in the right way, core values will help you significantly reduce many unnecessary management problems.

Many of the frustrations a leader encounters can be traced back to core values. I often find most companies have a defined set of core values, but most employees don't know what they are, don't understand them, or ignore them because management fails to hold anyone accountable. The drama between employees, client problems, poor teamwork, lack of communication, and improper behavior in companies around the world are problems that cost them billions with a capital "B." Many clients have significantly reduced wasted management time and dramatically increased growth and profits by removing people that refused to live the company's core values.

As mentioned in Chapter 4, when I consider all the leaders I've encountered, many people who do *not* make my "great" list are hard-working, determined, wealthy, smart, and considered successful in many ways. I have worked (as an employee) for three highly regarded Fortune 500 companies and three middle-market companies. Often, the wrong criteria were used when measuring the leaders' performance and effectiveness. Excellent leaders were fired and people with questionable character promoted. Unfortunately, my employers could not see the damage these wrong people were doing to their organizations by failing to live company core values when delivering results.

What is interesting is that these companies had clearly stated core values but were not applying them correctly! When these values are practiced daily, monitored, and used correctly in your business, they give you a competitive advantage over your competition. They help you recruit the right people and reject the wrong ones.

Accurately defining your core values causes everyone to act and think like a leader. Leadership is not a title. You do not need a title to lead, and you can have a title and not be an effective leader. This was illustrated after the mass shooting in Parkland, Florida, when students stepped up to mobilize action on gun control and voter registration, and parents stepped up to address student safety with local, state, and national political leaders. The fact is that people can lead every day of their lives. It is character that shapes leaders. Some people believe that you must only focus on excellent financial outcomes and that those "results" are all that matter. Such relentless focus on "results" has caused many to go to great lengths to produce outcomes at any cost. Thus, it is critical to center your core values around the character traits you expect from your employees.

I often find companies choosing things like "improving communication" and "innovative thinking" as areas for attention. While those are positive outcomes of good character, they are not areas where you should place your emphasis. You want to choose the values that are both important to you and serve as the foundation for making significant decisions, values that produce positive long-term results, enhance strong relationships with vendors and customers, and create the platform for an enduring company. Choose no more than five. I challenge you to select more moral character traits than performance ones. *Moral character traits* govern our relationships with others, and *performance traits* govern our relationship with ourselves. Here are some examples:

- **Moral Character Strengths** – Traits that govern our relationships with others
    - » Care for others, compassion, fairness, generosity, gratitude, honesty, humility, integrity, loyalty, respect for others, sense of responsibility, and truthfulness.

- **Performance Character Strengths** – Traits that govern our relationship with ourselves

  » Adaptability, ambition, commitment, competitiveness, courage, constructiveness, creativity, determination, focus, mastery, mental toughness, resiliency, and resourcefulness.

The primary reason why core values are not ingrained in many businesses is that their senior executives do not live them. If the top executives are not role models, their employees will likely not exhibit the company's stated core values consistently. Typically, the organization mirrors the values established by this core of executives. As an executive, if you do not like the behaviors you see from your team, be assured that you need to change your routine before you notice any changes.

It takes discipline and diligence to create a culture and to successfully instill core values. Core values reflect how you make decisions affecting:

- People (hiring, compensation, retention, benefits, promotion, demotion, firing)
- Customers (acquisition, retention, pricing, concessions, product changes, service, types)
- Vendors (selection, retention, proper controls, exclusivity, rotation)
- Products (quality, price, consistency, innovation, competition)
- Growth (mergers, markets, consistency, speed)
- Costs (controls, policies, discipline)

Four Lessons that Apply to Core Values

There are four fundamental rules to consider applying when driving culture in your organization. In fact, I realized that the same practices I learned them from being a parent apply to being a leader.

1. Less is more, and simplicity rules.

If it is not memorable, and a child can't understand it, then neither will your employees. This is not a swipe at employee intelligence. It's something learned in this age of text messaging, Twitter, and search engine marketing. Unless you capture your audience in a few words, you have lost them. In the not-too-distant past, we used themes, formulas, equations, and acronyms to get people to remember things that might otherwise be hard to recall. Today, people need sound bites. The rule of thumb: If your children cannot understand and remember what you want to teach your employees, then you are not ready to communicate your point.

2. Do not have too many rules.

This starts with core values. There should only be three to five of these. Essential values are those that, if consistently violated by someone, result in firing. They are the ones you will take a financial hit to preserve. By focusing the organization around those three to five values, you decrease complexity and increase the likelihood they will be followed. If you have too many rules, it probably means you have the wrong people. If you find yourself creating a lot of rules, stop and ask why. Many rules are created because of bad behavior by one perpetrator. Rather than fire the one person who should not have been in your company to begin with, you create unnecessary rules.

3. Repeat yourself often.

At the 2011 Fortune Leadership Summit in Houston, CCMP Capital Chairman Greg Brenneman said, "You should be tired of talking about your business plans over and over again." This applies to anything you want to have done. You need to repeat yourself daily, weekly, and monthly until you achieve your goals and expectations. What gets measured and discussed gets done. You can expand this to include process steps, values, and goals.

4. Stories make it stick.

People remember stories. If you tie a remarkable story to something you want people to recall, it is more likely that they will.

One illustration of this is a client of mine in the healthcare industry. When analyzing why revenue was falling so short of projections, they discovered a checkbox that their doctors were overlooking on a form. Failure to check that box was costing them millions in reimbursement from insurance companies. The box was not checked because doctors continued to miss it—buried in multipage forms. To remedy the situation, my client created a program called "Check the Box." By reminding doctors daily, training, measuring compliance, and discussing results in management meetings, this program was worth an additional $25 million for this company. Anyone can remember "check the box."

What Are Your Employer Brand Promises?

In addition to core values, companies should construct, plan, and grow their employer brand. This is different from your business brand—the external perspective of your customers on the quality and experience of interacting with your products and services. Your *employer brand* defines the relationship between leaders and employees. It tells prospective employees what they can expect should they want to consider working for you. You can have a strong business brand and a weak employer brand and vice versa. For example, if you are on a tight budget and need everyday products, you are likely to consider Walmart. However, if you are looking for the best place to work, that pays above-average wages and treats its employees exceptionally well, Walmart is not on your shortlist.

Remember that in most cases you are not just vying with your direct competitors for new employees. You are competing for talent with *all* other companies, and the companies with stronger employer brands and business brands win. Many companies find it challenging to recruit new employees with a weak or nonexistent employer brand.

The companies that work hard at being great employers not only find it easier to recruit new employees but also have higher retention rates and higher productivity.

After considering pay, benefits, and core values, how would your employees describe what stands out about working at your company? For many companies, that feedback would not be flattering, explaining the lack of extra effort from many employees. It is also why they get few candidates for each open position.

An example of this is a business services company whose employees tell a tale of a Dr. Jekyll and Mr. Hyde environment. Their company's top tier is made up of members of one family. A family member or a close friend of the family likely has a dream job. They are not held accountable, come and go as they please, are paid well above market value, and can treat everyone else as servants. They can take off as many days as they like, and love their jobs. However, the other 80 percent of employees are not treated with respect, are never good enough, are underpaid compared the other 20 percent, and must be available 24/7. Members of this underclass operate every day in fear, are micromanaged, and are frowned upon and considered not committed to the company if they happen to come in late, need to leave early, or take a paid day off. This company has severe problems finding new employees. Employee engagement scores are consistently meager, yet the owner is always surprised and blames the scores on an inept middle management team—which also continuously turns over. The employer brand for this company promises a hostile, unfair, and toxic work environment.

Now consider Salesforce's employer brand. In *Fortune* magazine's annual list of the 100 best places to work, Salesforce topped the list in 2018, for the second year in a row. [3] In 1999, the company was founded with a vision for a new kind of company—to leverage its technology, people, and resources to improve communities throughout the world. They call their integrated philanthropic approach the 1-1-1 model. According to their website, since their founding, they have given more than $240 million in grants, 3.5 million hours of community service, and provided product donations for more than 39,000 nonprofits and educational institutions. If you consider working for this company, you know you are going to be in an innovative and visionary company and that 1 percent of Salesforce's product and 1 percent of Salesforce employees' time goes back to communities around the world.[4]

Another client of mine—a global organization servicing top software developers—has a positive culture that attracts employees and deals decisively with nonperformers. What makes them interesting is that most of their employees work virtually from home. Their products and services reach a high percentage of elite software developers for leading-edge companies around the world. A core value that the founder and all the leaders are passionate about is learning. Not only is the purpose of the organization to educate their customers, but they also expect every employee to continue to learn and develop. Every employee is given a training budget, creates a development plan, and is provided one week of paid leave for training, including their first year of employment. They are serious about this. When I recently conducted a quarterly strategic meeting for their executive team, they were doing a talent review of their direct reports. One of those direct reports was failing for the second year in a row to use that budget or take any time off for learning. This person used too many excuses and was refusing to go out and learn. They decided at the meeting to remove this person from the company and to fill the position with someone who shared their vision. You know you can expect to learn and grow at this company.

Consider the employer brand promises that you want employees to tell others when describing your company. Why is it an exemplary place to work? Why should someone choose your company over another? If you do not have the right answers, it is time to craft your story and build an organization that lives that story. You develop your employer brand through a healthy culture. It is one in which employees are proud because managers take care of them, employees are put in a position to be their best, and people are in an environment that makes them feel safe and secure.

DEVELOP A STRONG CULTURE

- *Culture* starts with clearly defined core values that are consistently demonstrated by all your leaders and expected from every employee. It encompasses how leaders, managers, and coworkers treat everyone, working conditions in general, available tools and resources, and the physical workspace.
- For cultural transformation to take hold, an organization must be ready to make a two-to-three-year commitment to implementing it.
- *Core values* are the rules that, when practiced daily by employees, shape and define how you want people to behave in your culture.
- When we define our core values correctly, everyone acts and thinks like a leader.
- Construct, plan, and grow your "employer brand."
- Your *employer brand* defines the relationship between leaders and employees. It tells prospective employees what they can expect should they want to work for you.
- Many companies find it challenging to recruit new employees because they have a weak or nonexistent employer brand.
- The companies that work hard at being great employers not only find it easier to recruit new employees but they also have higher retention rates and achieve higher productivity.
- After considering pay, benefits, and the core values of your company, how would employees describe what stands out about working there?
- The number one reason core values do not get ingrained in many businesses is that their senior executives do not live them.

- There are four fundamental rules you should consider applying when driving culture in your organization.
    1. Less is more, and simplicity rules.
    2. Do not have too many rules.
    3. Repeat yourself often.
    4. Stories make it stick.

BUSINESS ACCELERATION CALCULATOR™

It is time to pause and determine how much the concepts discussed in "Develop a Strong Culture," if not followed, cost your company. Go to www.howardmshore.com/tools and request our *Business Acceleration Tools®* to gain access to the *Business Acceleration Calculator™*. This will help you keep track of all the company weaknesses identified in this book.

Anyone in your organization who is not living your core values is a nonperformer, including leaders. Leadership is a very costly issue, and the more senior the leadership, the costlier it is. Smart & Associates claims to have done more studies on the costs of mis-hires than any other organization. Based on their studies, they have determined the cost of a mis-hire to be as follows[5]:

LEVEL	COST VS. BASE SALARY
Supervisor	4 x base salary
Middle Manager	8 x base salary
Vice President	15 x base salary
Executive	27 x base salary

With this as a reference point, follow the instruction in the *Business Acceleration Calculator™* tool to fill in the row for Leaders Not Performing. We are being conservative by recommending you use a multiplier of 5 in the *Calculator* for leaders and 2.5 for everyone else.

PART III
HUMAN CAPITAL MANAGEMENT

ACQUIRING   **GROWING &**   **OPTIMIZING**
                        KEEPING

We use and dispose of resources.
People need to be treated as assets.
We want to find, grow, extend life,
and get a high return on the very best assets!

CHAPTER 8
Growth Accelerator #5:
OPTIMIZE
YOUR RETURN ON HUMAN ASSETS

As mentioned earlier, if you still rely on a traditional human resources mentality to grow and manage the people within your organization, it's likely keeping you from acquiring and retaining top talent. Effective organizations have transformed their thinking into a new paradigm: Human Capital Management. This chapter is about measuring how well you manage your most valuable asset—people—and will help you answer the question: "How good are we at acquiring, growing, and managing talent?"

As leaders, we have four primary roles to play when it comes to our workforce: acquiring, growing, keeping, and optimizing. These concepts are framed from different vantage points throughout this book. This chapter ties it together to help maximize profitability.

In most businesses, labor is the most substantial cost on an income statement, and the one over which you have the most control. It is also the one that is the most mismanaged. In addition, many companies fail to view independent contractors and vendors through the same lens as their employees. This is a huge mistake. Outsourcing or insourcing labor is a strategic decision, but one that should enhance outcomes and returns, not compromise them. Always include contractors and other third-party labor when working your way through this chapter.

What Is Human Capital Management?

Human capital management is an ideology recognizing employees as assets managed through a system of activities. It is imperative to home in on the concepts, "employees are assets" and "system of activities." These are crucial principles and are, I believe, only given lip service by most leaders. They need to be embraced by all leaders in your company.

Let's begin with the difference between a *resource* and an *asset*. Consider how differently you treat a resource versus an asset. We use resources, but we grow assets. Resources do not get the same amount of attention as assets. Resources are disposable—like garbage—and are not cared for in the same way as assets. When you purchase an asset, you look for the very best one to meet your needs. You do not want to overpay, but you will agree to pay top dollar for the right assets because you know what they can produce. You are willing to work hard to acquire a prime asset. Compare this to a resource where purchasing tends to be all about cost and convenience.

Once you have purchased an asset, you usually want to make sure it is taken care of. You make sure it has all that it needs, that it is nurtured. The goal is to extend its life and develop it fully. On the other hand, you do not give a resource much thought. A resource is there for you to use "as needed." Once it is used up, you move on to the next resource.

Finally, we expect a return or benefit from an asset. We are frustrated if we purchase an asset and fail to achieve an adequate return on investment. Would you invest in real estate, a stock, a bond, or any other entity and be happy with below-average returns? Do you measure those returns? Great investors expect above-average returns. With a resource, we are much more careless.

This is where systems come in. Great financial investors use a disciplined approach to systems and processes to obtain extraordinary returns. They understand that high returns are not achieved without great systems and processes. To become great requires mastery. You must master methods, update them, hire the best specialists to help you get them right, find the best tools, and measure results. In sales and operations, you rarely see a great leader cut a corner. The same should occur in the crucial function of human capital management. People are your most essential assets, one of your most substantial investments. But if I came into your business to evaluate how well you measure success in this function, I would likely find subpar and inadequate processes. Company growth suffers when this is the case.

There are four different systems and processes that require functional expertise, staying up to date on the latest techniques, improving your skills and talents, and continually raising the bar to keep you ahead of the competition:

1. **Acquire Great People** – This is how you find the right people. You need to master the concepts in Chapters 9–11.

2. **Growth and Development** – This is how you develop those right people and help them continuously grow throughout their careers. (This topic merits its own book. It represents a myriad of other, related topics, which are not addressed in this book.)

3. **Retention** – Master the concepts of stewardship (Chapters 4–7), implement planning and accountability systems (discussed in Chapters 16–20), and master strategy (discussed in Chapters 12–15).

4. **Optimize** – The proper use of measurement and management to get the optimal return from your human capital. This is addressed in this chapter.

After years of running my own companies, speaking to large audiences, and coaching, I have come to realize why human capital management is so tricky. It is a balancing act. We must balance the needs of many stakeholders at once: customers, owners, employees, and the community. Looking at all five plates (stewardship, human capital management, strategy, planning, and accountability) that must simultaneously spin, they sometimes conflict with one another. As tricky as that is, it's the difference between good and great leaders.

Labor Efficiency Ratio™

Business owners often ask, "Which book should I read to understand my numbers better?" I regularly recommend *Simple Numbers, Straight Talk, Big Profits!: 4 Keys to Unlock Your Business Potential,* by Greg Crabtree and Beverly Harzog.[1] Their The Labor Efficiency Ratio™ (LER) is not hard to calculate—*if you have clean numbers.* Clean numbers indicate that you keep your accounting records in accordance with generally accepted accounting principles as prescribed by your country. If that is not the case, it's imperative to address that issue first. Once that is done, everything you need to know about calculating labor efficiency is in Greg and Beverly's book. Frequently, however, when beginners apply an accountant's mentality to improve the LER, growth gets stunted rather than accelerated. That is where I want to help!

The LER expresses labor as a multiplier, not a fraction. In simple terms, it helps quantify how many dollars in gross profit is returned to you for every dollar you spend on labor. When you begin to learn how to look at LER, you may start calculating how to increase your multiplier instead of looking at labor as a cost of sales. When you look at labor as a cost of sales, you can observe each person in a role, see varying returns, and gain an understanding of why that return varies. It helps you get comfortable with paying one person twice as much as another in the same role—you can see that you receive a more substantial return from one person than the other. LER is also a crucial tool in forecasting and planning scenarios and makes profitability analysis much more straightforward than other methods. LER is the ultimate measure for helping management determine whether they are optimizing labor properly or not.

Commonly, we view high performers as outliers and remove them from our calculations to determine the right Labor Efficiency Ratio™ for a position. My challenge to leaders is to gain an in-depth understanding of why the outliers perform as they do. Usually, these people do not have exceptional talents, do not appear to work harder, and are not smarter than the rest of their team members, but they *are* doing something different. If you can identify that difference and disseminate it as a best practice, you will increase LER for a function or role.

There are three general categories of labor efficiency: direct labor, sales labor, and management labor. Many leaders make the mistake of trying to use one overall LER calculation, which can be very misleading. One of my clients was trying to use the one-size-fits-all method. After breaking down the calculation into the three categories, they learned that they were overinvested in the management-labor area, masking the fact that they were understaffed in indirect labor to handle growth. Had they not realized this, they would have instituted a hiring freeze and missed a big last-quarter surge in sales. Additionally, we find in the many organizations whose sales teams are not performing that instead of addressing the issue, they start cutting labor costs in areas such as customer service and product quality, unintentionally causing severe problems for those departments.

I strongly recommend making LER a key measurement on your management dashboard and regularly discuss it with your management team. Read Crabtree and Herzog's book for the details on how to calculate it. Rather than replicate the contents of their book, I want to use the content of *this* book to how you improve that ratio—to make increased labor efficiency a simpler task.

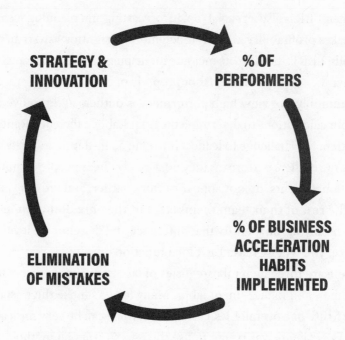

STRATEGY & INNOVATION

% OF PERFORMERS

% OF BUSINESS ACCELERATION HABITS IMPLEMENTED

ELIMINATION OF MISTAKES

There are four ways to improve labor efficiency. If you make improving it a focus every quarter, you will accelerate your growth.

1. **Percentage of "Performers"** – In the next chapter, we discuss this in depth. Every employee you keep on your team who is not living your core values and is not meeting reasonably high key performance indicators lowers your company's labor efficiency.

2. **Percentage of Business Acceleration Habits Implemented** – Throughout this book, we will teach you habits that help increase labor efficiency. These are compiled in our Business Acceleration Checklist, based on my previous book. The more of these habits you implement, the higher your labor efficiency will be. You can get this checklist by going to www.howardmshore.com/tools and requesting access to our *Business Acceleration Tools*®.

3. **Eliminating Mistakes** – When you develop priorities for your company and individual departments, consider where you find the most common and significant mistakes, the ones that cause customers not to come back or never to buy, and that destroy margin. These are priorities that should get the most focus. Once you address the biggest mistakes and eliminate them forever, labor efficiency increases dramatically.

4. **Strategy Strength** – Improve your strategy and its execution and use automation to give your company a competitive advantage and accelerate labor efficiency.

How Often Are You Hiring the Right Person?

How do you *measure* how well your organization hires the right people? I have found that most organizations have no such measures, and those that do are using mostly the wrong ones. For example, most leaders think turnover is a good measure for hiring effectiveness. While you should measure turnover and understand why it is happening, there are too many variables to make it a good test of whether you hired the right person or not.

The one measure all organizations should use to determine whether they've hired the right people is the percentage that are "performing" out of the total number of people hired. We define "Performing" as someone who is living all your organization's core values and achieving the reasonably high standards established for that person's role at that stage of employment. Some companies measure new hires at three-, six-, nine-, and 12-month intervals. If a person performs well throughout their first 12 months, then it was a great job of hiring. If a person is not performing well, then before assuming the hiring process has failed, determine whether something else is causing the problem. You may find that you did not provide your new hire with the proper training, direction, tools, or resources to do the job well. It may not be the person.

What Is Your Success Rate?

NUMBER OF PEOPLE TO BE REPLACED	YOUR CURRENT SUCCESS IN HIRING/ PROMOTING			
	25%	50%	75%	90%
10	31	17	11	10
20	67	35	24	20
40	141	72	48	40
100	357	179	120	100

Topgrading, by Bradford Smart [2]

In our estimation, the national average for hiring success is approximately 25 percent. Based on the chart above, if you have a 25 percent success rate in hiring performers, it will take 31 hires before you acquire ten good people. Further, if your success level is not 75 percent or more (three times the national average), then you have a gaping hole in your profitability. [3]

It is stunning how often a company will hire someone, realize within 90 days (the average probationary period) that they hired the wrong person, but allow that person to remain in place for years. Companies are full of mediocrity, and mediocrity has become the acceptable standard at most companies.

Keeping nonperformers (mediocre or worse) is a severe and costly issue. The extra management time expended and the *lack* of *productivity* (the gap between the performance standard and actual performance) creates a need for more people. The existing team plus the poor hire performs less work than the same number of people performing at prescribed levels. An even worse consequence you can observe is that keeping a nonperformer encourages other workers to slow down. Mediocrity breeds mediocrity. This is exacerbated by the increased number of mistakes that occur. We have found that a mis-hire costs you anywhere between five and 15 times the nonperformer's salary, depending on the employee's level.

Keep track of how many good performers you hire and make it a point of discussion at least once a quarter at your monthly meetings. When my clients start doing this, they are shocked by how low their success rate is. Most companies also underestimate how many people they've hired each year. I recently dealt with a client who was unaware of how much hiring the company did. At a quarterly strategic meeting, the CEO threw out "five" as the number of hires he thought there were during the year. The actual number was 30. His guess reflects their meager hiring success rate and a much higher turnover rate than he remembered. It is incredible how we can block out the facts.

Open Positions Are a Hidden Cost

One cost you are likely not capturing is that of open positions. Going back to the previous multiplier discussion, would you ever decide to hire someone for your company if it were not directly or indirectly going to contribute to helping your company grow and be more profitable? Of course not! However, every day a necessary position is not filled costs you a multiple of the salary that you do not have to pay. On paper, it may look like you are saving money, but that vacancy has a steep price.

Many of our clients that are growing at least 20 percent a year, and have a healthy 10 percent turnover ratio, typically have several open positions every month. When I press the issue, they acknowledge that even though they never stop recruiting, not enough is being done to address this shortfall. Only after we help them estimate the cost of the open positions do they take more action and fill positions with the right people in a timelier manner.

You need three numbers to calculate the cost of open positions: the number of open positions, the labor efficiency ratio, and the average salary for those positions. If you do not know what the labor efficiency ratio is for the open positions, we recommend that you use 2.5 as the multiplier. Most companies, when running optimally, can achieve labor efficiency higher than that, depending on whether it is direct, management, or sales labor. But 2.5 is a reasonable approximation, based on data collected from thousands of companies and compiled by Crabtree and Harzog, to determine the daily cost for open positions. Once you have the data in hand, here is the calculation for the cost of open positions:[4]

Cost of open positions = labor efficiency ratio × average salary × number of positions ÷ number of workdays in the year.

So, if you have one open position that pays $50,000, we estimate that it costs $576 a day to have that position open. If that position is open for 20 workdays (an average month), it costs you $11,520 for the month.

In our experience, until they calculate the cost of open positions, companies are not willing to hire internal or external recruiters to help them fill positions even though they have three to five open positions every month. It costs far more not to have those recruiters than it would to hire them.

Measuring Personal Development

Observe any organization that invests resources in growing their people. I can assure you that you will find lower turnover and higher labor efficiency. Our clients with environments that encourage and provide learning and development programs have a lower turnover than their industry peers and always have higher employee engagement. As a result, these companies consistently experience higher profitability in the long run. Companies that do not make the time to develop their teams lose ground to the competition. In the short run, they may be producing more, but in the long run, the learning-friendly organizations gain an edge.

Many of our clients make learning a requirement in their companies. All employees are expected to have personal development plans that are reviewed at least quarterly. Some firms set aside a specific development budget for each employee and allow several days of paid time off for an employee to use for personal development. Too many organizations do not measure and hold people accountable for a minimum amount of development. Not doing so has a negative impact on your turnover and employee engagement, which in turn lowers labor efficiency.

Your company's best interests lie in looking at the people in your organization differently and adopting an "asset" perspective henceforth. As leaders, we must master the skills to fulfill our roles in acquiring, growing, keeping, and optimizing our greatest assets. Only then can we unlock the full potential of our organizations!

OPTIMIZE YOUR RETURN ON HUMAN ASSETS

- We have four primary roles as leaders when it comes to our workforce: acquiring, growing, keeping, and optimizing.
- In most businesses, labor is the highest cost on your income statement and the one you have the most control over.
- Human Capital Management is an ideology that recognizes that employees are assets managed through a system of activities.
- We use resources and grow assets.
- Read *Simple Numbers, Straight Talk, Big Profits!: 4 Keys to Unlock Your Business Potential,* by Greg Crabtree and Beverly Harzog.
- The Labor Efficiency Ratio™ expresses labor as a multiplier, not a fraction.
- The Labor Efficiency Ratio™, in simple terms, shows you how many dollars in gross profit is returned to you for every dollar you spend on hiring employees.
- Make the Labor Efficiency Ratio™ a key measure on your management dashboard and regularly discuss it with your management team.
- Every employee you keep on your team that fails to live your company's core values and meet the reasonably high key performance indicators set for their position results in lower labor efficiency.
- The more of the habits on our Business Acceleration Checklist you implement, the higher your labor efficiency. You can get this checklist by going to www.howardmshore.com/tools and requesting access to our *Business Acceleration Tools®.*

- When the biggest mistakes get eliminated forever, labor efficiency goes up.
- Improve your strategy and its execution and use automation to give your company a competitive advantage, and labor efficiency will go up.
- The one measure that all organizations should use to determine whether you hired the right people is whether the people who have been hired are "performing."
- If you have a 25 percent success rate in hiring "performers," it will take 31 hires before you acquire 10 good people. If you are not hiring at a success level of 75 percent or more, you have a gaping hole in your profitability.
- Keeping *nonperformers* (mediocre or worse) is a critical issue that costs you dearly.
- Cost of open positions = labor efficiency ratio × average salary × number of positions ÷ number of workdays in the year.
- Observe organizations that invest resources in growing their people, and I can assure you that you will find lower turnover and higher labor efficiency.
- Not measuring development has a negative impact on your turnover and employee engagement, which in turn lowers labor efficiency.

CHAPTER 9
Growth Accelerator #6:

INCREASE THE PERCENTAGE OF PERFORMING TALENT

We've been discussing the importance of leadership to your company's overall success, but even great leadership cannot overcome the detrimental effects of "nonperforming" talent. Leaders can only go as far as those they lead. Let's examine that from a sports coaching perspective. A world-class coach, with a team of goofy players with mediocre athletic ability, will only get so far. The coach can draw up all the plays he wants, but it's the team that must execute on the playing field. Players must make split-second decisions and execute the plays as the game unfolds. Ultimately, the players determine whether you win or lose. Business is no different.

A great leader is like a gardener who plants seeds, makes sure that the soil has the right nutrients, and then nurtures the soil. The gardener cannot command the crops to grow; he can only provide the right seeds and right conditions for growth. Great leadership places subordinates in a position to excel and succeed, but those people still must do all the heavy lifting.[1]

When using our *Business Acceleration Calculator*™, you will find that much attention is given to people—and the losses we attribute to filling business with the wrong ones. This should be no surprise, given that between 60 to 70 percent of all internal costs on a company's income statement typically relate to compensation. The percentage is lower in industries where there are significant direct expenditures to external parties for the costs of goods (such as materials and finished goods). The most considerable cost you manage is for your human assets, and those human assets contribute to the perception of the value you create for your customers. It is also the cost that is usually the most mismanaged.

Leaders think they have done their jobs by focusing on the number of their people and the levels of their salaries. In our experience, this is the least important aspect of personnel problems. As mentioned earlier, costs that are essential to your acceleration are not present in a financial statement. No line in your statement shows the revenue you have lost due to poor employee performance, the added cost from an excess of mistakes, the fact that you may have more employees than you need, or the fact that the leadership team has less time to be strategic because of nonperformers.

It is imperative that each employee achieves the definition of performing to obtain optimal results. It takes leadership to keep all of them at that performance level. Don't think that this growth accelerator is about rating people. Instead, it is about establishing the standards by which you choose your team, and to which you hold your team accountable. It is about counteracting the detrimental results of hiring the wrong people, accepting low standards, and having poor accountability practices. It is about how seriously you and your company take your human asset investment—and how disciplined you are in demanding that it produces a reasonably high standard of performance.

Stop Labeling Employees *A*, *B*, and *C*!

Many of you have been taught to believe in the importance of labeling your employees according to their performance levels. The most popular ranking system is "A" versus "B" and "C" players. I used to be an avid user of that method, even writing about it extensively in my last book. Then I realized that the labeling process makes the improvement process too complicated and dehumanizing. There is a better way to handle the issue.

The way I was taught to assess employee caliber was that people fell into the different categories based on two criteria: whether they lived or did not live core values, and whether they met the performance requirements of their position. I eventually realized that while it is essential to measure both areas, it is neither essential nor desirable to label or rank people. A person labeled anything other than "A" needed to get feedback that would show him or her a path to reach "A" status and to be advised that failure to do so meant no longer being on the team. In other words, "A" equaled "performing," and anything else equaled "nonperforming." "Nonperforming" was and should be unacceptable.

One of my core values is *simplicity*. I am analytical and a "big thinker," but I am also good at cutting things down to the root. I pay attention to friction—that which interferes with progress and damages structure. When a process seems to cause a lot of resistance, I ask, "Why?" and "Is it necessary?" While the process of labeling employees as *A*, *B*, and *C* appeared to have a useful purpose, in practice, it only created a delay in getting to the task at hand, namely improving employee performance.

Consider this: When you hire someone, you expect the individual to live your core values. You have performance standards you want to be met. If a person were to say, "I am willing to accept the pay, but I am only going to live some of your core values and focus on some of your performance standards while I ignore or fail the rest," then hopefully you would not hire that person! You should not be willing to pay someone to *not* do what he or she was hired to do. So why not just say that? When employees are not performing, they should be dealt with, period. Why go through the trouble of applying a label to their level of nonperformance?

We ran into several types of friction when companies labeled people as *A, B,* and *C* players—versus "performing" or "nonperforming" employees. When companies discovered that too many of their employees did not meet the definition of "performing," it was embarrassing to the people who hired them. We also found that some of those implementing the assessments were equating "performing" with "unicorns." "Unicorns" are extraordinary people who exceed the norms of the rest of the universe, who always perform at a level that is in the top 1 or 2 percent of the field. Not finding unicorns is the least of your worries. Discovering that you have too many employees who fail to meet a reasonably high standard of performance and thus cause everyone else to slow down is a significant problem.

Another type of observed friction was that leaders became concerned with calling someone an "A" player when that person was not promotable. Some of the best performers in a role are not promotable and never want a promotion. There is nothing wrong with that scenario, but you need a way to show they are "performing" in your scorecards. Thus, the *A, B,* and *C* system caused distress for employers who wanted to use those ratings to identify who was eligible for a promotion.

We also found the type of friction that arose from employers being incapable of labeling an employee who was a family member, friend, or long-term colleague as a "C" player. How could you put a label on paper that you'd be uncomfortable saying to someone's face? This kind of friction raises another real issue: You should never hire someone you are not willing to hold accountable or fire. It only leads to mediocrity and puts your organization at a disadvantage to other companies that do not have to deal with such handicaps.

These observations led to an epiphany: *If someone is not performing, focus on the actions and not the person.* Don't label the person. Label the action. Therefore, I moved to "performing" versus "not performing."

Any other way tends to dehumanize the process and unintentionally classify, label, or brand people.

We must identify the actions that will help lead our companies to acceleration and quantify the gaps between required and actual performance. Your process must identify the gaps and force a discussion on how to address each employee's circumstance appropriately to accelerate productivity.

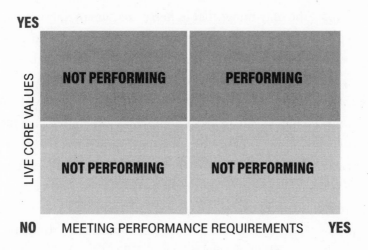

What Is the Definition of Performing?

Performing talent ("performers") are employees who consistently meet productivity requirements (performance standards) and always live your company's core values. Productivity requirements should be set at a high bar but be readily achievable. Do not place the bar so high that it takes a unicorn to fill your position. Regardless of their roles, strong performers can produce at two to three times the output of what your competitors usually accept in the market. I challenge you to identify the two most critical key performance indicators for every position and set the right standard of performance based on the level of experience of an employee. The standard should rise from continuous improvement and because of tenure.

Many organizations label the wrong people as performers. Leaders may favor people they identify with personally or have less conflict with, who have organizational tenure, who have the most institutional or industry knowledge, or who they consider loyal supporters. Many of these people are not performers. If you are like many leaders, you may be giving more weight to only a few attributes or qualities you find valuable. The only things that honestly matter are the core values and key performance indicators that drive real value for your organization. Everything else may seem critical but is not essential to the actual mission, purpose, or success of your organization.[2]

I want to push the point of maintaining reasonably high standards. I have witnessed mediocrity in every company, even among high fliers. It destroys growth and profits, one position at a time. You are better off with a vacant position than having a mediocre person filling the seat. Imagine yourself as part of a team of 10 people out on a cross-country hike through the wilderness. Two of your teammates are mediocre hikers; we will call them Tommy and Mike. You start in a straight line, and away you go. Predictably, once an hour, eight of you will have to stop to wait for Tommy and Mike to catch up. Of course, they are distressed because everyone else walked too fast and were inconsiderate, and the other eight are upset because they had to sit around doing nothing while Tommy and Mike lagged. When they finally catch up 10 minutes later, they are exhausted and ready for their break and are offended when the rest say, "Let's go!"

Apply the hiking analogy to your company. You have too many Tommys and Mikes; while they seem to be walking with the group, they are holding everyone else back. It is destroying employee engagement. Tommy and Mike are not happy, and neither are their colleagues. High performers do not like walking at the speed of mediocre walkers. They enjoy being challenged to go faster. Laziness breeds laziness. Mediocrity breeds mediocrity.

For far too long, a client of mine kept a leader and longtime employee named Jerry, who had worked for him for more than 10 years. Jerry knew a lot about the company's clients, had worked in almost every role in the company, and—you guessed it—got promoted to a level beyond his capacity. He did not get along with his coworkers. Several people, one level below him, were more skilled than he was. Jerry also lacked some critical character traits essential to working in a team environment. He did not treat others with proper respect, and believed he was entitled to more respect than anyone else because he had been with the company for so long. He knew he'd been promoted past his competence level and was over his head, and the CEO and his colleagues knew it too!

The CEO let Jerry stay on despite the many problems he was causing. I heard every kind of excuse. "It is too hard to find people with Jerry's knowledge and experience." "Clients love him." "We have too much work to let Jerry go." The CEO was committed to transforming Jerry. He was determined to turn a duck into an eagle—which would be some transformation!

By letting this situation go on for so long, the company lost some key employees. The CEO spent far too much time dealing with weekly employee drama Jerry caused. His failure to act was very costly, as the time would have been better spent working on higher-value opportunities.

After Jerry quit (yes, he quit) there were several revelations for the CEO:

- He felt relieved.
- The company did not skip a beat and was running at a higher speed.
- As soon as Jerry quit, a former employee who was much more talented returned to work.

Leaders should categorize an employee as nonperforming (a "nonperformer) when he or she:

- Consistently lives all your organization's core values but does not meet 100 percent of their position's productivity requirements, or
- Performs at the required levels but does not consistently demonstrate one or more core values, or
- Fails to meet both the performance *and* values standards.

Talent Checkup

We recommend doing a talent checkup at least once per quarter. The talent checkup is not one of those complicated performance appraisals. Go to www.howardmshore.com/tools and request access to our *Business Acceleration Tools*®. You can gain access to the *Talent Checkup*™ tool, which I developed to provide leaders with a simple framework for identifying nonperformers, creating a dialog among the senior management team, seeing critical patterns, and taking swift actions.

The purpose of doing a talent checkup is to help you understand what actions to take to make sure that everyone can and will excel in their current roles. If these checkups are mishandled, you risk causing good performers to decline or not improve by failing to offer them the proper training, coaching, feedback, and measuring tools. You could also negatively affect your culture by overweighting or underweighting individual team members.

The talent checkup aims to create affirmative action by helping a person find a role in your company where he or she can achieve peak performance. It helps develop a culture of accountability, making sure that everyone knows what is expected of them. It clarifies that everyone will be held accountable and what objective criteria performers must meet. It provides a simple framework for identifying when remedial actions need to be taken for an employee who is not performing.

Eight Questions to Ask When Someone Is a Nonperformer

1. Have you adequately communicated to the person what is expected of him or her?
2. Has this person been a performer in the past? If so, what has changed?
3. Does the person have the skills and knowledge necessary to perform his or her job at a high level?
4. What training is required to get this person to peak performance?
5. Has the organization created unnecessary barriers to this person becoming successful?
6. Do you believe this person will achieve productivity within a reasonable amount of time?
7. Does this person believe in your core values, and is he or she willing to live them?
8. Which processes, if fixed, would lead this person to better success in the future?

Answering these questions will help you diagnose the issue(s). Sometimes, team members are well past the rebound zone; that is, you simply cannot resuscitate their performance. Other times, with a little redirection and emphasis on coaching, mentoring, or training, a former performer who is underperforming, can bounce back. Either way, you must determine the exact problem and then take great strides to address it.

Should You Ever Keep Nonperformers?

Keep a nonperformer when you confidently believe he or she can and will become a performer within a reasonable amount of time. If you cannot define how and when that will occur, stop fooling yourself and cut the cord. With that said, you may *have to* keep a person on board until a suitable replacement is found because having a vacancy would be too disruptive to the business.

Leaders have lots of excuses for not replacing their nonperformers. Most of their reasons boil down to laziness or poor leadership. Let's again clarify the definition of the *performer*. They are not extraordinary. They are people who meet the requirements of their positions and fit your culture. In other words, they consistently do what they are getting paid for! Anything less should not be acceptable to any employer.

Every company leader I have met with a cash flow problem or was dissatisfied with growth or profits also had a people problem. Growth problems attributable to a lousy strategy are also people problems because companies that choose the right people (including advisors, consultants, and coaches) are less likely to have strategy problems. Think about it. The employees of any business are like the cogs that keep a machine running. Doesn't it make sense that the device won't operate at optimum performance when you have broken, incorrect, or rusty pieces inside of it?

Research shows that replacing even one nonperformer with a performer has a significant impact on a business. In our experience, the amount is at least two-and-one-half times and five times their annual salary for team members and leaders, respectively. In real numbers, if you have a team member who you pay $60,000 who is not performing, it costs you at least $2,884 a week (2.5 times salary). If the person is doing *some* work each week, you may be thinking, "How can that be?" What you are not considering is the fact that the person is dragging down the performance of the others, causing mistakes, taking up yours and other leaders' time, and costing you customers. It is far more than you are paying in salary. The 2.5 times is just a conservative estimate that is the net of what that person produced.

Some companies do not understand what *could* happen if they commit to having performers in every position in their company. Instead, they create walls or personal obstacles, which sound like this:

- There are not enough performers out there.
- It will take much longer to hire people.
- It is too complicated.
- It takes too much workforce.
- It can't happen in our industry.
- I must fire everyone who is a nonperformer.
- Performers must be paid more than nonperformers.

These are all myths and limiting beliefs, allowing leadership to continue to justify poor hiring practices and maintain the status quo.

The Container Store provides one of the best examples of how to build an organization with performers. I was fortunate to hear company founder Kip Tindell share his formula for building a great organization, building the company from a small start-up to one of the most respected businesses in the country. At the time of his talk, with the help of his "performers" mantra, the company was still growing at 20 percent a year, as it had done since its inception. His formula has five important keys to success:

1. **Pay**. The company pays between 50 and 100 percent above the industry average. Tindell knew that one great person could do the work of two to three average people. Performers pay for their extra salary threefold, so overall labor costs are lower than the competition's. His people are proud to be part of the company and of their performance.

2. **Recruiting and Retention**. To win, he knew he must only hire great people. He knew performers only like to work with other performers. They do not want to be surrounded by mediocrity. To be on a great team, they would choose his company. This means his recruiting process had to be phenomenal—to find and select the right people and never settle. They wanted more of the best and brightest right out of school. They've been rewarded with less

than 10 percent turnover in an industry that typically experiences over 100 percent turnover.

3. **Training and Onboarding.** Tindell provides 84 hours of formal training in the first year compared to the industry average of only eight hours.

4. **Real Transparency and Communication.** Leaders and managers thrive with clear dialogue and transparency. If they don't feel sufficiently informed, they feel left out, and their performance will suffer.

5. **Culture.** Culture is everything. Free the employees to choose the means to the ends but instill the foundational principles to use in making those decisions. All employees will give you 25 percent of their efforts, considered to be the bare minimum amount of productivity required to keep a job. To get the other 75 percent, they must love their manager and culture.[3]

From each of these steps, you'll quickly come to a singular conclusion: Great leaders invest enormous time and energy in their teams. They create a culture that not only invites performers in but also demands that they perform.

Drive Accountability through these Seven Steps

1. Clarify the mission of each role in your organization.
2. Identify two to three key performance indicators for each role and establish a high (but realistic) standard for each indicator.
3. Communicate points 1 and 2 to each employee.

4. Establish a process for continually reinforcing your core values with every employee.
5. Every quarter review how consistently each employee measures up to points 1 through 4.
6. Put employees who are not living your core values or meeting performance expectations on concrete performance plans designed to direct them toward achieving the desired performance.
7. Take immediate action to help employees who are not meeting their requirements. Those who cannot meet your standards should be replaced.

Succession Planning

A critical issue with the process described above is that just because someone is performing does not mean he or she is promotable. Someone can be highly productive and a great organizational fit but lack the qualities to move into a leadership role. Also, some people are crucial to the team and crucial to the company in their current positions. Losing them would create a huge void. You must have a process that helps you understand where your organization has vulnerabilities. This important topic needs to be addressed as a potentially high risk in your organization.

Many companies are stuck because they are not considering this exposure as they build their organization. It may be a bigger issue for smaller companies than it is in bigger ones. For example, you may have one person who has the knowledge and experience to complete specific vital tasks or lead certain teams. Some of these people are aware of their power and act like terrorists, making sure that no one else captures that knowledge and experience. They hold your company hostage. You may be fostering this hostage situation by filling their teams with inexperienced, junior, and inferior people to keep payroll down, or by not cross-training someone to fill their roles.

Once or twice a year I recommend creating or updating a succession plan. Identify how important each person is to the team and the company. How difficult would it be to replace each of these people? For each team member, determine who has the capacity to fill different positions at the same level in your organization, and are promotable one or two levels up. Also, determine which ones will never be able to move from their current positions. For those who can eventually move, identify the training and development necessary to make these moves possible and where those employees' interests lie. You need to map this out for each role in your company. If you do not have at least two people you can visualize back-filling every role in your company, you have a risk that can significantly slow your growth in revenue and profit in the future. Consider how ready each of these people is to back-fill each role.

As for people you consider not promotable, consider the implications. You have likely determined this for one of two reasons. First, they may be content in their current role and have no desire for change. Some people want to become the very best in their existing role and lack ambition. We need such people in our companies. The second reason is that the person appears to have reached the limit of their capabilities. It is possible that they can move to roles at the same level and expand their knowledge and experience, but they have reached the top in your organizations—at least from what they have displayed. If they have higher ambitions, it may become problematic as they expect and seek promotions. When this occurs, they become less engaged and possibly disengaged. You must communicate effectively with each employee so that there is clear alignment of expectations. When there is a gap, be sure that if you can't find a resolution, the person will be leaving one way or another. You need to account for this in your staff planning.

Nothing gets done without your people. An effective manager hires the right people and expects them to perform. The largest and most crucial asset and expense that a manager manages is people. You must regularly track the performance of every employee, identify those that are not performing, and take corrective actions. Failure to do so is irresponsible management!

INCREASE THE PERCENTAGE OF PERFORMING TALENT

- How well your employees make decisions and act on the front lines, determine how profitable and fast your company grows.
- Wrong hiring and accountability practices, not putting people in the seats where they can excel, and failure to hold them accountable to key outcomes, are the results of poor leadership.
- Do not confuse reasonably high performers with "unicorns" or set mediocre performers as the performance standard.
- If someone is not performing, focus on the actions and not the person.
- When should you categorize someone as nonperforming (a "nonperformer")? A *nonperformer*:

  » Consistently lives all your organization's core values but does not meet 100 percent of their position's productivity requirements.

  » Performs at the required levels but does not consistently demonstrate one or more core values.

  » Fails to meet both the performance *and* values standards.

- Anyone who is *not* classified as a performer should only be kept on your team if management believes he or she can become a performer with proper training and coaching within an acceptable period.
- You are already paying every one of your employees to be a performer.
- Your productivity requirements should be set at a high bar but be readily achievable by everyone.

- Regardless of the role, strong performers can produce at two to three times the output of their peers.
- The *Talent Checkup*™ aims to create affirmative action by helping a person find a role in your company where he or she can achieve peak performance.
- Ask the eight questions when someone is not performing.
- By not requiring a specific level of performance, monitoring that performance, and holding employees accountable, you are allowing your employees to establish their own performance requirements.
- Every company leader I have met who had a cash flow problem or was dissatisfied with company growth or profits also had a people problem.
- Practice the seven accountability steps identified in the chapter.
- Every company needs to perform a succession plan at least once each year.

CHAPTER 10
Growth Accelerator #7:

ADDRESS VACANT
POSITIONS

Creating an organization of performers will put you on the fast track to success. However, other important people issues aren't caused by hiring or keeping nonperformers. Some problems occur when your people are not in the right place or not in place at all. You invest the most substantial part of your budget in human capital, so investing the wrong way can create some of the biggest challenges to your future growth and current profitability. However, many leaders are too focused on individual salaries and myopic when staffing their companies. While cost management is essential, it can become a trap, causing missed opportunities for growth and profit. Consider how having people in the right seats, and filling the empty ones, brings value and growth to your business.

As an example, one of our clients that increased revenue by 70 percent in just nine months by identifying where they had failed to fill and under-invested in positions. The company was growing and profitable but could not turn profits into cash quickly enough. Had they continued to operate with inadequate staffing, they might have become insolvent. Instead, they invested in growing their team and their cash flow mushroomed. Only when you invest wisely can you maximize your return on investment.

Weigh your business against the competition on a player-by-player, position-by-position basis—just as you do when comparing your favorite basketball team against its competitors. How ready is your organization to compete? How would it affect your team if it had to play with only four people on the court while your opponents have five? How does it affect the team's performance when positions are not filled correctly because the owner is trying to keep payroll down? Would your best player only be a backup player on most other teams? How does it affect the team when a performer has to leave his or her "real" position to make up for the inadequacy of that shooting guard on defense? Imagine your competition has 10 eligible players and you have only seven because you did not fill your roster. What happens when your team lacks depth, so two or three players score 70 percent of your points each game? The average business deals with these issues regularly, and I probably have an idea of what your answers to those questions look like. Take some time to explore each of these questions. Addressing them will help you accelerate your growth rate and increase your profitability.

Five Phases of Growth Are Related to People

As your organization grows, so must its structure and people. A critical factor to scaling is understanding the challenges at each phase of growth and what adjustments to the personnel they will require. I have started six companies and have been on leadership teams in companies as large as $20 billion in revenue. I can tell you firsthand: running a business dramatically changes based on the number of employees it has, how many locations it occupies, and geographic proximity of people to the business and each other. As you increase the number of people you deal with—employees, customers, and vendors—operational complexity grows as well.

The central element to success is getting people and structure adjustments right. Many organizations get stuck in one phase of growth and do not realize what is occurring. These growth stages are always related to employees, not revenue. From observing hundreds of companies and my own experiences, I have identified five developmental stages where many companies get stuck. (To be clear, I have no outside data or research to back up these observations, just my own stated experience.)

1. **Survival Stage** – This describes companies consisting of 10 employees or less. I am intentionally not calling this the start-up stage. Many organizations never grow past 10 employees. Some do, but they can't sustain the momentum; they slip back into the survival stage throughout their lifetimes. Frequently, this kind of company revolves around its founder, and its structure is often a circle— everyone reports to the founder. The structure may be defined differently, but no one is fooled. The top person makes all the decisions. Employee selection tends to focus on cultural fit and a person's willingness to do whatever it takes, rather than specific competencies. People are asked to function in multiple roles, some that they are ill-suited for, but the mantra is to do your best. The founder is usually someone who created a product or service, left his job to carry on and expand that product or service, or was just plain not employable and thus became a business owner. Typically, the founder's main concerns are how to make money and create a legitimate, sustainable business model—one where the company has a market out in front of it instead of just a few customers. Founders usually do a lot of heavy lifting, spending as much as 80 to 90 percent of their time on developing their products and services and serving customers. No more than 10 to 20 percent of their time is spent managing people. Survival and having enough cash to continue are constant concerns. This is a stage that "visionaries" want to get out of as quickly as possible.

2. **Sales Stage** – This stage is typical of businesses with approximately 11 to 29 employees. For most visionaries, this stage is the most fun. There is usually plenty of cash, and the CEO's focus is on ramping up sales and marketing. The company has found a place in the market where it can be successful. Visionaries tend to be starters and not finishers. In this stage, it becomes clear that the company needs to bring in someone to drive operations and finish all the visionary's ideas, which seem to sprout by the hour. Another vital hire at this stage is a good controller. The Sales Stage is typified by very little structure—just the way an entrepreneur likes it. Selecting the right people, defining roles well, and holding people accountable are not traditionally strong capabilities for companies at this stage. They tend to hire too many people to support their surge in sales. Another common mistake is to throw more people at problems rather than recognize that some of the original employees are the cause of those problems. If the company has the right implementer on its team, this stage may later be remembered as one of the most profitable times from a net margin perspective because so few people were used to get everything done.

3. **Systems and Process Stage** – This stage describes organizations that have grown to 30–50 employees, and it may be the most challenging level. It is where most visionaries decide they are no longer having fun, determine growth may not be relevant to them anymore, and want to sell the business and move on. This is where a company's lack of structure in people, process, and systems shows up. Complexity seems to have snuck up on you. More products, services, customers, employees, and vendors have made your business a convoluted mess. For the founder, learning how to move from department-, customer-, job-, and task-centric to enterprise-centric is the most challenging part of this stage. One now must bring on leaders who know what systems and processes are missing and how to attract and hire process-oriented people to build them. The

CEO role must shift to delegating to other leaders (something rarely done before), team building, and clarifying vision and values for the organization. If you try to continue to do business the old way, you are going to burn out. This stage is very challenging for those who prefer to operate with no processes or systems. They will clash with the new, process-oriented people. Consequently, this stage often leads to the turnover of the old guard. Not many early-stage people will want to continue or have what it takes to adapt.

4. **Strengthening the Administration Stage** – This stage takes over at the 50–99 employee level and is about sharpening the company's tools. At this stage, you need to departmentalize and raise the game in each department you create. Additionally, this is where you learn to value and respect the administrative functional roles, such as human resources, finance, information technology, and marketing. Previously, those roles were taken for granted, but now it's time to hire and defer to functional experts who know more about their specialties than you do. If you do not hire people that you believe know more than you do, you've either failed to hire the right people or need to look in the mirror and check your ego. These departmental experts should bring their 10,000 hours of honing and learning their specialties—experience that you do not have. You may be the expert in your industry and have dabbled in these roles, but they are the functional experts. Repeatedly, I see entrepreneurs hire functional experts and then interfere with and prevent those experts from doing their jobs well (or at all). To be sure, entrepreneurs should ask questions about suggested changes, but they should understand that they must make changes to grow.

5. **Scale-Up Stage** – This most often happens in companies with 100 or more employees. Your company is no longer a flat organization and has been building layers of management. This period is all about taking on the challenge of spreading your culture, possibly across

many locations. The Scale-Up Stage is where most of our clients achieve lift-off. A major problem at this stage is how to hire and onboard many performers at one time, and do so throughout the year. You will need to have layers of leaders delivering the message of why your company exists and fostering the culture it has built. You must have all your people offering your products and services with equal passion, and going "all in"—living all your core values. You need to have every employee "all in," so your primary job as a leader is to create that environment. You are going to want to develop your team to support you as you build your most important asset: people!

There are more and different challenges as enterprises grow past 1,000 employees, and again when they become Goliaths. Right now, however, you should be thinking about how your business structure, roles, and people need to evolve based on the stage of your business. Have you developed your structure appropriately, and fast enough? Do you have the right people in the right seats to help you power through to the next stage? If yes, congrats! If you are approaching the next stage, it is time to start making the shift so you can move swiftly and seamlessly into it.

Do You Have the Right Structure to Succeed?

After looking at your organization's structure based on the growth stage you've reached, you should also consider whether that structure supports your strategy. Strategy has two dimensions, internal and external. Do you have the structure best designed to serve your ideal customers' problems better than any of your competitors? Are you set up to acquire those ideal customers? Can you do that in a way that will make you highly profitable?

Innumerable businesses are very focused on products and services, yet their structure has been formed by accident rather than by design. Not surprisingly, this results in failure to see where that structure causes unnecessary complexity, underinvestment in critical roles, and inadequate accountability.

For example, the CFO of one firm failed to see the crucial importance of adding the human resources function to the company's organizational structure. Rather than invest $75,000 in creating this one essential position and $90,000 to engage a qualified consultant to set up its procedures and help to hire its director, the CFO opted to spread the operational responsibilities for human resources among numerous unqualified people within the existing structure.

Failing to have a trained human resources manager cost that business $1.6 million. The organization was growing rapidly and had to replace several nonperformers. They had several open positions and a long history of making poor hiring decisions. The CFO's refusal to take the appropriate action resulted in several epic mis-hires over a six month period. They could not fill positions quickly enough and had to keep several nonperformers. That resulted in several operational shortfalls. They had to pass up significant growth opportunities because their operation couldn't support them.

In my experience, not appreciating the role of human resources managers (and the many variations of that position) is a crucial mistake many companies make. Clients often underestimate the complexity of human resources and the value a qualified person can bring to the organization. They often ask if they can train one of their existing people to do the job. I answer that it wouldn't be a problem *if* the person they want to train is a certified and trained human resources professional. Companies that want to grow intelligently need a professional who already has the education (there *is* a certification), has the requisite experience, and can teach them what needs to be done. It takes 10,000 hours to become an expert at anything. Do you want an amateur helping you find and select your most expensive and critical asset—your people?

Furthermore, the term "human resources" describes a real function, and there are quite a few roles within that function. These include:

- Recruiting and staffing
- Employee relations and culture
- Training and development
- Compensation and benefits
- Diversity
- Compliance
- Payroll

Depending on company size, these roles become more complex and crucial to the success of your business. The person you hire must have the requisite experience in the areas where you need them to do well. In the early years, your company dabbled in all the roles and likely did each of them poorly. Each role drives value for your organization and should have two or more key performance indicators to indicate mastery by the person performing it.

When you reach the Systems and Process Stage—the level where you need to establish a human resources function formally—you should decide which one or two roles you want your initial human resource person to master. In a company's early days, we recommend hiring a great recruiter who can increase the speed of attracting suitable applicants, help to avoid some critical mis-hires, develop an infrastructure for getting new employees on board and training the newly hired, and aid in building systems for accountability. Having the right person in this function can accelerate your ability to grow and scale, and it takes a tremendous amount of pressure off the other leaders. Frequently, organizations fail to create and fill this position because they believe they can't afford the cost of a competent, let alone talented, human resources person. What they fail to recognize is that you can never recover revenue and profit lost by not adding that person to your infrastructure in the first place. Each vacant position that your human resource person successfully fills provides at least 2.5 times the value of that position's salary in gross margin. In other words, failing to fill a $60,000 salaried position costs you $5,000 per week for each week you have been unable to fill it.

You should be expanding your human resource function by filling the HR specialist roles as you continue to add employees to other segments of your organization. As I said earlier, every role in the human resource function has multiple accountabilities and responsibilities that can be measured. Imagine that you are one person in a smaller entity of 50 employees. You are likely to have six roles (and thus 18 key performance indicators or KPIs). Ideally, no employee should have more than two roles, and it is best for an employee only to have one. A reasonable expectation is for people to be great at only three KPIs and for their performance level to start falling beyond that. The further you spread their focus by expecting them to fill more roles, the lower the performance you can expect. The same is true for each of your employees. If you are a smaller organization that expects people to fill many roles, help them prioritize and determine which ones are the most important.

When asking if you have the right structure to win, you are trying to answer these questions: "Where are our structural weaknesses?" and "How are they causing our strategy to fail?" The Human Resources function is just one example of areas where you likely have role failures. We commonly see role failure in other administrative functions like marketing, technology, and financial areas that do not touch your products, services, or customers.

We have a great tool that can assist you in determining where you may have structural deficiencies. If you are not sure where they are or want a tool to consider what you need, you can use our Role Accountability Worksheet, available as part of our *Business Acceleration Tools*®. Go to www.howardmshore.com/tools to download.

Right People in the Wrong Seats

We work with many companies that experienced significant growth in a short time, hired the right people to address that growth, but put them in the wrong seats. This means they acquired people with great aptitude and personalities who shared their core values but did not possess the knowledge, skill sets, or experience for the roles they were hired to fill. Let's dive deeper into understanding how the "right people in the wrong seats" issue occurs:

1. **Growth**. When a company is growing rapidly, its leaders often scramble to fill the necessary roles. They tend to hire the first available candidates or fill the positions by assigning them to current employees who "know the business." Essentially, they "plug holes" with people instead of hiring the right people for the proper roles.

2. **Overconfidence**. During growth, leaders may believe their team can simply "pull it together and make it happen," no matter what. Such a company shifts people around or asks them to pull double duty because it seems like the most natural solution.

3. **Comfort**. Leaders mistakenly think they can shuffle top performers from one position into another. Past success in one position equals proficiency in another, right? Wrong.

4. **Understanding**. The leader fails to step back and take the time to understand what attributes are required to succeed in specific roles.

5. **Capacity**. As companies expand, they may outgrow some of their original people. These employees either lack the desire or ability to keep up with their companies' growth.

Let's be honest; this is a natural challenge. Anyone who has grown a company has put the wrong people in the wrong seats at one time or another. Some have done it more than others, as I've witnessed time after time. However, there are a few more factors I have found that may be exacerbating the problem:

- Most people do not successfully ascend to more than two leadership levels in your company. (I do not have the data to back this up, just my observations and those of my clients to corroborate this.) Be careful not to set your team up for failure.

- There is a tendency to want to promote from within. I am a huge proponent of this but I have a rule about when to do so. Ask yourself, "If the internal person I am considering applied from the outside, would they be a strong candidate compared to others?" Far too often, the answer to that question is, "Hell, no!" If the answer is not yes, you are setting that insider up for failure. It is not fair to the person, the person's manager, the company, and your customers. A person's career is a long-distance run, not a sprint. There will be other appropriate opportunities. Let this one pass.

- You also get lazy. When we're tired and have too many things on our to-do list, it seems easier to work with the unqualified insider versus trying to find the right outsider. Do not ignore prior experience. It will take far longer to train an unqualified person than to find the right person. Worse, you will turn a good employee into someone who becomes more likely to leave—a double negative.

- Rather than figuring out what is wrong with the recruiting funnel, some blame the market. Before you start to cutting corners, putting the wrong people in the wrong seats, improve your marketing for candidates. Have you done all it takes to find the right people? Have you been willing to hire great recruiters? Have you hired more than one recruiter? Have you placed enough advertisements in the right places? Have you enlisted all your employees to help you find candidates? You get the picture!

How Long Are Positions Vacant?

Do you measure the length of time a position remains open in your company? Promptly filling a vacancy is especially problematic when the job market is as tight as it is right now. For some roles, companies look for specific, hard-to-find requirements that only "unicorns" could fill. In our experience, these companies can take from nine months to a year to hire someone who often turns out not to fit the bill. The old saying, "Hire slow and fail fast," is wrong. Amend it to say, "Hire a performer fast."

Policies and organizational pressure can force an organization to hire the wrong person. They can make it more critical just to fill the seat than to fill the position *right*. In some cases, leaders make unproductive comments that cause team members to cut process corners, hire friends and family, and make other unwise choices that lead to bad hiring decisions. Ironically, after the dust settles, the first person to get blamed for the wrong hire is the manager or human resources professional who succumbed to the pressure.

For all these reasons, hiring the wrong person is a costly mistake. Vacancies may be bad, but you are better off with an open seat than a wrong fit.

Seven Questions to Help Address Position Vacancy

1. What is your strategy for finding the ideal candidate?
2. How many quality candidates applied this week for each open position?
3. If you are not getting enough quality candidates each week, how will you adjust your strategy?
4. Does that strategy match the reality of where candidates will be found?
5. Is your offer going to be attractive to your ideal candidate?
6. Have you created a position that requires a "unicorn"?

7. Will engaging a quality recruiter increase the number of qualified candidates, improve the quality of candidates, and speed up your process? Bearing in mind that time costs money, will using a quality recruiter cost you less than continuing on your own?

These questions will help you sift through potential candidates and make an educated hiring decision. There is no perfect equation for finding the optimal candidate, but this vetting process will help you succeed. Remember to review vacant positions over time to see if the company was able to perform well without that position being filled for a quantifiable time frame. This can help determine whether that position is integral to the success of the business or if it can be fully eliminated to allot resources elsewhere.

When you consider your strategy, you must consider building your candidate pipeline and have a candidate "bench-in-waiting." There is a saying in sales, "Always be closing." In talent management, the saying is, "Always be recruiting." I believe it should be a required KPI for every leader in a company to meet with at least 10 people every quarter who would be great candidates to join their teams. They need to find those candidates through their networks. Also, the person accountable for recruiting needs to make sure that all business-model-critical positions have candidate flow coming in every week, 52 weeks a year, through a series of candidate funnels. It costs your company too much to have anything less. Consider your recruiting funnel to be as important as your sales funnel. After all, who is going to get, keep, and grow your customer base?

ADDRESS VACANT POSITIONS

- You invest the most substantial part of your budget in your people. Investing it the wrong way can create one of the biggest challenges to your future growth and current profitability.
- A focus on cost control may cause you to hinder your organization by underinvesting in people. Do you give enough consideration to how hiring the right people brings value to and helps you grow your business?
- Know which stage of growth your organization is in, and make sure you are making the proper adjustments.
- Many organizations that grow quickly have the right people in the wrong seats. While these positions are filled, they might as well be vacant.
- Do you have the structure best designed to serve your ideal customers' problems better than any of your competitors? Are you set up to acquire these ideal customers?
- Each quarter, evaluate your organizational structure and ask yourself how your structure may be failing to support your strategy.
- Glaring weaknesses in many companies are the lack of strength in human resources, marketing, and finance.
- A poor hire is a hidden vacancy. Research has shown that a wrong hire can cost you up to 15 times their salary.
- There are eight steps to addressing position vacancies.
- A "Role Accountability Worksheet" is available as part of our *Business Acceleration Tools*®. Go to www.howardmshore.com/tools to download.

BUSINESS ACCELERATION CALCULATOR™

It is time to pause and determine how much vacant positions cost your company. Go to www.howardmshore.com/tools and request our *Business Acceleration Tools*®. This will give you access to the *Business Acceleration Calculator*™. It will help you keep track of all the deficiencies this book has helped you discover in your business. There are two types of vacancies that you must account for in the *Business Acceleration Calculator*™.

CHAPTER 11
Growth Accelerator #8:
INCREASE HIRING
SUCCESS

I n the previous chapter, we discussed how to accelerate your business by addressing vacant positions, identifying and filling the gaps in your organizational structure, placing employees in the right seats, and measuring hiring success. Hiring the wrong people for the job, or cultivating the wrong environment for the right people, can result in either excessively low or excessively high turnover. These issues affect a company's ability to achieve the maximum acceleration.

Low turnover is often considered a measure of success. Management assumes everything is excellent if employees are not quitting their jobs. However, on too many occasions, low or no turnover is a sign of organizational complacency, weakness, or low standards. On the other hand, high turnover is sometimes considered an industry norm for some positions. Acceptance of high turnover makes your organization *mediocre*, which is another word for *average*. Great companies know addressing this issue gives them a strategic advantage over their competition since high turnover is a significant drain on profitability. The Container Store is a great example; they average 10 percent turnover in an industry where the norm is over 100 percent.[1]

Is Your Turnover Too Low?

Let's examine and address your turnover situation. No exact number can gauge whether your turnover is too low. However, if your turnover is below 10 percent, you need to take notice. You can evaluate turnover for the company as a whole and by function.

Some turnover is healthy, and there is always natural turnover. You might realize you made some hiring mistakes. People move, have life-changing events or career needs that may not match what you offer, and some people just need a change. Each of these occurrences is par for the course. Extremely low turnover is often a sign that you are willing to accept mediocre performance, not measuring the right indicators, or don't hold people accountable for their work productivity.

More importantly, bringing new people into your organization can have excellent benefits. The right mix of new people shakes things up because they breathe new life into your business. New employees come in with a desire to prove their worth. They are excited about their new positions and company. They bring fresh ideas and new perspectives and ask, "Why?" often. Without them, an organization can get stale and fall behind its competition. People can get too comfortable with each other and the way things have always been done.

How Does Culture Affect Your Hiring Success?

In Chapter 7, I discussed the importance of culture, aspects that contribute to it, and how important culture is to accelerate the growth of a business. Culture is critical when discussing employee retention; it is one of the main reasons why they leave. It has been said that employees do not quit companies; they quit managers. And they not only quit cultures, but they also look for or avoid certain cultures when seeking employment.

A classic example is a real company, a beverage manufacturer and distributor we'll call XYZeco, that seriously underperformed against its competition. Its curse: its performance level, which always provided an adequate income for its main shareholder, resulted in leadership complacency.

XYZeco did not want to address what everyone who visited the company could see: the organization's culture could not attract or keep performers. Worse, its culture fostered high turnover of performers and low turnover of nonperformers. The people who were not performing made sure that the performers could not survive.

Although it had approximately $1 billion in sales, XYZeco was looking for someone to conduct training with their sales force, which was experiencing high turnover and had a high number of nonperformers. While it would be nice for a company such as XYZeco to be committed to developing its own 150 salespeople, training and development were not the company's core issues.

The facts were alarming. The company did not have clear goals, did not fire nonperformers, did not have good hiring policies, and did not tie compensation to performance. Finally, the sales training company lead asked the magic question, "What are your company's core values?"

Silence followed. The leadership had never defined and implemented core values to make this company great. What resulted instead were some highly unflattering, unwritten core values:

- **Mediocrity:** Salespeople were not working hard or trying to be their best. When selling to customers, they would give in on price because they believed they were second-rate compared to their competition. Very few proactively sought training, and when the company offered training, they did not show up.
- **No Accountability:** If people did not hit their sales targets, there were no consequences, particularly if they had been with the

company for several years. They were just forgiven—and still paid handsomely.

- **Mistrust:** The organization did not follow through on initiatives. They talked big and acted small. Consequently, when they said they wanted to create change, nobody took them seriously.
- **Disrespect:** Senior management would begin initiatives only to have the CEO step in and usurp them.

XYZeco was growing more slowly and had lower margins than their competition, even though their product was just as good as others, and in some cases, better. While they thought sales training would solve their problem, they were not facing the core issue: company culture. Do you think ideal performers would want to stay in such a work environment? Would anyone operate at peak performance here? Could they attract top talent with this reputation?

If you do not plan your core values, they happen anyway, and the results can be devastating. The longer you wait to define and instill the right core values in your organization, the more difficult it will be to achieve your ideal culture and thus maximize performance.

But what does this have to do with turnover? The reality is that if you do not create a strong culture, you probably won't attract quality team members. True performers will not stay with you because they will not find passion or happiness within your business. Performers need the right environment to thrive. They like to work with other performers, be challenged, and to know they are working toward excellence.

The Position Profile Is the Secret to Hiring Success

Given that hiring the right person is such a critical decision, one that costs dearly when you get it wrong, we realized it would be prudent to consider all the factors when evaluating a job candidate. We have developed a comprehensive process that leads to a high success rate, and one factor has been crucial.

After working with thousands of leaders over the years, our team realized that in too many cases leaders fail to hire the right person because they missed a key step in the process. This step requires a much better job of clearly defining your ideal hire before you start looking. Most started their searches with only a vague idea of who they wanted and what they were willing to pay. Consequently, when we compared the opinions of the multiple people in the hiring process as to what the ideal person looks like, we usually got different answers. There's no wonder that the average hiring process yields only a 25 percent success rate.

After realizing this, I asked the head of our Human Capital Management division, Albert Noa, to determine what tool we could create to help clients hire the right people for the right seats. We needed a tool that would be owned by the hiring manager and could be worked on together with all stakeholders, to make sure that all agreed on the DNA of their ideal hire. The *Position Profile* was born.

The *Position Profile* has more depth than a job description. When completed correctly, this document serves as the framework for creating a job advertisement, a compensation plan, an onboarding process, a job scorecard, and interview guides. It crystalizes for all interviewers precisely what you are looking for in a candidate. While you may not want to use ours, I recommend you define the following for every role in your company:

1. **Position Mission:** One or two sentences summarizing why the position exists.
2. **Job Description:** Collection of tasks and responsibilities that an employee is responsible for.
3. **Key Accountabilities:** For what and to whom does this person have primary accountability? Essentially why they will get paid.

4. **Responsibilities:** Unit of work or set of activities needed to produce some result (e.g., answering phones, writing a memo, or sorting the mail).
5. **Competencies:** Abilities (skills) and capacity required to perform the job successfully.
6. **Critical Success Factors:** Provide focus on the influences that impact the performance of the job.
7. **Key Process Ownership:** Identify the critical processes owned by the position.
8. **Key Performance Indicators:** Provide visibility to performance using metrics and established performance targets, thereby giving context to vague concepts.
9. **Career History:** The background experience typically required to have gained the level of knowledge and competency required for the position. The *Career History* form clarifies the outcomes they have produced in the past that would provide confidence that they will be successful in your position.

Without definitions for those essential position attributes, how would you be able to write a job advertisement? How would you know where to look for candidates? Would you be able to choose between job candidates with similar resumes? Of course not! Your human resources team cannot know what will make the ideal candidate if you do not prioritize the qualities most important about the person you want to hire. Such a person will not know what they need to accomplish once they are on board. As a result, they will be working hard, but with no targets in mind and little direction. The results will be less than optimal.

This is the paramount failure in the hiring process. Either this step has not been performed, performed improperly, or the person hired did not match the criteria developed in the process. When interviewers decide to focus on some, but not all, of the characteristics identified in the *Position Profile*, it comes back to haunt them in reduced efficiency and increased turnover.

Are You a Good Interviewer?

When I ask leaders how they learned the interview process, most tell me they learned on the job, through trial and error. Most consider themselves very good at this, but their track record proves otherwise. Before working with me, one client consistently chose the wrong people because *attitude* was the all-important employee trait. She felt that one could accomplish anything with a good attitude. As a result, her company had rampant turnover. The people who stayed were friends and family, and they were far from top performers. Because of their relationships, it didn't matter.

To ensure your company's turnover remains as low as possible, you need an excellent interviewing process. *Topgrading* by Brad Smart includes an interview process that boasts a 90 percent success rate in hiring a performer for any position in your company. Even then, you must be disciplined in your hiring practices. The *Topgrading* process can fail for those who are inconsistent and do not follow all the procedural steps.[2]

Another issue is that some people simply should not be interviewing job candidates. Some interviewers spend more time talking than listening to the actual interviewee. They can't help themselves; they are always selling. They overconfidently believe they only need 10 minutes to spot talent. But what candidate can't fake it for 10 minutes? If someone is not usually a good listener or has a lousy track record, that individual should be excluded from the primary process. If such a person needs to be in the process because of his or her title, schedule them for the end of the process, after talented interviewers are confident they have the right candidate. Then you can let the "heavy hitter" close the deal.

There has been much written on interviewing and selecting talent. As I speak with clients—even those who use some of the best interviewing techniques—our talks reveal they often miss the main point. Finding the ideal person for each position requires understanding what constitutes talent for that position. The people tasked with filling a position need to ask themselves, "What talents are required to perform this job very well?" That is the crucial question.

When filling a job, interviewers often look for:

1. Education
2. Experience in the role
3. Experience in the industry
4. Personality
5. Aptitude

While these are important considerations, if the applicant lacks the core talents specific to the position, then they can possess all the above and still not perform well. For example, if you want to hire a head of strategic planning for a large company, you should consider a person whose talents include the ability to:

1. Ask questions that most others do not think to ask.
2. See patterns in data that most others cannot see.
3. Persuade others who want to continue with the status quo to consider alternative possibilities.
4. Present information in a way that others can't.
5. Ask tough questions of organizational superiors.
6. Have the self-confidence to go against the grain and not be a yes man.

The applicants may have had experience in strategic planning, have worked in your industry, have great personalities, and be smart. The problem is that unless instructed to do so, most interviewers would not even identify the other key talents as necessary, let alone probe for and get a sense they exist in the applicants. Ironically, if someone has more of the latter (i.e., key talents) and is light on the former (i.e., education, experience, personality, and aptitude), this individual will outperform the people who have more of the former on their resumes.

How Robust Is Your Onboarding Process?

If you bring your new employees on board in the wrong fashion, you may permanently destroy the relationship. First impressions matter! Many new employees leave within their first six months.[3] As I mentioned earlier, 67 percent of your employees are either actively disengaged or not engaged.[4] At the root of these problems is the failure to bring them on board properly in the first place. Obviously, organizations with strong onboarding processes save themselves a lot of time and money. But it is also true that they typically need fewer employees—because their people perform better and faster than those in other organizations.

Most leaders know the importance and value of a strong onboarding process, yet some who conceptually develop one does not use it. Why, you might ask, do they not act on their own wisdom? One reason has more to do with a mindset than a process. If a leader fully subscribes to the approach that people are assets rather than resources, as discussed earlier, they would treat them as such from the moment they are hired.

Lack of attention to the onboarding process boils down to a failure to see it as a top priority. Managers who should be accountable and responsible for much of the onboarding see themselves as too busy to do it properly. Co-workers—who have a lot to gain by helping their new colleagues succeed—have full-time jobs to perform, have been carrying the added weight of position vacancies, and feel that assisting in onboarding a new hire takes away from their ability to do their "real" job. Onboarding co-workers is not in their job descriptions, and they are not rewarded for doing it. Leadership fails to motivate them to make it a top priority. Therefore, when given the task to assist in the process, they do not give it their primary attention.

In such organizations, new people get second-rate attention at best. As a result, the typical onboarding process involves meeting with a designated person to help them with standard paperwork, such as that required for them to receive payroll or gain access to the computer systems. Upon completing their paperwork, they get basic training on how to do a specific task and use the company's proprietary computer systems. They are introduced to a few people and told which ones they can go to with any questions.

Essentially, new people are thrown into the pool, and the manager watches to see whether they sink or swim. If they are not swimming as intended, they are pulled out of the water and given feedback on how to kick harder or improve their stroke. Eventually, and often with much frustration, the new employee figures out how to do their job. It usually takes longer than anyone wanted, and the experience makes them less than enthusiastic about their manager and the company. They resent the lack of attention and support, causing these bright and capable people never to want to give their full engagement to their employer. Trust has been broken, with little chance of repair.

Onboarding processes in companies that have the highest employee engagement, lowest turnover, and high levels of performance look very different from this. In such companies, we find that most positions have defined onboarding activities for 90 days (the most common probationary period). The first 30 days are usually intensive, with much reinforcement over the next 60 days. The activities include:

- Learning about the vision and values of the company
- Identifying long-term and short-term goals, key priorities, and how the new employee will contribute
- Clarifying the key expectations for the role
- Visiting and learning about all departments in the company
- Shadowing someone who performs the same role
- Someone else shadowing them as they perform their role
- Meeting with vendors
- Meeting with customers
- Training to help them understand how the business works
- Daily huddles at the end of the day with the supervisor to discuss key observations
- Weekly coaching from their supervisor

- In-depth training on each task they need to perform and testing to ensure that they learned what they were taught

You go to great lengths to find and attract the very best people to your company. It is your job to create conditions where they can flourish. Onboarding is the first step toward creating bright futures and is the first impression a new employee has of the company culture. Investing the time upfront in preparing employees to excel in their new roles, will yield huge dividends!

INCREASE HIRING SUCCESS

- Do not accept high turnover, even if it is common in your industry for a specific position.
- Very low turnover (usually below 10 percent) shows you are complacent, willing to accept mediocre performance, not measuring the right indicators, or don't hold people accountable for their work productivity.
- New employees come in with a desire to prove their worth. They are excited about their new positions and company, and they bring fresh ideas and new perspectives.
- Your culture has a direct impact on turnover.
- Failure to define positions well is the number one reason for hiring mistakes.
- The *Position Profile* is more depth than a job description. When prepared correctly, this document serves as the framework for creating a job advertisement, a compensation plan, onboarding process, job scorecard, interview guides, and crystalizes for all interviewers exactly what you are looking for in a candidate.
- Implement Brad Smart's *Topgrading* interview process to achieve an 80–90 percent success rate in hiring the right person.
- If the applicant lacks the core talents specific to the position, then they can possess educational experience, role experience, industry experience, culture, and aptitude requirements but still fail in the role.
- If you bring your new employees on board in the wrong fashion, you may permanently destroy your relationship with them.
- You go to great lengths to find and attract the very best people to your company. It is your job to create conditions where they flourish.

- Onboarding is the first step toward creating bright futures and is the first impression your new hire will have of your company culture.
- Investing the time upfront to prepare employees to excel in their new roles will yield huge dividends!

BUSINESS ACCELERATION CALCULATOR™

It is time to pause and determine how much not increasing your hiring success costs your company. Go to www.howardmshore.com/tools and request our *Business Acceleration Tools*® to gain access to the *Business Acceleration Calculator*™.

The impact of this issue is reflected in the line items called Number of Leaders and Team Members Not Performing. As a result, I did not create a separate line item in the *Calculator* for fear of double counting.

PART IV

STRATEGY

BUSINESS MODEL   **SEGMENTATION**   **DIFFERENTIATION**

"However beautiful the strategy,
you should occasionally look at the results."

— Unknown[1]

DESIGN A
PROFITABLE
AND SCALABLE
BUSINESS MODEL

As I mentioned at the beginning of this book, you must consider strategy from three perspectives. The first perspective—the external dimension—considers strategy from where you compete with other companies who want to attract the same customers. The second perspective—the internal dimension—considers the way you make business model choices so that you can acquire momentum and turn your revenue into a sizeable profit and produce enough cash. The third perspective considers your ability to sustain growth. We will address the internal dimension in this chapter, the external dimension in Chapters 13 and 14, and continuous growth in Chapter 15.

Many leaders allow their business models to happen by accident rather than by design—especially in the early days. Rather than carefully considering the options you have and making conscious choices about the design, you act instinctively and determine the consequences of your actions by reviewing your income statement after the fact. When you like or don't like what you see, you start tinkering with the model. If the architect who built your house or offices engineered your project in such a manner, how safe would you feel? Would your electric bills ever be as low as they could have been had the architect adequately planned and designed this part of your house? What if the architect did not consider that you were in a hurricane-prone area like Miami and built your home with the wrong materials and not to code?

This example may seem ludicrous but, if you are honest with yourself, you probably have not put enough thought into the design of your business. If you haven't, then you are a lot less profitable. And when you reach the point of wanting to grow and scale dramatically, you are likely to find your business ill-prepared.

When you design your business correctly, you will grow faster than your competitors and have at least three times their profitability. Sharp entrepreneurs find models that produce enough cash, so they do not · have to give away too much equity to outside investors. You know you have a great business model if you have an abundance of cash and your net profit margin is two to three times the industry average.

If you believe you are the next Amazon, Airbnb, or Peloton, realize that you are attempting to create a unicorn—which I do not want to discourage. But to create one, you need to understand that there must be a business model behind it, not just a product, technology, or service. Alternatively, when we drive products, technologies, and services through our ideologies and business models, that is what produces the unicorn. To date, all unicorns have involved a lot of capital, so your investors will want you to be able to describe your unique business model. They need to know how it will leverage technology, and how it will provide a product or service that will produce unprecedented value for shareholders.

Whether you are creating a unicorn or just a great company, you must understand how to develop the correct business model, how to clarify the components that will make your model different from the competition, and how cash will flow through your model. By having this understanding, you will be in a better position to make the adjustments needed along the way to create a sustainable and highly successful business model.

If your vision requires raising money, it will be vital that you have a transparent business model and can show that you can deliver on crucial assumptions. Far too many leaders have little substance to demonstrate how they will get from *A* to *B* to *C* and *D*, or they tell the story but do not perform. This chapter will help you succeed, whether or not you need to raise capital.

What Is Strategy?

I love asking this question. Whenever I sit with leaders and ask them to tell me what strategy *is*, I get an array of fascinating responses. However, I rarely get one that resembles a good definition of *strategy*. Even though most CEOs and leaders pride themselves on being strategic, you can see from their replies that there is little or no strategic thinking in their companies.

The essence of the problem lies in the delineation between *strategic thinking* and *execution thinking*. The subtle difference is that when we speak of significant objectives and changes to be completed *more* than one year from now, it is strategy. If they are to be completed *within* one year's time, it is execution. However, if your company is a start-up and is growing 100 percent each quarter, your quarters are equivalent to a year in most established companies in terms of how fast the world moves. In that case, your execution thinking needs to be faster. Strategy is always long-term thinking.

Strategy is also about choices. As the head of strategic planning for Ryder System (a $5 billion company at the time), I had the pleasure of working with Monitor Group. This company was founded by Michael Porter, a well-known professor at the Harvard Business School. When working with Porter's team, I realized how our company had not been rigorous enough when considering our choices. For example, during Ryder strategy sessions, we discovered that all the largest companies in the industry, including ours, were failing to make choices that were important and valuable to a large segment of the market we were targeting. While working with Monitor Group, our market research uncovered the fact that only 40 percent of the companies with large fleets were outsourcing truck leasing and maintenance to companies like Ryder. This figure had not changed in more than 30 years. We were all fighting for the same pie, yet none of us had demonstrated enough value to get the other 60 percent of the potential market to want to outsource to us. In those companies' minds, we offered them no real value. Using Michael's Choice Analysis Process, we drove through many iterations of choices to choose a new course for Ryder, which proved to be invaluable.

Let's use a military analogy. Would you ever want your country to take a military course of action before it considered all its options? We may not agree with or understand the actions they ultimately decide to take, but what if they did not weigh all the possible outcomes? There have been many military actions averted because someone found an alternative path that was less expensive and destructive. They need to correctly assess the situation at the *preparation phase*—something critical to the success of any team. They must understand the assault team's capabilities, how to best position them to win, and what choices they need to make to outflank their adversary. Without that preparation, slaughter ensues.

Similarly, every business has a preparation phase that we refer to as *strategic thinking*; that is, thinking and collaborating through a process to determine a winning strategy against your opponent in the business arena. After setting a strategy, the next step is preparing for the action phase, which we refer to as *execution planning*. As a basketball coach for my kids when they were younger, I successfully took a team that had one of the worst records in their league to the finals, and I can assure you it was a combination of strategy, execution planning, and those kids playing their hearts out.

Strategy is about adding value. Once you clearly identify the customer segment you want to dominate, you need to create a unique mix of value for that segment. If you feel and act like a commodity, that's all you are. When you do not add that unique mix of value, you will always find growth challenging, and profit will never be exceptional. (This is addressed more deeply in Chapter 14.)

The Business Model Canvas

There are many approaches you can use, whether it is Porter's Choice Analysis Process or the one that I prefer using—the Business Model Canvas. In *Business Model Generation,* Alexander Osterwalder and Yves Pigneur developed the Business Model Canvas as a tool to help you look at the nine elements (building blocks) of a business model and to make significant choices to make your business model uniquely different and preferable to that of your competition. [1]

1. **Customer Segments.** This building block describes the different groups of people or organizations that an enterprise aims to reach and service. You can better serve customers by separating them based on common needs, behaviors, and other attributes. The simplest way to understand the choice set is to look no further than the dining industry. The number of segments in this industry can make your head spin. Understanding *your* segment is crucial. Here are some ways to break it down:

   » Style of dining (Fine, fast, fast-casual, etc.)
   » Cuisine (Japanese, Mexican, Italian, etc.)
   » Experience (High service, low service, family-friendly, take-out, delivery, etc.)

   (I address this in more detail in Chapter 13.)[2]

2. **Value Propositions.** This element describes the bundle of products and services to unusually solve customers' problems or needs. You must decide on what is most important to them and how they are underserved. The critical question for you to ask and answer is, "What unique value can we offer our clients that allows us not to have to compete with our rivals on the same dimensions?"[3]

Consider Peloton. Instead of competing with many other companies to add a stationary bicycle to your home gym, they took advantage of technology and professional instructors to create the ability to live-train thousands of people at one time, all around the globe. It gives people around the world the ability to take a class together without being in the same room. It provides access to vast numbers of training programs of various lengths—not just cycling, but also yoga, running, and spinning. You can take any class, anywhere, at any time. Customers are willing to pay more than they would for a regular gym membership—and in many cases, have both. Peloton vastly extended their market and have created a $4.2 billion company in a relatively short period.[4] (I delve further into this in Chapter 14.)

3. **Channels.** This component addresses how a company communicates with and reaches its customer segments to deliver its value proposition. Often, I find that there is not enough thought put into sales and distribution channels. One must truly understand one's customer segment before one can understand the best channel or channels to master.[5]

A key question you must ask is, "Which channels work best for our ideal customer?" Your job is to master owning those channels. Are you "spraying and praying" at too many channels and not doing particularly well at any of them? I recommend that you focus on the top two and come up with one or two measures of traction.

Those will gauge whether you are gaining speed and velocity in your chosen channel. When you increase acceleration in these channels, your cost to acquire leads and your cost per customer drop. If either cost is going up, it signals that something is wrong. Do your measures demonstrate that you are leading in your industry? For example, we know our coaches are speaking on the right stages and delivering value to our audiences when we get a lot of leads from the participants. Another key channel for us is referrals. We work hard to perfect these two channels.

4. **Key Activities.** Your company is made up of many activities. Your job is to identify the key activities that will give you an advantage over the competition. What are the three to five processes in your business that would cause exponential growth for your company if you were better, faster, and cheaper at doing them than everyone else is? Who is the one person who owns each process? How do you measure that you are the best in the world at doing these activities?[6]

Key activities are where you need to think about innovation! How can your technology do things differently than everyone else? I suggest you look at this from two perspectives: 1) internal activities that drive your business and 2) outside activities that influence your end customers. Think about how you can radically reduce your internal cost structure or increase your ability to scale by changing how you go about conducting activities. The same approach should be used when considering how you radically improve customer experience. Because the use of technology is so transformative, these questions have forced every business to become a technology company.

Think about how we recruit people today. If you understand how to use Facebook, Instagram, LinkedIn, and other online services correctly, you can reach millions of potential job applicants faster and in a more targeted way compared to only 10 years ago. This has dramatically increased the ability of both employers and job applicants to find each other in surprising ways from anywhere with a few mouse clicks or touches on a smartphone.

5. **Customer Relationships.** This building block describes the types of relationships a company establishes with specific customer segments. We commonly find that there is not enough thought put into finding the right mix of personal versus automated interaction with customers. This should not be based on your own preferences. You need to get out in the market and understand your ideal customer. Each segment is different, and preferences are evolving.[7]

   Do you interact with customers in the same ways you did five years ago? If you do, it is likely that they are frustrated and that you are not meeting their expectations. If you told me five years ago that I would interact as much as I do by smartphone, I would have said, "no way." I use WhatsApp, Slack, Yammer, text, and email to communicate with people. My doctors have portals that allow me to chat with them directly. I buy almost everything online.

6. **Revenue Streams.** This block represents the cash a company generates from each customer segment. What pricing mechanism options do you use? Fixed, bargaining, auction, volume, yield? What are your revenue streams? Free, asset sales, subscription, advertising, usage, licensing, brokerage, leasing, renting, lending, product sales? A lot of money is left on the table in the pricing area for most industries. For example, retail has started getting traction by using artificial intelligence. But many of you have no strategies or policies on how and when to change pricing.[8]

7. **Key Resources.** These are the most valuable assets required to make a business model work. You need to give more thought to which assets must be owned because they constitute your competitive

advantage and will be what makes you different. Which ones should you give up to avoid the hassle? These same considerations apply to people. Which ones do you need as employees because they give you a competitive advantage, and which ones can be independent contractors? When making these decisions, consider which assets and people are essential to your differentiation strategy.[9]

8. **Key Partnerships.** This element describes the network of suppliers and partners who make your business model work. At Xcelerate Restoration, we identified strategic alliances between noncompetitors that helped us add clients faster and add more value for our clients. It was a win-win for both our alliance partners and ourselves.[10]

In some cases, it may be a smart idea to create strategic alliances with your competitors or vendors. One of my clients in the construction industry just arranged special terms with suppliers—for two reasons. He had problems in his business, both in finding enough capital and with the cost of capital. The special terms with suppliers provided him access to unlimited purchases on 60-day terms. He gained access to significant capital for free. His company will now be able to double sales, better serve clients, and improve his cash-flow model.

9. **Cost Structure.** This last building block describes the most significant costs incurred while operating under a business model. You need to understand and be able to forecast your business model. You will need to know how much of your cost structure is fixed and how much is variable. At what points will you need to add to fixed costs? Break these down between the direct cost of sales and indirect costs, so you understand the scalability of your business model.[11]

Strategy is essential to building a growth company. It necessary that you and your team consider choices from a market perspective—to construct your activities in a way that provides a unique and valuable position in the market. When you do, it allows you to compete in a different landscape than your rivals, giving you a competitive advantage. The Business Model Canvas is a tool designed to help you look at the nine elements of a business model and to make meaningful choices to make your business uniquely different from and preferable to your competition.

DESIGN A PROFITABLE AND SCALABLE BUSINESS MODEL

- Too often, leaders allow their business models to happen by accident rather than by design.
- When you design your business properly, you grow far faster than your competitors and have at least three times their profitability.
- Sharp entrepreneurs find models that produce enough cash, so they do not have to give away too much equity to investors!
- When you have a proven business model and think you need outside capital to scale, challenge yourself as to whether that capital is a real necessity. Most people raise money for the wrong reasons, and it happens because of their business models.
- If you are speaking about initiatives to be accomplished more than one year from now, you are talking about *strategy*. Within one year, it is *execution*.
- *Strategy* is also about choices and adding value.
- In *Business Model Generation*, Alexander Osterwalder and Yves Pigneur used "The Business Model Canvas" to help you work through the nine essential business model building blocks that form the basis for your business.
- The Business Model Canvas is a tool designed to help you look at the nine elements of a business model and to make meaningful choices to make your business uniquely different from and preferable to your competition.

BUSINESS ACCELERATION CALCULATOR™

It is time to pause and determine how the content discussed in "Design a Profitable and Scalable Business Model" affects your company. Go to www.howardmshore.com/tools and request our *Business Acceleration Tools®*. This tool will give you access to the *Business Acceleration Calculator™*. It will help you keep track of all the deficiencies this book has helped you discover in your business.

The same section applies to Growth Accelerators #9 – #12. In section 2 of the *Calculator*, entitled Ways to Improve Revenue (Volume or Price), the first line is dedicated to helping you calculate the impact of having a subpar strategy. In our experience, a company has a subpar strategy if it is **not** growing at a rate of at least 20 percent annually. The caveat to this is that your company should also be growing at three times your industry's average. If 20 percent is **not** more than three times the industry average, you must bump it up. If your company is not growing fast enough, you have a strategy problem.

There is one added effect from Growth Accelerator #9. It relates to profitability. If your profitability is **not** three times that of the industry, it may relate to the business model. Beware of this issue and be honest with yourself. If you know your profit issue is really a strategy issue, make sure to address it. Remember that "Revenue is vanity, profit is sanity, and cash is king!" If you find that you are not producing an exceptional profit, develop ideas to innovate in the areas of how you acquire customers, deliver your product or service, or create leverage in your business model. This will then go in the appropriate section in the *Calculator*.

CHAPTER 13
Growth Accelerator #10:
NARROW YOUR TARGET MARKET

I n the last year, I helped found and joined the board of Xcelerate Restoration. Eager to gain insight to apply to our start-up, I recently talked with Ron Antevy, President and CEO of eBuilder. Ron had sold his company to Trimble Company for $500 million in February 2018.[1] He gave me several key nuggets of advice, most importantly, how he narrowed his target market.

eBuilder is a cloud-based, enterprise project management solution for capital projects. It delivers insights in a way that causes its clients to save huge amounts of money. The company's software has not always been as sophisticated and world-class as it is today, but the strategy and business model have remained the same. Rather than trying to build software that catered to a broad audience, the leadership team narrowed their target market. While many leaders viewed the market too generically, this team realized that less is more. Capital project needs are very different, depending on the industry and the size and nature of projects. Ron and his team recognized that the more differences they tried to capture, the more complex the software they would need.

Additionally, widening the net to capture clients would complicate marketing and sales strategies. The team considered all their options and then identified a narrow segment with tremendous potential. They decided to focus on a specific set of 800 hospitals across the United States. From inception until he sold the company, they acquired 130 of those organizations as clients. Narrowing the focus was worth $500 million.

Segmentation is a huge opportunity for many organizations and doesn't get the right amount of attention. Typically, segments are not defined correctly. Companies target too many segments and often have no strategy related to segmentation. In my last book, I referred to this as chasing revenue everywhere and anywhere. Great companies quickly learn that by accurately segmenting the marketplace, they can perfect their business model and own their segment.

What Is Segmentation?

As Ron Antevy demonstrated, *segmentation* is all about becoming the best at serving your slice of the market. Ron told me that once he got a client, he never lost that client. Strange as it may seem, his was also the highest priced company in the market. His clients did not dare move to a cheaper provider because they felt they had too much to lose if they were wrong. If another product could not deliver what Ron's did, it would cost far more than what they might save in monthly license fees. Every month, competitors contact eBuilder's clients with cheaper offerings, challenging them to save money. Hospitals, a low-margin industry always looking for ways to save money, steadfastly refuse to switch. The offsetting cost savings are not as attractive as eBuilder's platform.

What I typically see in companies is the opposite situation. Not to insult anyone reading this book, but too many of you have the commodity mentality that views sales as a numbers game. While salespeople do need to play a specific role, that role is different when a company has a good strategy versus a bad one. When you try to be all things to all people, chasing too many segments with a generic product, it becomes a numbers game. In essence, you have decided to offer an average product that has little to no exceptional qualities. You call enough people until someone who doesn't know any better buys it. Sometimes your product matches a specific kind of client, but because you did not take enough time to understand segments, you did a lot more work than necessary to convert a sale. Either scenario is a bad strategy.

Restoration is an industry I have worked with a lot. The average company in this industry grows 5 percent a year, and most get stuck once they reach approximately $5 million in revenue. By narrowing their segment, our clients grow more than 25 percent per year. The average restoration company has too many sales channels and dabbles in both residential and commercial restoration. Our clients who have few sales channels and focus their energy on either residential *or* commercial restoration—but not both—experience mushrooming sales and are the most profitable.

The need to choose specific client segments is essential in every industry, but is more evident in some industries than others. Consider the food and beverage industry. If you are going to create a restaurant, before you even create the concept, you must decide to whom you are catering. There are four basic styles of dining: fast food, fast-casual, casual dining, and fine dining. Once you pick the style, you must choose the type of food within that style. After you make those decisions and construct your restaurant, acquiring loyal customers will depend on some variables within each segment:

- Food variety
- Food quality
- Portion size
- Range of service
- Beverage availability

- Entertainment value
- Décor
- Cleanliness
- Speed of service
- Price

Restaurateurs who are uncertain about the segment they want to own will have difficulty constructing their strategy among these different dimensions. As a result, they try to please everyone and likely please no one. They will end up with marketing, operations, and cash-flow problems.

Narrower Is Better

Why did eBuilder's strategy of narrowing the market to 800 hospitals work so well? The narrower you can make your customer focus, the better. This seems counterintuitive to the typical entrepreneur who naturally wants to see revenue go through the roof. Conventional thinking is that having more potential clients gives you more revenue opportunities. However, that is only true if those potential clients are part of the same segment.

In small businesses, focusing on a segment can be scary. It is especially hard to consider in the Survival Phase I described earlier in the book, when revenue may be hard to come by, and you may be losing money daily. However, three factors can help you understand the importance of choosing your customer focus:

1. Time is Limited.

You must consider the purpose you are trying to serve your customer base. As previously stressed, your company needs to be purposeful. Apple has done a great job of keeping a very focused product line. At the time of this writing, they had become the most valuable company in US markets by having a very concentrated product line with very few options to a very select market. While their competitors arguably went after much larger numbers of people, Apple focused on a narrow slice of people they knew would become loyal fans. By owning that segment, they have achieved a profit per employee of $393,853[2] compared to the average profit per employee of $36,916 for the entire S&P 500[3]; 10 times the profit.

Each targeted segment requires you to spend time to gain their attention. Time spent with one segment takes time away from another. In most instances, to properly dominate a segment, you must market and sell to different people in different ways in different places, and all these people have different expectations and needs. It takes time to sell to different segments and use different channels, but time is finite. By not focusing, businesses harm their growth instead of improving it.

2. Cash Management.

Regardless of the size of your business, cash needs to be rationed. The more cash you have, the more options you have. But I have seen some clients get sloppy because they have a lot of cash. Going after too many customer segments is not using your cash wisely. You need to understand each segment and which channels clients buy from. Not mastering these is a sign you do not understand the client. Unfortunately, most leaders do not realize this until it is too late. They throw their cash in lots of directions hoping something will stick. Then they run out of cash or must settle for a lesser path because they lacked the foresight to choose their ideal customer base correctly.

Another way to look at this is to treat it as an investment portfolio. If you treat customer segments the way you make other investments, you will allocate cash based on the expected return on capital. When I look at investments, I look at the return percentage and the energy it will take to obtain that return. I like investments that have low energy requirements and a high return. But companies too often spend high energy for lower returns. They could spend less energy to incrementally expand their share within an existing segment; their dollar return percentage would be higher if they would stay focused. But they love the idea of selling their products and services everywhere. They go after additional segments, not recognizing that it's diluting the value of their brands.

Brand dilution is the highest, unaccounted cost that occurs when companies go after too many segments. It is essential to understand what you want to be known for and to whom!

3. Complexity.

For each additional segment you target, each channel you use to sell, and every additional product and service line you offer each segment, you will increase the complexity of your business model. An excessive number of revenue-oriented leaders focus so much on the revenue opportunity that it blinds them to the complexity each additional segment will cause within their operations. To avoid this, sit with your operations team and understand the implications of adding new revenue streams to the mix. Consider the impact on the process, technology, sales channels, pricing, and value proposition. An entrepreneur's natural tendency is to say yes, to downplay every obstacle. They do not listen to their operations people's explanations of how the additional sales create real, new complexity that will layer on existing complexity. If you often catch yourself saying, "that is simple," your organization may be an example of what I've just described.

Time, cash management, and complexity come into play in a myriad of ways. The narrower your market, the easier it becomes for you to stand out in the market. eBuilder's segmentation strategy made it easy for them to say, "If you are a hospital, frustrated by your inability to get your arms around the cost and complexity of capital projects, it is time to call eBuilder. They are the pros." Can your marketing message be that clear? Is it easy for your target audience to know that you are the primary company for them?

There is also a speed factor. When you narrow your market, it simplifies product and service offerings, allowing you to go to market faster. Your minimum viable product is much simpler than that of a company that is trying to solve all the world's problems. You can do it with fewer employees, and you can cut unnecessary features. By narrowing your segment, you can lower the time, energy, and cost of acquiring customers. When you master a marketing channel, your cost to receive leads goes down, the volume and quality of leads increase, and sales conversion rises. Having a clear and simple message with the correctly priced product puts your company in the driver's seat.

How Do You Find Your Segment?

Hopefully, I have inspired you to act! So let's address that nagging question, "How do I find my segment?" Many companies already have a competitive advantage hiding in plain sight, but have failed to capitalize on it. Assuming you are not a start-up, a good place to begin is to analyze your client database. If you allow yourself to open your mind, you will discover a trove of information. Start by grouping clients in different ways to find critical patterns. Here is a list of good questions to ask:

- How did we acquire each one of these clients?
- Why did these clients choose us? (It is never about the price.)
- For each grouping of clients, make a list, rank-ordered as to what service attributes they considered when making their decisions. What product attributes are most important to them?
- Which clients are the most loyal, and why?
- Which clients are the most difficult to service, and why?
- Which clients do you find more of your competitors vying for, and why?
- Which client segments are shrinking, and why?
- Which client segments are growing, and why?
- Which groups are more profitable for you, which ones are less profitable, and why?
- Who is the decision-maker in each of these groups?
- What are the characteristics of each decision-maker?

- What are the circumstances that your decision-makers face?
- What are the specific problems each decision maker is trying to solve with your product or service?
- In the scope of importance, which group finds your product most important to them?

Your goal must be to have most of your client base filled with those you love to serve. Great companies commit to identifying the best clients and building their strategies around owning that market. By doing so, you will find that your operation is custom-built toward serving that ideal client, so you have a competitive advantage. Ideal clients are loyal, so they give you referrals to more ideal clients. These clients are more profitable for you, and as you become the leader in the niche, it ultimately becomes easier to attract additional ideal clients. This leads to a more profitable and stable business model.

NARROW YOUR TARGET MARKET

- Too many leaders look at the market too generically.
- Great companies quickly learn that by segmenting the marketplace, they can perfect their business model and own their segment.
- While salespeople do need to play a specific role, the role is different when a company has a good strategy versus a bad one. When you are trying to be all things to all people, chasing too many segments with a generic product, it becomes a numbers game.
- The need to choose specific client segments is essential in every industry.
- When it comes to segmentation, less is more!
- Three factors can help you understand the importance of choosing your customer focus:

  1. Time is Limited
  2. Cash Management
  3. Complexity

- The narrower your market, the easier it becomes for you to stand out.
- By narrowing your segment, you can lower the amount of time, energy, and cost to acquire customers.
- When you have mastered a marketing channel, your cost to acquire leads goes down, the volume of leads goes up, the quality of leads increases, and sales conversion rises.

BUSINESS ACCELERATION CALCULATOR™

It is time to pause and determine how the content discussed in "Narrow Your Target Market" affects your company. Go to www.howardmshore. com/tools and request our *Business Acceleration Tools®*. This tool will give you access to the *Business Acceleration Calculator™*. It will help you keep track of all the deficiencies this book has helped you discover in your business.

The same section applies to Growth Accelerators #9 – #12. In section 2 of the *Calculator* entitled, Ways to Improve Revenue (Volume or Price), the first line is dedicated to helping you calculate the impact of having a subpar strategy. In our experience, a company has a subpar strategy if it is **not** growing at a rate of at least 20 percent annually. The caveat to this is that your company should also be growing at three times your industry's average. If 20 percent is not more than three times the industry average, you must bump it up. If your company is not growing fast enough, you have a strategy problem.

CHAPTER 14

Growth Accelerator #11:

DIFFERENTIATE
PROPERLY

A s I indicated earlier, this book is not sequential, and it is iterative. There is no engraved-in-granite, step-by-step manual to follow covering how to build a company. *Strategy* is a process where you continuously look at your business from various points of view. You must maintain both a rookie mentality and a watchful eye for what you might not have seen in the past. Your job is to discover ways to create value for clients that you and everyone else missed before. It seems impossible, yet it continues to happen.

Chapter 12 helped you consider strategy from an internal perspective when you design a profitable and scalable business model. In Chapter 13, we viewed strategy from a segment perspective to show how narrowing your focus facilitates and strengthens your strategy. In this chapter, we look at strategy from an *external perspective*, where you incorporate a client's viewpoint in your strategy construction. This chapter raises the question of how you differentiate your business from others in your industry.

Differentiation is about learning how to stand out from the competition. Doing so simplifies and increases the velocity of client acquisition, reduces client turnover, and maximizes your profits per client. Failing to differentiate has reverse effects.

Failing to differentiate equates to having a commodity mentality. Typically, leaders can't or won't make an effort to find a way to be different from their competitors. Leaders who take that position spend more to acquire clients and make less money serving them. It also leads to decreased enjoyment of being in business.

As you work through this chapter, download the Vision Worksheet and Attribution Framework tools from our *Business Acceleration Tools®* at www.howardmshore.com/tools). These tools were designed to help you assess, identify, create, and effectively communicate your unique and valuable position in the market. The Vision Worksheet addresses clarifying questions essential to differentiation. The Attribution Framework enables you to assess how your competitors positioned themselves in the market so that you can choose a unique and valuable position for your product or service. Your results should prove how effective your differentiation is by delivering revenue growth rates that are two to three times faster than the industry average. Our best clients, even those in slow-growth industries, grow a minimum of 25 percent each year. If this is not true for your organization, you have a strategy problem and are leaving great potential on the table.

Great Differentiation

Many leaders think they must be in a "hot" industry or use technology to create differentiation. Nothing could be further from the truth. Differentiation starts with doing a great job of understanding all the market segments. Figure out how those segments are serviced, how they are underserved, and how they are changing. Determine which segments are untapped. Study and understand the competitive landscape. It is critical that you know your competition, how they operate, and what their strengths and weaknesses are when viewed from the vantage point of your target clients.

The best way to help you understand differentiation is to tell you about a company that has completely distinguished itself from its competition in a remarkable way. Picture this: I ask you to be an investor in my grocery chain, and I tell you the following about my concept:

- Our aisles are going to be narrow.
- Parking lots will be small, and clients will probably have to wait for parking.
- The staff, who we will refer to as our crew, will wear cool Hawaiian shirts.
- We will do no television advertising, no social media, and no advertising in the Sunday newspaper.
- We will never have anything on sale and won't accept coupons.
- No self-check-out, and, by the way, we will have a ton of employees at the checkout lines—one telling you which register to go to, one pulling you out of the big line and into a shorter one, and one or two holding up handmade signs marking the middle of the queue and the beginning—three or four employees doing a job that most stores use zero employees to do.
- We do not believe in loyalty programs.
- While typical supermarkets have 35,000 stock-keeping units (SKU), we will average 3,000.
- We will stock our shelves during business hours instead of at night.
- We will make little use of technology and not harness big data like our competitors.

I just described Trader Joe's, which with fewer than 500 stores nationwide was crushing the competition with more than $13 billion in revenue in 2015.[1] The sales-per-square-footage estimates are unbelievable—three and four times better than some of the leading players in the industry. They also have been ranked as one of the 100 best American workplaces.

The Trader Joe's model belies the belief that some industries don't allow for much differentiation. The grocery industry is going through massive changes and is under siege by two different trends. After years of trying to overcome increasing competition, the grocery business has had to address the "Amazon effect"—a considerable problem given that the grocery industry has always had low margins. If that was not enough, a new problem has emerged. For the first time in history, American consumers are spending more money in restaurants and bars than they are in grocery stores.[2]

Trader Joe's has bucked the trend by growing but not being a low-margin business. What gives? First of all, they know their core clients well, so much so that they have what amounts to a cult following. With fewer than 500 stores, there is a good chance there is not one near you. Store openings receive coverage as significant news events. Some people claim that they bring an extra suitcase when they travel to a city that has a Trader Joe's. There are Facebook pages posted by superfans all over the country who want Trader Joe's to put a store in their area. They build up a potential clientele, hoping to get noticed by Trader Joe's. It's crazy. Imagine achieving this in your industry.[3]

Amazingly, Trader Joe's has generated this momentum with no traditional advertising of their own. Until recently, they did not even have a decent website. Their explosion has all come from word-of-mouth advertising. How loyal would you be to your supermarket if you moved and they were not in your town? Would you put up a fan page and fight to get them to put up a store in your location?[4]

Trader Joe's secret to success starts with their human capital management strategy. Every employee must be an extrovert. They look for friendly, helpful, and enthusiastic people. When they onboard employees, managers aren't too worried about teaching people how to operate a grocery store. They give them the necessary training and focus most of their efforts on teaching the company's values. Essentially, the most significant portion of new employees' orientation is about how to treat clients. Lastly, they pay employees above the industry standard. Crew members make about $50,000 per year, and "captains" make more than $100,000, with better-than-average benefits, as of 2013.[5]

Their ideal clients look forward to shopping as an experience. It has been reported that Trader Joe's puts a great deal of effort into scouting, sourcing, and producing food that their clients truly love. However, one of the keys to improving the client experience—and the brand's allure—is their package design and descriptive salesmanship. Their marketing director is called the "Director of Words & Phrases & Clauses." They publish an old-fashioned newsprint bulletin, *The Fearless Flyer*, with in-depth descriptions of new products. Roughly 80 percent of their products are private-label items. When you walk into a Trader Joe's, there's a playful vibe, and they want employees in the aisles who have sampled the products, will talk about them, and walk their clients around, encouraging them to try new things.[6]

My goal here is to give you a taste of what it looks like to be different. Most supermarkets look and feel nothing like what I just described. In fact, the rest look predominantly the same. Trader Joe's has done a fascinating job of identifying a specific client niche and catering to it in a way that no one else has.

By identifying your differentiating niche, you can accomplish a little bit of Trader Joe's formula, and a portion of its scale and success overall. This is what I want to help you perform in your business.

Do You Know What Your Clients Want?

For your company to maximize its profitable growth, it has to create the right differentiation. To do that, you must identify the small but impactful differences in what you offer that will give you a substantial competitive advantage. There are many ways to add value to your product or service to distinguish your company from its competitors, but few right ones.

Creating your unusual value proposition takes creativity and a real understanding of the needs, wants, and desires of your target clients. When leaders work on intuition rather than facts when attempting to create their differentiators, it severely hampers the growth of their businesses.

A good example is a client in the business services sector with a long history of high client retention. They knew this retention meant they were doing something right, and that something prevented competitors from stealing their clients. But they had been unable to define what that "something" was. Like many companies, their definition of what made them different was too broad. They would say it was service. This helped them keep clients but made it challenging to acquire new ones. The marketing department and the sales team could not articulate to prospective clients why they were the best option.

To make matters worse, the CEO decided to pivot the organization toward a unique value proposition without validating it with existing and potential clients. This turned out to be a huge mistake for this 30-year institution. Many clients they acquired over the next few years did not value the extra effort and moved on quickly. Although the organization invested extra money to deliver additional services, those new customers did not believe they had received fair value for their money. Sadly, the organization lost several of its long-established and marquee clients for the same reason.

This scenario is a widespread one. The key to gaining knowledge lies outside of your building. Often, our experience becomes our enemy. We look for information that validates our current beliefs instead of examining all the data available to us. The company I mentioned was advised to hire a third party to help understand the market soon after experiencing a slowdown in growth and client turnover. However, once they learned that it would cost over $20,000 to hire a competent consultant, they decided not to get help. They continue to experience average growth.

One of the tools that I asked you to download at the beginning of this chapter to help you determine what factors to focus on in terms of differentiation is the Attribution Framework tool. It enables you to identify and prioritize factors your target clients use to choose your company over your competitors. It then allows you to compare your company against your competitors along each dimension. When we fill this out with clients, we find that many do not know much about their competitors, nor have they collected substantive market research to support their hypotheses on what matters to a client. Acquiring such knowledge is crucial to gaining dominance in the market. It teaches you how to walk in your ideal prospects' shoes—from their perspective instead of yours.

What Elements Constitute an Unusual Offering?

To help your business grow, let's talk about the notion of creating an *unusual offering*. There may be an obvious opportunity before you, but you must have an open mind to grasp it.

Consider Trader Joe's. The typical supermarket has more than 35,000 stock-keeping units, and yet Trader Joe's only has 3,000—items that people will drive or fly with a suitcase to purchase. Think about an aisle of jam or chocolate in a typical market. There are many choices, but no one to vouch for brands you don't know. At Trader Joe's, you have very few options, but the company has built its reputation on carrying and recommending only high-quality products. If you love jam or chocolate, you will be excited to see what they have and buy some. Even better, at Trader Joe's, prices are 32 percent cheaper than at Amazon Whole Foods.[7]

Depending on who your core clients are, and what options are available to them, you need to consider how the following elements add value to your unusual offering:

- **Price.** What is the total cost of your product today? Do your customers know what their total cost is? What would additional features, benefits, and services be worth to your potential clients in terms of time, value, doing more business with you, or reducing their stress? If you added new features, services, and benefits, would you increase prices, or would you just be increasing your cost of doing business? Think about your process for purchasing a printer for your office or home. The cost of the machine may be irrelevant. The cost of the consumables and many other factors may make or break the deal. How many pages per ink cartridge are you going to get? How long is the machine going to last? Is the engine fast enough for your needs, or are you going to sit around unproductive all day because it tends to break down or takes too long to finish printing?

- **Cost/Risk Reduction.** How can you modify your offering in a way that substantially reduces client costs? How can the design of your product or service minimize the risk for your client? Many companies give 30-day free trials and money-back guarantees as inducements to allow clients a chance to experience their product or service. Your company should not make such an offer without being able to back up its promises. The risk you remove must be one of the critical deterrents to the buyer trying your product or service.

- **Trends.** What industry-wide trends are occurring—technologically, economically, and environmentally—that call for a new advancement to sell, deliver, distribute, or market your product or service? Uber and Lyft took advantage of people being frustrated by poor client experiences with taxis. Their technology makes it easier to hail a ride in nicer vehicles and with people with better attitudes. Also, it's essential to understand what was different for clients today may no longer be different tomorrow. FedEx used to have an advantage by promising to deliver by 10:00 a.m. tomorrow. Now, the US Postal Service offers that same delivery promise. You need to understand what competitors are doing and update your business model to stay ahead of the competition.

- **Performance.** What are the performance enhancements to your product or service that are most valuable to your clients? Would your clients pay more for these enhancements, and would you lose clients to a competitor that added them while you did not? Is the enhancement necessary to keep up with minimum expectations? At what point does the performance improvement no longer make a difference in clients' buying patterns? Many times, people think this is only a product issue, but I find it is equally critical in business services. For example, recently, many marketing firms have failed to meet the needs of their clients. The world of marketing has been shifting from traditional advertising to interactive and social media. Business owners need marketing to build, nurture, and preserve their brands and generate leads using these new platforms. But while there is a proliferation of firms offering services in the modern marketing spaces, many fail to provide the results they led their clients to expect. Proving performance can be a crucial differentiator.

- **Customization.** To what extent does customization of a product or service significantly enhance its value? Many of my clients offer different bundles of their products and services to change their perceived value to clients. For example, Activate Group, Inc. bundles services to drive a better impact for clients. We do this through Bronze, Silver, Gold, and Platinum business coaching programs. Our Gold and Platinum clients experience better and faster outcomes than Bronze and Silver clients. These higher levels give clients a much more comprehensive experience. Our coaches have more touchpoints with more leaders and employees, allowing us to help unlock the full potential of more employees.

- **Design.** To what extent does the design make a difference in the usability of your product or service? Can design make your product more appealing or usable? Technology and "people intensity" are the two key levers here. Some businesses guarantee you will always talk to a human being. In others, you will never speak to one. How do you use technology to increase the speed of a critical aspect of the product or service—or add convenience, functionality, integration, accuracy, or consistency?

- **Brand/Status.** To what extent does brand or status influence the buyer? The internet has allowed some companies to rise to the top and achieve national and international recognition for a fraction of the cost that was once required. Dollar Shave Club was purchased by Unilever for $1 billion. Founded in 2011, this company used YouTube videos to acquire 3.2 million members and was on track to reach $200 million in revenue in 2016. Dollar Shave Club has come a long way since it posted its first quirky video that poked fun at the razor-buying experience eight years ago. While its customer growth has slowed, it currently has 4 million subscribers, including myself.[8]

- **Accessibility.** How can you make your offering more accessible to your target clients? What channels do you use to access clients? Netflix stole significant market share from Blockbuster once DVDs became the primary medium for home viewing. Now that they've determined that clients prefer streaming video over DVDs, they are doing the same to cable companies.[9]

Evaluating each of these elements will help you realize and truly define your unusual offering. It is also important to note that you must make choices. When leaders take the position that they will offer the lowest price, best service, and the highest quality, they are embracing a business model that is guaranteed to fail. In reality, a business may focus on two out of the three but only be best at one.[10]

It is likely that you already have some of the necessary frameworks in place and now need to identify what truly makes your company unique and why clients should choose your company. Use the Vision Worksheet and Attribution Framework tools to increase your confidence in your strategy. Failure to be differentiated in the eyes of the market is a sure-fire way to maintain an average growth rate.

DIFFERENTIATE PROPERLY

- Your job is to discover ways to create value for clients that you and everyone else missed before. It seems impossible, yet it continues to happen.
- *Differentiation* is about learning how to stand out from the competition, simplifying the acquisition of clients, increasing the velocity of client acquisition, reducing client turnover, and maximizing your profits on clients.
- Download the Vision Worksheet and Attribution Framework tools in our *Business Acceleration Tools®* at www.howardmshore.com/tools.
- The Vision Worksheet will help you address clarifying questions essential to establish differentiation.
- The Attribution Framework tool will help you assess how your competitors are positioning themselves in the market so that you can choose a unique and valuable position.
- To maximize your company's profitable growth, you have to create the right differentiation.
- You must identify the small but hugely impactful differences in what you offer that will give you a substantial competitive advantage.
- There are a lot of ways to add value to your product or service to distinguish your company from your competitors, but few right ones.
- Creating your unusual value proposition takes creativity and a real understanding of the needs, wants, and desires of your target clients.
- The key to gaining knowledge lies outside of your building.

- The Attribution Framework tool will help you determine what factors to focus on in terms of differentiation.
- The Attribution Framework tool will also help you identify and prioritize which factors your target clients use to choose your company over your competitors. It then enables you to compare your company against your competitors along each dimension.

BUSINESS ACCELERATION CALCULATOR™

It is time to pause and determine how the practices discussed in "Differentiate Properly" can affect your company. Go to www.howardmshore.com/tools and request our *Business Acceleration Tools*®. This tool will give you access to the *Business Acceleration Calculator*™. It will help you keep track of all the deficiencies this book has helped you discover in your business.

The same section applies to Growth Accelerators #10 – #12. In section 2 of the *Calculator* entitled, Ways to Improve Revenue (Volume or Price)?, the first line is dedicated to helping you calculate the impact of having a subpar strategy. In my experience, a company's strategy is subpar if it is **not** growing at a rate of at least 20 percent annually. The caveat to this is that your company should also be growing at three times the industry average. If 20 percent is not more than three times the industry average, you must bump it up. If your company is not growing fast enough, you have a strategy problem.

CHAPTER 15
Growth Accelerator #12:

LAY THE FOUNDATION FOR CONTINUOUS GROWTH

Leading companies must play to win and strive to grow. Otherwise, they will find themselves left behind when the competition creates a new product or service with more appealing features and benefits, or new technology makes your process obsolete, or a foreign firm aims at your client base.

Just a few years ago, we featured Blockbuster as a leader because they had developed a then-revolutionary approach to distributing video content to consumers. They did this by negotiating a new way to license and use studio content in a flat-fee-plus-revenue-share (upside) economic structure. Less than a decade later, Blockbuster no longer exists. Similarly, Jim Collins, in his famous book, *Good to Great,* used Circuit City as one of 11 featured companies. They no longer exist. Toys"R"Us was a company that every kid in America knew as the place to go when they were good boys or girls. Kodak, founded in 1888, stayed focused on producing film, got complacent with their dominance, and failed to understand that they were in the business of helping people capture "moments." New and better ways emerged to accomplish this, and Kodak failed to evolve. Borders, once an internationally franchised bookseller, went out of business because they were unable to position themselves correctly for online retail the way Amazon and Barnes & Noble had.[1]

Great strategic thinking is much like optometric refraction, the test your eye doctor uses to determine your exact eyeglass prescription. During refraction, the doctor puts an instrument called a *phoropter* in front of your eyes and shows you a series of lens choices. They then ask which of the two lenses helps you see the eye chart more clearly. The same thing happens with strategic thinking. We continuously examine data, and with an open mind, can see the marketplace from different vantage points. With this clearer and evolving view, we realize that without change, we too may become obsolete.

Build a Valuable Company

Leaders can become so focused on products and services that they forget their main priority—to build a great company. In his book *Built to Last,* Jim Collins dedicated a whole chapter to this issue. He referred to it as the difference between "clock-building" and "time-telling." He said the distinction between visionary companies and the others in their field is that visionary leaders build great companies that can live and continue to thrive after the initial leader leaves. He called that *clock-building*. He compared the visionary companies to other well-regarded organizations whose claim to fame was having more charismatic leaders or being founded on a single great idea. He referred to those as *time-telling*. His research showed that companies founded on the clock-building philosophy outlasted and far outperformed the time-telling companies.[2]

While all the case stories in *Built to Last* are remarkable, I favor the Hewlett-Packard (HP) story because of my intense focus on culture. HP continued to thrive after founders, Bill Hewlett and Dave Packard, stepped aside. In contrast, Texas Instruments almost self-destructed after Pat Haggarty retired. If you looked at HP's beginning and compared them to Texas Instruments, you'd have thought that the latter would be the stronger of the two. Most of the early products created by HP either failed or had lackluster success. It was over time, by following "the HP Way," that the company became known for great products. Bill and Dave's focus on designing and building a great organization rather than making the products led the company to exceed Texas Instruments.[3]

I understand that not all leaders are trying to develop an enduring or billion-dollar company. We all have different aspirations and definitions of success. The key is to be aware that you deserve a return for taking on the risk and stress of building a company versus taking a job. Strive for much more than a good paycheck. Leaders who build their companies to last not only have higher valuations but also more fun and satisfaction along the way.

My career includes a successful exit from Ryder System, Inc. I had helped build and sell the Ryder Public Transportation Division through mergers and acquisitions. I was fortunate to have this experience and to participate in an executive education program on this subject at the University of Chicago. Both experiences gave me insights into how to sell a company and what makes a company valuable to a prospective buyer or investor.

To increase your business's valuation, consider the following factors:

- The consistency, growth rate, and amount of revenue your business generates
- The consistency, growth rate, and amount of earnings before interest, taxes, depreciation, and amortization (EBITDA) your business generates
- The depth and strength of your leadership team
- The depth and strength of the rest of your team
- The strength of any proprietary intellectual property that can be acquired

- The size of the definable market you have captured and how much more runway there is in that market
- Trends and their impact on your current position in the market

Although creating an enduring, billion-dollar company may not be your current goal, I'm sure you don't want to end up like Blockbuster—or any of the other companies that have disappeared for failure to implement the right strategies. While this book aims to help you maximize your business valuation, I wrote this chapter because so many businesses fail to realize that the ground beneath them is always moving. This is why I want you to become a "clock-builder"—and build a great company!

The Past Is No Indication of the Future

Those who invest in the stock market know the universal disclaimer, "Past performance is not an indicator of future results." The same is true for your business, yet leaders continue to buy into the misconception that if they've grown by 20 percent per year for the last three years, they can expect to do the same for the next three years. This brings us to the subject of *forecasting*.

Many organizations we've worked with were weak in this area. Planning for growth should not imply that there will never be a slowdown. When you know what to look for, you can predict when these inevitable slowdowns in growth will occur. To improve their forecasting skills, every business owner must be aware of and understand the concept of the S curve. This awareness will show you how to find opportunities for continued growth.

The *S curve* is a business concept that defines the growth of company sales for a product's lifecycle. A product's sales lifecycle, when charted on a graph, will look like the letter "S." When a product enters the market, it shows a rapid, and in some cases, exponential sales growth, followed by tapering or leveling off. The tapering occurs when the population of new customers declines or too much competition has entered the market, causing a supply versus demand imbalance. At that point, growth becomes slow or negligible and is sustained mainly by existing customers who continue to buy the product. Eventually, you hit a decline phase. In some cases, like Blockbuster, that can seem like falling off a cliff. In most cases, it is not so rapid.

As we will discuss in Chapter 17, you must maintain a rolling forecast of your revenue and expenses, which you will find very instructive. As a company, you must view each product, segment, and geography choice through its lifecycle lens.

As a leader, your job is to extend the growth portion of the S curve. You do this by expanding geography, market segments, and incrementally bundling the product with additional product and service features and benefits. But eventually, your ability to grow will start to diminish. A great case example is the frozen yogurt and ice cream market.

I worked with the franchisor of a successful ice cream chain. He wanted to continue to grow in a market that is mostly standing still. He currently has about 300 locations and is encountering significant headwinds in adding stores. Considering that he's still growing, he has a much better story to tell than TCBY. He had worked for TCBY during its high-growth period. For almost two years, they opened the equivalent of a new location every 17 hours. TCBY peaked at 1,800 locations and is now down to 300–400 sites.[4]

In his current business, it appeared that the S curve for my client's product had hit the top of the S. The market is saturated, and consumer preferences are changing. Unless he discovers something to do that is dramatically different from his model, he will see only modest growth at best. At this stage of the S curve, his best option for achieving exceptional growth is to steal market share, which is still a possibility.

Build Your Next S Curve

Great companies don't focus on products. They build companies that develop products and services that address needs, problems, and challenges for client segments. Average companies focus on products and services and stay oblivious to the risks. So, what can be done if you want to hedge your bets?

Apple is an excellent example of building a go-to S curve. Had Apple focused only on computers, they would be a much smaller entity today. Revenue would have flattened a long time ago. However, they realized that they are a software company that integrates great software with hardware and finds better solutions for end consumers. If you examine Apple's revenue streams, they never stopped building computers and have done everything they can to extend the lifecycle of their products. However, using the cash flow from computer sales, they found other market opportunities and became one of the pre-eminent platform companies in the world. They built one of the world's largest platforms from which consumers purchase and download music and applications affordably and conveniently. The iPhone now makes up most of Apple's profit. The device itself represents a small percentage of the mobile phone market but accounts for most of the industry's profit. This diversification has propelled Apple to become one of the most valuable companies on the planet.

Just as Apple built a great company around its core competency in software innovation, you and your team must understand and develop a core competency to use in creating new products and services. Your core competency provides a runway to gaining a competitive advantage. Note that I am not identifying specific skills. Some companies we work with have no core competencies or are focusing their efforts on factors that are of little consequence in providing a competitive advantage in their market. Jim Collins aptly pointed out in *Good to Great* that a company can likely only be "best in the world" at one capability. This is true for Apple and any other great company.

For the first time since launching the iPhone, Apple's revenues are currently dropping. Their current agenda is to build their next S curve in the entertainment industry to include producing their own original content, taking on Netflix, Amazon, and HBO. According to a *Wall Street Journal* report that cited anonymous individuals, the tech giant has targeted $1 billion in spending for original television series and films over the next year, looking to establish itself as a buyer of premium entertainment. It remains to be seen if they are too late to this game and if this plays to their strengths. They have a platform and a strong customer base. But if there is any company that can pull this off, it's Apple. They have a balance sheet and cash flow that allows them to place a big bet such as this one.[5]

Embracing diversification and learning how to innovate is difficult for most companies. It requires a willingness to accept failure. When studying highly successful companies, you will find that they failed more often than they would like to admit. They put their best people in charge of new opportunities and risk significant capital. In some cases, they bet the entire company on the next new product or service. Apple faced insolvency and fired Steve Jobs before he came back and made the company great. Their products failed before they worked. They lost a lot of money before they made a profit. Some Apple products never even came to market. I don't advise you to take foolish risks, but I do suggest that continuing to take the risks you chose when you started your company is necessary to building future greatness.

Again, past and current success is not a guarantee of the future. You need to keep your phoropter ready and keep looking at the market through different lenses. It is hard to continue to look at the same eye chart and challenge yourself to see something new. If you don't keep your eyes open, you may wind up like Blockbuster, Circuit City, and other formerly great competitors that failed to see and address the opportunities, risks, and challenges right before their eyes. If you are content to be a one-hit-wonder and not willing to develop new S curves, I advise you to create a plan that helps you determine the right time to exit. Every industry and product can become oversaturated, hit maturity, or encounter obsolescence. There are many stories from owners who have ignored their S curves, only to watch their valuations drop 50 percent or more.

LAY THE FOUNDATION FOR CONTINUOUS GROWTH

- Excellent strategic thinking is much like an optometrist's refraction process.
- We continuously examine data and, with an open mind, can see the marketplace from different vantage points. With this clearer and evolving view, we realize that without change, we may become obsolete.
- Leaders can be so focused on their products and services that they forget their main priority is to build a great company.
- Past performance is not an indicator of future results.
- The *S curve* is a business concept that defines the growth of company sales for a product's lifecycle.
- Your job as a leader is to extend the growth portion of your S curve. You can do this by expanding geography, market segments, incrementally bundling the product with additional product and service features and benefits.
- Great companies don't focus on products; they build companies that develop products and services that solve problems and challenges for customer segments.
- You must understand and develop a core competency that you can use to create new products and services.
- Embracing and learning how to innovate is difficult for most companies. It requires you to be willing to accept failure.
- Highly successful companies put their best people in charge of the new opportunities and risk significant capital.
- If you are content to be a one-hit-wonder, not willing to develop new S curves, I advise you to create a plan that helps you determine the right time to exit.

BUSINESS ACCELERATION CALCULATOR™

It is time to pause and determine how following the suggestions in "Lay the Foundation for Continuous Growth" can affect your company. Go to www.howardmshore.com/tools and request our *Business Acceleration Tools*®. This will give you access to the *Business Acceleration Calculator*™. It will help you keep track of all the deficiencies this book has helped you discover in your business.

The same section applies to Growth Accelerators #10 – #12. In section 2 of the *Calculator* entitled, Ways to Improve Revenue (Volume or Price), the first line is dedicated to helping you calculate the impact of having a subpar strategy. In my experience, a company has a subpar strategy if it is **not** growing at a rate of at least 20 percent annually. The caveat to this is that your company should also be growing at three times your industry's average. If 20 percent is not more than three times the industry average, you must bump it up. If your company is not growing fast enough, you have a strategy problem.

PART V
PLANNING

3 YEAR   1 YEAR   1 QUARTER

"If you fail to plan, you are planning to fail!"

— **Benjamin Franklin**[1]

CHAPTER 16
Growth Accelerator #13:
COMMIT TO AN
AUDACIOUS GOAL

I f you have been working through this book sequentially, then you have established a clear and compelling purpose, narrowed your target market to a particular segment, identified how you want to own that segment, and clarified your business model. If you are like most leaders, you want to put all of this into action. In order to win, however, we must have a plan, whether it be in war, sports, business, or anything of substance.

I don't know what your behavioral style is. My natural style can be described as "fire, ready, and aim." I mention this because many leaders have a similar profile. This style serves me well in my role as a coach because my value to a team is that I get things done. I am a quick decision-maker, an innovative thinker, and a change agent. The problem is that people who embrace this style tend to be impatient and don't think things through.

The bigger the business opportunity, the more it requires that we think things through. I found that when people with *my* style failed to plan, a lot of activity occurred, but that did not mean it was productive. That technique can cause a whole organization to work harder than necessary, only to fail in accomplishing anything significant. Meanwhile, their competitors put in the same effort, or less, and are growing faster and becoming more profitable. Chapters 16 through 19 will help make sure you get maximum productivity with less work.

Planning is all about *alignment.* Your plans need to be aligned with your strategy. In other words, everything in your plans must be aligned with the work you did in the strategy Chapters 12 to 15. If you did not do the work in those chapters, or you developed a poor strategy, then expect your plans to yield suboptimal results. If you have a great strategy and no plans, you will also yield suboptimal results.

Have you ever been asked the question, "What is more important, your short-term plan or your long-term plan?" Pause for a moment and think about what your answer would be. Of course, it is a trick question. They are equally important. If you fail at your short-term plan, you will not achieve the long-term plan.

This chapter is about the very long term. It is about creating and committing to a crucial goal that sets the wheels in motion to help your company on the path toward greatness.

What Is an Audacious Goal?

We start our long-term planning with a concept author Jim Collins calls the "Big Hairy Audacious Goal" (commonly referred to as BHAG™). Our firm decided to remove "Big Hairy" from the phrase, believing that, while it may bring more emphasis to "audacious," it certainly does not fit into our modern-day, gender-neutral environment. Politically correct or not, Jim's concept has been critical to helping companies plan for greatness, and you must introduce it into your planning vernacular. Use whatever name for this concept that suits your organization.[1]

In his books, *Good to Great* and *Built to Last*, Jim Collins identified the "Audacious Goal" as one that visionary companies developed and pursued through time. The goal was so challenging that while leaders might not know precisely how to accomplish it, it would inspire the company to pursue and achieve greatness. The Audacious Goal is expressed as a number that arises out of the intersection of three key considerations:

1. A company's Core Purpose (its reason for being—or "Why We Exist");
2. A company's area of focus, something that they can be the best in (their) world at providing. We call this their Leading Customer Brand Promise;
3. A "Profit per X" that is the central increment or building block that drives their profit.

What is so compelling about this goal is that when you get it right:

1. It challenges you to greatness because it is a big stretch, audacious but doable. To achieve it will force your organization to make changes and not be complacent.
2. It reinforces your business fundamentals and causes you to address chokepoints today.
3. It will take at least 10 years—in many cases, 25 years—to achieve.[2]

What Makes for a Strong Audacious Goal?

The Audacious Goal is the essential number showing progress toward the purpose of your company. If you are not the best in the world at what you do, you will make little or no progress toward this number.

But when you move this number, your "Profit per X" increases. In Jim's research, they found more evidence of this powerful mechanism in the visionary companies and less evidence of it in the comparison companies in 14 out of 18 cases.[3]

All companies have goals. But there is a difference between merely having a goal and becoming committed to a huge, daunting challenge, like a big mountain to climb. Consider your Audacious Goal to be your Mount Everest. When Jim Collins and Jerry Porras discussed the Audacious Goal in *Built to Last*, they used the example of the moon mission in the 1960s. President Kennedy and his advisors could have drafted something like, "Let's beef up our space program," or some other vacuous statement. In 1961, the most optimistic scientific assessment of a moon mission's chances for success was 50-50. Most experts were more pessimistic.[4]

Nonetheless, Congress agreed (to the tune of an immediate $549 million and billions more in the following five years) with Kennedy's proclamation of May 25, 1961. Famously, he said, "That this Nation should commit itself to achieve the goal, before this decade is out, of landing a man on the moon and returning him safely to Earth." Given the odds, such a bold commitment was, at the time, outrageous. But that's part of what made it such a powerful mechanism for getting the United States, still tired from the 1950s and the Eisenhower era, to move vigorously forward.[5]

When you are developing your Audacious Goal, make sure you consider the following:

1. Your Audacious Goal is never revenue. If you find the right goal, however, you will have extraordinary growth in revenue and profit.
2. It must be compelling and serve as a unifying focal point of effort, often creating an immense team spirit.
3. It has a clear finish line so the organization can know when it has achieved the goal.
4. It takes 10 years or longer to reach.[6]

The moon mission didn't need a committee spending endless hours wordsmithing the goal into a verbose, meaningless, impossible-to-remember "mission statement." The goal itself—the mountain to climb—was so easy to grasp, so compelling, that it could be said 100 different ways yet was easily understood by everyone. When an expedition sets out to climb Mount Everest, it doesn't need a three-page, convoluted "mission statement" to explain what Mount Everest is.[7]

Think about your organization. How clear is your Mount Everest? Do you have such a clear and compelling mountain you are trying to climb? Is everyone in your organization rallying around a clear goal that causes them to drive change, all in the same direction? If not, I encourage you to start by creating a genuinely Audacious Goal.[8]

COMMIT TO AN AUDACIOUS GOAL

- Planning is all about alignment. Your plans need to be aligned with your strategy.
- If you have a great strategy and no plans, you will yield suboptimal results.
- In his books, *Good to Great* and *Built to Last,* Jim Collins identified the concept of the "Audacious Goal" as one that visionary companies developed and pursued through time.
- The Audacious Goal is expressed as a number that arises out of the intersection of three key considerations:

  1. A company's Core Purpose (its reason for being—its "Why We Exist");
  2. A company's area of focus, something that they can be the best in (their) world at providing—we call this their Leading Customer Brand Promise;
  3. A "Profit per X" that is the fundamental increment or building block that drives their profit.

- What is so powerful about this one number is that when you get it right:

  1. It challenges you to greatness as it is a big stretch, audacious but doable. To achieve it will force your organization to make changes and not be complacent.
  2. It reinforces your business fundamentals and causes you to address chokepoints today.
  3. It will take at least 10 years and, in many cases, 25 years to achieve.

- The Audacious Goal is the essential number showing progress toward the purpose of your company. If you are not the best in the world at what you do, you will make little or no progress toward this number, but when you move this number, your "Profit per X" increases.
- Consider your Audacious Goal as your Mount Everest.
- When you are developing your Audacious Goal, make sure you consider the following:

  1. Your Audacious Goal is never revenue. If you find the right goal, you will have extraordinary growth in revenue and profit.
  2. It must be compelling and serve as a unifying focal point of effort, often creating an immense team spirit.
  3. It has a clear finish line so the organization can know when it has achieved the goal.
  4. It must take 10 years or longer to reach.

CHAPTER 17
Growth Accelerator #14:
ESTABLISH A
LONG-TERM PLAN

O nce you have established your Audacious Goal, you are ready
to plan. With the strategic work in the previous chapters and
the Audacious Goal, you now have the foundational elements
necessary to go through the planning process. Effective organizations
link their plans to their strategy and plan before they execute.

I often ask leaders which they find more important, long-term goals
and plans or short-term ones. Whenever I do so, I hear arguments
defending both positions. As I've said earlier, it is a trick question. Both
are equally important. Without the longer-term plans, the shorter-term
plans will likely be insufficient as stepping-stones to get us there. We
must plan our way to the finish line.

You and your team need to excel at planning your future and executing
the plans you make. So, let's talk about the key considerations in establishing a long-term plan and how to prepare your organization for success.

Strategic Thinking versus the Planning Process

Distinguishing between strategic thinking and planning is essential. *Strategic thinking* is the time you set aside to discuss factors outside your company, consider what opportunities and threats they create for your company, and weigh the various options to address them—to best position your company versus the competition. To make the right decisions (as discussed in Chapters 12–15), you must look externally. As in a game of chess, when contemplating key moves, you must consider the response and acceptance of all stakeholders. Your best moves will meet the least resistance from stakeholders *and* steer you clear of the competition. Strategic thinking is a weak point in too many organizations. Great companies have not only faltered but failed by taking strategic thinking for granted.

Planning processes bring your strategy to life, when done correctly. We repeatedly see companies contemplate a strategy and never actualize it. Someone once told me that the difference between a dream and goal is an action plan. This holds true for running any business. As entrepreneurs, we are dreamers. We all have different dreams—impacting our community, changing an industry, creating a legacy, creating many jobs, or becoming a billionaire. Some dreams may not be so glamorous, but everyone has them.

For someone like me, who has ADHD, new ideas sprout daily. I love chasing challenging opportunities. Articulating the torrent of ideas in my head to everyone else has always been a real challenge. Now envision trying to manage a whole leadership team facing this same reality. If we do not have a process to extract what is in our team's heads, agree on what we will do, and make sure that we are all saying the same thing, then the rest of the organization and our customers are in for a wild ride. An excellent planning process helps extract these ideas in an organized manner.

You will notice that I specified the *process* when referring to planning. Your leadership must recognize this as a never-ending, iterative process of making your company great. It is not a retreat, a meeting, or an event. It includes:

- Long-term planning:
  - » Gathering external data
  - » Gathering internal data
  - » Establishing your Audacious Goal
  - » Setting aggressive targets for three years
  - » Identifying three-year focus areas
  - » Clarifying what else needs to happen to achieve those aggressive targets:
    - ▸ Expansion to new geographic territories or new segments
    - ▸ Mergers or acquisitions
    - ▸ Acceleration or expansion in client acquisition channels
    - ▸ New revenue streams
    - ▸ Possible use of a catalytic mechanism

- Annual company planning:
  - » One-year aggressive goals
  - » Annual company prioritization
  - » Critical numbers

- Quarterly company planning:
  - » Quarterly goals
  - » Quarterly priorities
  - » Critical numbers

- Department priorities:
  - » Quarterly goals
  - » Quarterly priorities
  - » Critical numbers

Of all the clients working with Activate Group coaches, those experiencing the most success are the ones who have learned the importance of strategic thinking and planning. They double their revenue and profit every three years. They understand that it is all about clarity and alignment. In this chapter, I will help you develop your long-term plan. Chapter 18 will cover the one-year plan, and Chapter 19 will help you establish your quarterly plan.

Voices of Customers and Employees

A critical component of the planning process is *gathering data*. It is a process that should happen 365 days a year. You need a process for collecting market, client, competitive, and employee intelligence. Interestingly, addressing the voices of customers and employees is done poorly by average leaders, which gives great leaders a competitive advantage.

The *voices of employees* is your way to connect with your front line to adjust strategies and priorities based on strengths and weaknesses employees identify from their internal perspective. The *voices of customers* is a way to examine your organization from the external world's perspective. It gives your leadership team a clear and broad view of opportunities, threats, and your position in the market. It is essential to validate your assumptions regarding each customer segment's wants and needs and how these are changing. You must use your current and potential customers to understand the competitive landscape.

The voices of customers concept is similar to the voices of employees, in that they are multifunctional—serving both the needs to collect data and manage relationships.

I am going to rant a bit on this subject. Unextraordinary leaders think that their industry longevity, interactions with customers, and thriving businesses allow them to skip this all-important focus area. These average leaders usually have an anecdotal but false understanding of their competition and inflated beliefs about the strengths of their products and services. They make many false assumptions about their customers. In my experience, the great leaders take their employees' and customers' voices seriously and, in many cases, hire a third party to make sure they get it right. You know you have a strong understanding of your customer when you have the lowest cost of customer acquisition in your industry, your growth rates are astronomical, your salespeople are mostly order takers, and your biggest challenge is scaling fast enough. You have likely failed if that last sentence does not describe your company.

The critical goal of gathering the voices of customers is to identify valuable information to differentiate yourself from your competitors in a substantial manner—so that you own 70 percent of your target market. When you do this correctly, you have the key differentiators to cause your ideal prospect to buy, to retain your existing customers, and to increase your market share.

In the end, most companies only collect incremental data, or data that helps validate their high self opinions. You must be a heat-seeking missile for targeting patterns in the market that invalidate your beliefs, help you identify the next trend, see preference changes, and spot competitive shifts. If you are not getting this type of data, then it is time to find a new method of collection or expand the sources from which you collect data.

Strengths, Weaknesses, and Trends

To establish a long-term plan, we must collect the external and internal data and conduct a strengths, weaknesses, and trends survey. *Strengths and weaknesses are internal data, and trends relate to external data.* If you want to use our tool, go to www.howardmshore.com/tools and download it. It is important to know that it is only necessary to fill out the entire tool one time per year, and update trends once a quarter. Your internal strengths and weakness are not likely to change much in 12 months. Trends, on the other hand, form weekly. It is crucial that the leadership team review trends to make sure that the company is not on any collision courses based on their understanding of the data.

You must take completing the Strengths, Weaknesses, and Trends tool seriously. Over the years, several of my clients have had extreme "A-Ha!" moments. Others averted catastrophic events because they were able to see approaching issues and shift their businesses beforehand. For example, many companies tie themselves to a few clients that make up a large percentage of their revenue and profits. If a company is unable to procure a lot more clients to reduce its dependency and concentration on too few, it needs to address that weakness. Too many organizations do not place enough urgency on resolving this problem—until it is too late.

Sadly, some companies have no core competencies. A core competency must meet three tests:

- Your competition would want to replicate it and would have difficulty doing so;
- The competency can be re-used widely for many products and markets; and
- It must contribute to the most essential benefits and values of your products and services in the eyes of your ideal customers.

While you must have one or more core competencies, we usually see that items written in the core competency section of the worksheet are weak in form or not validated. Your belief that you are stronger than your competition may exist only in your head rather than being a reality. When that occurs, it means you need to implement proper differentiating activities to allow your company to thrive in the marketplace. Not dealing with the issue makes getting and keeping customers costlier and more difficult, and pricing tends to be weaker.

On the trends side, we help clients see and avert danger. One of these clients competed in the online media market. They noticed that some of their competitors were massively outperforming them. Combined with changes they observed at Google, YouTube, and other platforms crucial to their business, this caused them to stop and reconsider all their current priorities, just as Steve Jobs did with the iPhone. Jobs' team was working on the iPad when he realized it was much more critical for the company to be in the mobile phone business. He focused all their best people on the iPhone—one of the most significant strategic decisions in the history of Apple. The iPhone became the majority share of the company's profits and catapulted Apple to being the most valuable company in the world.

While not on the same scale, my client experienced the same result. They were working on perfecting a product that was already showing signs of obsolescence. It was equivalent to trying to make a better DVD player today or to concentrate on developing a better way to deliver printed newspapers. While there were still people using my client's product, evidence indicated that their ideal customers had already moved to a different platform to consume that product. Trying to perfect their existing platform would be a waste of time and resources. My client's new direction helped his company continue to grow at more than 25 percent a year, and its future remains bright.

Three-Year Aggressive Targets

If you have not already downloaded the *Business Acceleration Tools*®, this would be an excellent time to go to www.howardmshore.com/tools and download the toolkit. Open the Long-Term Plan Worksheet so you have a visual idea of what I am about to describe.

I strongly suggest that leadership teams not overthink targets. We create targets to help teams realize which key assumptions require the most work. I find that leaders spend more time focusing on the numbers than on what it would take to achieve them. Every company, especially those with less than $1 billion in revenue, should be able to double in revenue and profits every three years. We recommend you adopt this as your minimum target and then challenge your team to develop a plan to get there.

Please note that we call the three-year-plan numbers *targets,* not *goals.* With a goal, there is a high certainty we will achieve it in a relatively short amount of time. Reaching a target will take three successive years of elevating the business in a significant way. In my experience, our clients either crush their three-year target or fall well short of it. Crushing it occurs when you substantially elevate your strategy, innovate your operations, and dramatically improve execution. Some of you are going to crush it. Others will get the strategy all wrong. Flawlessly executing a lousy strategy is like repositioning deck chairs on the *Titanic.*

The last point on this subject I want to address is forecasting the target. Do it before you conduct your planning session. It bolsters the confidence of the team to know you have already built out the forecast and understand what it takes to get there. There are usually three to five critical assumptions in a forecast that will drive it. You don't want to start figuring this out in the room, which takes too much time. For example, the critical assumptions for an advertising agency we helped were:

1. Number of retainer clients, net added each month—needs to increase continually
2. Average retainer amount—needs to go up
3. Monthly project revenue—needs to average a certain amount per client
4. Labor Efficiency Ratio™ (see Chapter 8)

Once my client knew these numbers, creating the forecast did not seem so daunting, and it became clear what they needed to do to get there.

Three-Year Focus

It is time to identify the key focus areas that your company will elevate over the next three years. My colleague, Shannon Susko, author of *3HAG Way,* calls these "swim lanes."[1] Every quarter, look at these areas when setting your annual and quarterly priorities. You will want to focus and move across these lanes. They are focal points where you need to make significant progress in elevating your company in order to have a competitive and sustainable advantage.

The next tool, derived from Jim Collins' work, is the *3-Year Focus* tool. This tool is the next step in helping you fill out the Long-Term Plan Worksheet. Great companies realize that no one single event catapults a company into greatness. Instead, it's a series of cumulative actions that add up to sustained and amazing results. In *Good to Great*, Jim Collins refers to this as *the flywheel effect*. Picture a huge, 5,000-pound flywheel, a 30 x 2-foot metal disk, mounted horizontally on an axle. Imagine your task is to get the flywheel rotating on its axle as fast and for as long as possible. It takes time to get the flywheel moving to make the first revolution. After a continuous and concerted effort, it starts to pick up speed, making rotation after rotation until, at some point, it's its own weight continues its progress. That's the breakthrough. Getting the company's "flywheel" to move at the desired speed takes more than just an initial company meeting, a motivational speaker, and a party to announce your plans. It takes substantial effort to get the wheel turning.[2]

I found that for my company to have a good long-term plan, it was important to distill the business model down to its rawest components to make ours the most successful company in the industry. On the surface, this seems simple, but it isn't. We concluded that the starting point to help shape strategy is first to identify your flywheel.

Here is Amazon's wheel. From its founding until now, Amazon has had only one flywheel from which it has grown into the large company it is today. It has used the same five key levers to make the company great.[3]

First let's ask, what type of company is Amazon? The correct answer is a technology company. As a technology company, Amazon lists the following targets on their website:

- Builds algorithms that find ways to offer more of the right offerings at lower prices

- Has more offerings that increase customer visits
- Has more customers; that attracts more third-party sellers
- Has more sellers; this expands the store, and they find ways to extend distribution so that customers can have the convenience of receiving everything faster
- Has a business model, the last part of which is to grow revenue per fixed cost[4]

Then they repeat the cycle. Increasing revenues per fixed costs is how Amazon has crushed everyone in the online retail business. How did they do it? Their technology platform was very large—their largest cost structure. They developed a way to turn this core company asset into a revenue source. Customers pay to use Amazon's infrastructure, lowering Amazon's fixed costs per dollar of revenue.

You need to construct your own flywheel. How does your cycle work? Most organizations do not take the time to dissect their business models into no more than five components that they must master. Those that do take time to examine their business models have a distinct advantage over those that don't.

Once you identify these components, you will be ready for long-term planning and to create your "swim lanes." For each element of your flywheel, you and your leadership team must develop a vision of what "awesome" can look like in three years. For each component, what can you do differently that will help you grow faster or be significantly more profitable? Where are the choke points in each part of the wheel? How can you remove them?

Do not get all caught up in the details. Stay "big picture" on systematic and structural changes that need to be made in each swim lane. With this discussion, you will formulate how to identify your first doubling in revenue and profit. This is the time to eradicate incremental thinking. Your goal is to have no more than five (ideally only three) focus areas for the next three years that you will use to elevate your company toward your Audacious Goal and greatness.

Expansion

The brunt of long-term planning is the three-year focus. However, we did set some lofty goals, so there are moves you may be able to make that either will help you achieve larger targets or are necessary steps to achieving your objectives. A vital component of the Long-Term Plan Worksheet is *expansion*. This was a critical move in my achieving success in the past.

In my early days as a corporate planning executive at Ryder System, I was assigned to help Ryder Public Transportation Services achieve its strategic plan. This was one of our highest-return businesses, but growing it was challenging. This had a lot to do with the construct of the industry and the state of the economy. We identified that our best strategy would be to grow the business by acquiring smaller companies across the country. We could buy companies for four times their earnings before interest taxes depreciation and amortization (EBITDA).

The goal after acquisition would be to get immediate cost savings and a valuation bump by consolidating them under our umbrella in a national footprint. It would be much more difficult and time-consuming to grow these organically. Throughout the next three years, I helped the division grow from $400 million to over $600 million, and we sold it for almost $1 billion, over eight times EBITDA. This was a significant cashflow story for Ryder. That division could never have come close to this sale multiple without our acquisition strategy. To my knowledge, no other public transportation company in our industry and of our size had ever sold for that multiple.

Another consideration for growth not captured in the three-year focus is geographic expansion. Many companies spend too much time in too small a geographic area, and would find it much easier to grow if they looked at new markets. A property management client of ours spent its first eight years doing deals only in Florida. For several reasons, they were no longer finding good deals in Florida. It was at that point they realized they needed to expand their horizons and have now done deals in several new states. This significantly increased their prospects. In the last two years, the company has doubled its number of units and is a lot more profitable, and a key reason has been their expanding geography.

Client Acquisition Channels

Are you correctly measuring the success of your client acquisition channels? Do you excel in two or three channels—or even one? In my experience, many companies are not reliable in *any* client acquisition channels.

The first issue to understand is the difference between marketing and sales. Simply put, *sales* begin when someone actively enters the buying process. Interaction before that is *marketing.* If your salespeople are cold calling, networking, speaking to a group, or engaging in any activity other than taking someone through the buying process, then they are marketing. Your salespeople probably spend far more time marketing than selling. How much assistance do they get from talented marketing people to help them master marketing activities? Many firms have a marketing problem and never resolve it. Many of the companies we work with, have a marketing channel problem but misidentify it as a sales problem.

Segmentation defines the best channels used to acquire clients. This is important for several reasons.

1. **Cost of Acquisition** – You must align the cost of acquiring a client with the lifetime value of that client.

2. **Motivation** – You must make sure that the people in the channel are motivated to move your product. A company that manufactured mirrors was trying to sell them to the hotel and cruise ship industries, but used independent representatives who also sold other goods to the same buyers. It wasn't working. We discovered that the representatives earned much better commissions for selling rugs and other products than for selling the mirrors. Since they were not as motivated to represent the mirrors, it was always the last item they discussed.

3. **Customer Preference** – Each customer segment may have a distinct buying preference. Some may be willing to pay a higher price for added service. Others want the lowest possible price and will go online to save a buck.

It is best to choose no more than three marketing channels, and then master those channels thoroughly. Examples of channels include Facebook, Amazon, LinkedIn, a direct sales force, events, and tradeshows. Each of these is a separate marketing channel that requires people and financial resources. By mastering the three channels best suited to your segment, your inside sales team (if you have one) will have more than enough leads to convert.

My aim in this chapter is to help you see that planning your road to success is different from strategic thinking. We must have both a strategy and a plan. We need a long-term plan and a short-term plan. The team must know that the actions they take today are sufficiently substantive to lead them to where they expect to be in the long-term. You cannot reach a destination without knowing where you are headed. We start by establishing three-year aggressive targets. Once you have those targets, you then identify how your company must transform itself to reach such heights. If you look at those targets and feel you can operate the business "as is," then one of two things is occurring: 1) you are not stretching yourself or your organization; or 2) you have a small plan. Either way leads to mediocrity.

ESTABLISH A LONG-TERM PLAN

- Without a long-term plan, shorter-term plans will likely be insufficient for use as stepping-stones to get us to our target.
- *Strategic thinking* is the time you set aside to discuss factors outside your company, consider what opportunities and threats they create for your company, and deliberate about the various options to address them to best position your company versus the competition.
- When done correctly, the *planning process* brings your strategy to life.
- Your leadership must recognize that planning is a never-ending, iterative process of making your company great.
- You need a process for collecting market, client, competitive, and employee intelligence.
- The *voices of employees* source is your way of connecting with the front line to adjust strategies and priorities based on strengths and weaknesses identified by employees from the internal perspective.
- The *voices of customers* source is a way of examining your organization from the external world's perspective.
- You know you have a strong understanding of the customer when you have the lowest cost of customer acquisition in your industry, your growth rates are astronomical, your salespeople become order takers, and your biggest challenge is scaling fast enough.
- The critical goal of gathering the voices of customers is to identify highly valuable information to differentiate yourself from your competitors substantially, so you own 70 percent of your target market.
- If you have not already done so, download the Strengths, Weaknesses, and Trends tool at www.howardmshore.com/tools.

- A core competence is one that meets three tests: 1) your competition would want to replicate it but would have difficulty doing so; 2) the competency can be re-used widely for many products and markets; and 3) it must contribute to the most essential benefits and values of your products and services in the eyes of your ideal customers.
- Two more tools to download if you have not already done so are the Long-Term Plan Worksheet tool and the 3-Year Focus tool at www.howardmshore.com/tools.
- Distill your business model down to the rawest components to make it the most successful company in your industry.
- Consider expansion using either mergers and acquisitions or geography to help you achieve your lofty goals.
- You must choose no more than three marketing channels and master those channels.

BUSINESS ACCELERATION CALCULATOR™

There is no specific exercise to complete for this chapter. However, it is essential to make sure that innovation and removing mistakes in process initiatives are aligned with your three-year focus. When you choose items that are aligned with the long-term, they tend to have a more significant impact on your business.

ESTABLISH A ONE-YEAR **PLAN**

Develop a roadmap for your business the way your GPS builds a roadmap for a trip. You need a beginning and endpoint. A journey is misguided and apt to take longer if it's missing either one. Now that you've established an Audacious Goal, a clear strategy, and long-term goals and focus, it's time to bring your attention toward the present. You need to create a clear picture of what must happen in the current year to get you well on your way to a successful trip.

Download the *Organizational Focus Tool* at www.howardmshore. com/tools. We use this tool both for annual and quarterly planning. I named it the "focus tool" because I've found that we entrepreneurs have trouble staying focused. I am always stunned to see how often plans are created and never looked at again. That is why you must bring the *Organization Focus Tool* to leadership's attention at your weekly, monthly, and quarterly meetings. By doing so, you will keep the main things in your plan as the main things you're all doing.

Establish Aggressive Goals

When you set annual goals, I recommend that they are both *realistic* and *aggressive*. I'm sure you have gleaned by now that I believe leaders should challenge everyone on their team to strive to reach their own, and thereby the company's, full potential. I also believe your potential is unlimited, so this is a more of an odyssey than a lap around the track. My colleagues at Activate Group and I have helped clients far exceed what they thought they could achieve. The keys to their success were having an open mind and playing to win. I believe you are reading this book because you want to achieve remarkable outcomes and greatness.

High achievers do not ask what average achievers are accomplishing. They want to study the top performers and measure themselves against the best. I own a Peloton exercise bicycle, and since the first day I used it, I've looked at the leader board and challenged myself to move closer to the top. I don't care that some of the people on that board are in their 20s while I'm in my 50s. Nor do I care that I'm a beginner and ride infrequently. Every time I get on the bike, I look at what my last highest results were, expect to do better, and put in the effort to do just that. I expect to push higher up the leader board, and my Audacious Goal is to one day be first. In other words, if you want to be great, you can't set safe goals.

When you establish aggressive goals, consider that you are likely to face less than optimal conditions that are consistent with prior year experiences. Experienced leaders know they should not plan for perfect conditions. However, you should plan to address controllable conditions. Your job when setting goals is to understand which conditions are controllable and which are not.

For example, if historically, you have lost growth because of weak human capital management practices, address that issue so you can have better control over it.

However, some conditions may be outside of your control. Key employees leave, and it may take longer than you wanted to fill positions. Large customers leave, and new competitors enter the market.

A supplier may shut its doors. Customers fail to cooperate; mistakes happen; people get sick. When was the last time a year unfolded as you thought it would? Never! Statistically, the probability of all of those setbacks happening in one year is low, but the likelihood is high that something can happen each day to disrupt smooth sailing—so plan for less than optimal conditions.

After you establish revenue goals, I suggest you set goals for gross margin, net profit margin, days receivable, payable days, and inventory days, if applicable. In all cases, you should set aggressive targets. Average results are for the mediocre. We have established that you are reading this book because you want and expect to be great. Therefore, you must determine what the best companies in your industry are achieving and set your bar accordingly. If you are far from achieving excellence, use the *Business Acceleration Calculator*™ to challenge your team to find and make remarkable improvements this year. There is no better time than the present.

Critical Numbers

I've been involved in the development of too many annual plans to count, so I was perplexed by the frequency with which knowledgeable and well-intentioned people consistently created solid plans yet failed to yield their desired results. I believe the answer lies in the choice of their *critical number(s)*.

Whether your company uses our tools or others, you must still consider the same issues. At the bottom of the 1-Year Aggressive Goals column of our *Organizational Focus Tool* is the Critical # section. The selection of your critical number(s) is essential to the success of your year. Whether you are planning the year, the quarter, or your priorities, it is crucial to pick the one or two critical numbers that need the most attention at present.

If you are not sure which critical numbers to select, you'll find some clues by asking questions like:

- What is the critical weakness in our business model?
- What is the biggest weakness in our operations?
- Which key performance indicator would we be most embarrassed to show to industry peers?
- Which key performance indicator is the main culprit in not gaining customers?
- Which key performance indicator is the main reason we are losing customers?
- What key performance indicator has the most significant impact on our cost structure?

While revenue is the most commonly chosen number, it is NOT a good choice for a critical number. If you are faced with weak growth, you need to go deeper and find the leading indicator at the root of that problem. For example, most companies have a marketing problem, not a sales problem, because they do not generate enough leads. Does your company create enough quality leads?

I have mentioned that we consistently achieve remarkable revenue growth in the restoration industry. Much of that growth can be attributed to the fact that we identified the one critical number that seems to be a weakness in all restoration companies. (I am not going to share the specific number here because it is a secret sauce we only share with our clients.) So far, we have yet to find a restoration company that has not had to make significant improvements in this key performance indicator. By addressing and growing this one number, our clients consistently grow at least five times the industry average and become far more profitable. Even if it is not *your* company's weakness, addressing it is the secret to dramatic growth.

Once you find your critical number, ask the question, "If we focus too much on this critical number, what could go wrong in the company?" If the answer is nothing, then you only need that one critical number.

However, if you determine that focusing on that number hurts other areas of your business, you will need to balance that first critical number with a second one. By having such a balance, you will avoid hindering your progress. For example, if your key performance indicator focuses on getting a lot of new customers, you may need a secondary indicator to make sure that quality, on-time delivery, or service does not suffer in a way that defeats the benefits of your efforts.

Setting Annual Priorities

A common problem in many organizations—one I experienced at times—is becoming overwhelmed by the sheer number of things to be done. Average leaders spend most of their lives working too hard and find themselves increasingly unhappy. They know they have 50 things to get done but complete few, if any, of them. The greatest leaders I have worked with may have the same 50 items, but they choose only the very few, important ones, and make sure those get done first. Right priorities always have the most significant impact on overall success.

Leaders have very little discretionary time, and addressing the priorities they've identified in their plans only occurs during the discretionary time. Think about that. A typical executive works 50 or more hours per week. How many of those hours would you consider discretionary? The urgent, important daily issues of their day job suck them in. Usually, I find new clients struggling to set aside time to work on priority projects that will have the most significant impact on their organizations. They find themselves too busy with the daily fight. When I ask such clients to set aside five hours per week to work on a high-impact project, I often find them struggling to make the time. It often goes back to learning how to say no!

Given our limited time, we must use planning to help prioritize the few things that must get done and, more importantly, decide what *won't* get done. Planning well enables you to send the right message to your team and prevent wasted time and resources. I recommend no more than five annual priorities—preferably three. Our most successful clients have learned that less is more and avoid the temptation to cram too many things on everyone's plate.

When developing annual priorities, it is essential to use the information from the other tools to make your decisions. Priorities should not be developed in a vacuum. First, you must consider your three-year focus. How will you address the areas identified during those exercises? You need to start now if you are going to achieve a three-year plan. Second, consider which priorities must be accomplished to reach this year's critical number(s). Lastly, review previous annual goals and discuss what needs to change from last year to achieve these new goals.

As stated at the beginning of this chapter, whenever we start a journey, we need to have a clear idea of the endpoint. The annual plan is our sketch of what we believe it is going to take to complete this journey. It is the blueprint of what the company will look like after our one-year journey. It clarifies what key goals will be achieved, the critical numbers that must be accomplished to drive those goals, and the annual priorities that will position the company to succeed in its three-year journey.

ESTABLISH A ONE-YEAR PLAN

- If you have not downloaded our tools yet, you will find the *Organizational Focus Tool* at www.howardmshore.com/tools.
- You must bring the *Organization Focus Tool* to your leadership's attention at your weekly, monthly, and quarterly meetings. By doing so, you keep the main things in your plan as the main things you're all doing.
- When you set annual goals, I recommend they be both realistic and aggressive.
- If you want to be great, you can't set safe goals.
- Selection of your critical number(s) is essential to the success of your year.
- If you are not sure which critical number(s) to select, you'll find some clues by asking yourself questions like:

  1. What is the critical weakness in our business model?
  2. What is the biggest weakness in our operations?
  3. Which key performance indicator would we be most embarrassed to show to industry peers?
  4. Which key performance indicator is the main culprit in not gaining customers?
  5. Which key performance indicator is the main reason we are losing customers?
  6. What key performance indicator has the most significant impact on cost structure?

- It is critical to understand that leaders have very little discretionary time, and your priorities will only be addressed during discretionary time.

BUSINESS ACCELERATION CALCULATOR™

It is time to pause and determine how applying the practices in "Establish a One-Year Plan" affects your company. Go to www.howardmshore. com/tools and request our *Business Acceleration Tools*®. This tool will give you access to the *Business Acceleration Calculator*™ in both Excel and printable formats. I prefer the Excel version for this tool because it does all the calculations for you. The *Calculator* will help you keep track of all the deficiencies this book has helped you discover in your business.

The *Calculator* is the ultimate planning tool. As you have priorities you believe you should consider, we recommend that you put them in the proper section of the *Calculator*. By putting values next to each priority, you will understand the real impact of each. You will find that many items that may seem important have minimal effect on your business. Organizations tend to choose lower-impact projects because they know they can get them done. Learn to focus on the big ones!

CHAPTER 19
Growth Accelerator #16:

ESTABLISH A
QUARTERLY **PLAN**

As we think about acceleration, we have constructed our trajectory and connected to it from different levels. We started at the peak of acceleration by establishing an Audacious Goal, stepped down a level to develop your long-term plan, stepped down another level with an annual plan, and now it's time to move to the starting line. We know where we want to go; we've identified milestones and landmarks on the way to the destination; and your quarterly plan will be the starting line for the first 13-week race of your 36-month journey.

As we've noted earlier, *planning* is about the alignment of priorities, and there are two steps to creating a quarterly plan. We aligned your annual plan for your long-term plan. Now we align your quarterly plan to your annual plan. We must also align departmental and personal plans to your company quarterly plan. This last piece is usually bypassed, an oversight that can doom the effectiveness of the entire plan.

For this chapter, you will need to download both the *Organizational Focus Tool* and the Department/Personal Planning Worksheet at www.howardmshore.com/tools. You must bring along the *Organization Focus Tool* when you review the Department/Personal Worksheets at your weekly and monthly meetings. By doing so, you will keep the main things in your plan as the main things you're all doing.

Establishing Quarterly Goals

When setting quarterly goals, I recommend that you think about the *drivers* of your business plan rather than its end numbers. When working on quarterlies with clients, we found it unhelpful to focus on revenue, gross margin, and net profit budget numbers. Focusing on the correct drivers will enable you to achieve those numbers.

It is important to identify no more than four to six critical drivers of your plan. Whenever I help a client build a forecast model, I find that the key drivers essential to achieving their plans are also the areas where they usually have challenges, obstacles, and uncertainty. We must spotlight those areas and make sure that everyone who can contribute to improving them is paying attention.

Activate Group is all about scaling, and our needs and obstacles change from time to time. Last quarter, one of our quarterly goals was to add two unicorn coaches within 60 days during one of modern history's most challenging recruiting markets. From my experience (see Chapters 9 and 10), I knew we needed 100 candidates for each position. Our daily metric was to consider 10 candidates per day and screen them down to six great final candidates. We met those objectives and filled the seats in our 60-day time frame.

Two metrics that never leave our dashboard are leads generated and sales renewal dollars. In our forecast, we have a renewal expectation and new sales dollars expected. The renewals number is manageable because we know which accounts are up for renewal, who we hope and want to renew, and the dollars associated with those accounts. Over time, we gained a firm grasp on how to estimate our new sales funnel. For us to close a new account, we need 13 new leads, and we know the value of a new account. We track new leads, which is essential to achieving our sales goals.

Another critical item on our quarterly goal dashboard relates to public speaking. Our primary source for obtaining leads and closing new business is referrals from existing clients. We found this to be not scalable, so although we track the leads, we do not separate them on our dashboard. I consider it more relevant to track how many new people we reach through speaking engagements. This has become our second-best growth vehicle and an effective way to build our brand for the right audience. As a result, we set a quarterly goal for the number of new clients we expect to gain through speaking engagements.

You must choose your key drivers according to how they affect both revenues and costs. Here are some examples our clients have set for quarterly goals:

- Number of open positions filled
- Percentage of performers
- Number of attendees
- Number of new business relationships
- Average job size
- Number of contracts signed
- Number of projects sold
- Property expense percentage
- Number of "Followers"
- Close ratio
- Number of new outreaches
- Increase in pipeline

As with annual goals, quarterly goals help you see whether you have the right actions in place to achieve them. Many times, there is a big disconnect between a client's current activities and its goals. By identifying this discrepancy during the planning process, you can create an initiative to close the gap.

Critical Numbers

Your quarterly critical number(s) may not be the same as your annual critical number. Often it is, but sometimes we find that the quarterly number is a building block toward the annual critical number. It's essential to understand whether we need to make progress on the annual number or if there is an additional number that is a critical weakness affecting the overall annual number.

If you are unsure that you are looking at the correct critical number(s), ask the same questions as we did in the last chapter:

- What is the critical weakness in our business model?
- What is the biggest weakness in our operations?
- Which key performance indicator would we be most embarrassed to show to industry peers?
- Which key performance indicator is the main culprit in not gaining customers?
- Which key performance indicator is the main reason we are losing customers?
- What key performance indicator has the most significant impact on cost structure?

You must identify the correct critical number to determine which is the most crucial, current priority for the company.

Setting Your Quarterly Priorities

Think company priorities first, department, and personal priorities afterward. I frequently see leaders worrying that every other leader has priorities that they've failed to disclose and that conflict with the company's main priorities. My recommendation is to create a list of potential priorities and then decide which you are going to do.

Make sure you do not confuse priorities with *action steps*. Priorities (nouns) are the main things that need to get done. However, these are big projects and sometimes take many quarters to complete. They require initiative actions (verbs) to get done. Action steps define how you will accomplish your priority. We start with the company priorities—the big picture. You must determine what needs to be done from a total company perspective before you figure out what you want from each leader and department. Then take those company priorities and break them down into department and personal (individual) priorities. For example, one of my clients recently decided that they are not standing out in their market. Their annual priority is to "consistently communicate to our 100 target clients a clear brand message that helps separate us from the competition." Their first-quarter company priority is to "hire an advertising agency and to develop initial collateral that supports penetrating target 100." An initial action step is to develop a precise needs document that can be submitted to agencies to communicate what they are looking for. Another action step is to identify three advertising agencies capable of serving their needs and set up the initial meeting to determine fit.

In my experience, you will find an overlap when developing the company and department priorities. As you try to clarify what needs to happen during the quarter, you may see several projects that add up to a big company priority. Many times, the best company priorities transcend departments. There also will be priorities that may be necessary for the company and are critical to a department but will not make it onto the company's top priority list. A good example is a case where the accounting department was failing to deliver timely financial information. While this function must get back on track, it was not a priority that would elevate the company to another level. We would put it in the department's priorities but not the company's priorities.

In the end, remember that less is more. What is the lowest number of company priorities required to drive its annual priorities, achieve its near-term needs, and not overwhelm its executive team?

Department Priorities

As you move into department priorities, determine how each leader contributes to the company's main priorities and goals first. There must be no department priorities that overly strain the organization. It is a common mistake not to appreciate a support department's influence and the work they must do to assist in your key priorities. You must understand the impact of these interdependencies. You also must consider that any time you bring new procedures, tools, technology, and people into your organization, it represents that scary word—*change*. If you attempt to bring in too many changes at once, you are apt to meet wholesale resistance that negates the benefits you aimed to achieve.

Consider how realistic your goals and initiatives are, as they relate to a person's current circumstances, the seasonality of your business, and the plan. If a person's department typically has six people, is down three, and its leader must recruit and replace those three people this quarter, then it is unrealistic to expect much from that person beyond his or her day job. The department leader already needs to make up for the work of three people and find time to interview, hire, and onboard three new hires. If the company is entering its busiest season, where everyone works 60- to 70-hour weeks to service the business, you should not pile on much in the way of priorities. There may be no discretionary time to address those special projects.

The quarterly plan is a critical step in acceleration. Your team must understand the mechanics of goals, critical numbers, priorities, initiative, and action steps. These terms are often confused, and understanding them makes a real difference in the outcomes you achieve. First, identify the company goals and priorities. Then establish department and leader priorities that align to them. You will achieve much faster acceleration in your business with less effort.

ESTABLISH A QUARTERLY PLAN

- Just as it makes no sense to start on a journey without knowing where you are headed, if we don't know where we are starting the first leg, we can't expect to reach our destination.
- *Planning* is about the alignment of priorities, and there are two parts in your quarterly plan. We must also align department and personal plans to our company plans. This second dimension is usually bypassed, an oversight that can cause your quarterly plan to fail.
- Download both the *Organizational Focus Tool* and the Department/Personal Planning Worksheet at www. howardmshore.com/tools.
- When setting quarterly goals, I recommend that you think about the drivers of your business plan rather than the end numbers you are trying to reach.
- Your quarterly critical number(s) may or may not be the same as the annual critical number(s).
- Make sure you do not confuse priorities with *action steps*. Priorities (things/noun) are the main things that need to get done, while action steps define how you will accomplish your priorities.
- Many times, the best company priorities transcend departments.
- As you move into the department's priorities, it is essential first to understand how each leader contributes to the company's main priorities and goals.
- There must be no department priorities that can cause the organization to be overly strained.
- Consider that any time you bring new procedures, tools, technology, and people into your organization, it represents

change, which is disconcerting to many. If you attempt to bring too much change at the same time, it is likely to be counterproductive.

- Consider how realistic your goals and initiatives are as they relate to a person's current circumstances, seasonality of your business, and the plan.

BUSINESS ACCELERATION CALCULATOR™

It is time to pause and determine how the recommended procedures in "Establish a Quarterly Plan" affect your company. Go to www.howardmshore.com/tools and request our *Business Acceleration Tools®*. This tool will give you access to the *Business Acceleration Calculator™*. It will help you keep track of all the deficiencies this book has helped you discover in your business.

The *Calculator* is the ultimate planning tool. As you identify priorities, I recommend that you put them in the proper section of the *Calculator*. By putting values next to each priority, you will understand the actual impact of each. You will find that many items that may seem important have little effect on your business. Organizations tend to choose lower-impact projects because they know they can complete them. Give the most attention to the big ones.

PART VI
ACCOUNTABILITY

KEY PERFORMANCE   **COMMUNICATION**   **TRANSPARENCY**
INDICATORS

"Accountability breeds response-ability."

— **Stephen Covey**[1]

CHAPTER 20
Growth Accelerator #17:
CREATE A **CULTURE** OF ACCOUNTABILITY

So far, we have talked about stewardship, human capital management, strategy, and planning. However, all of the adjustments and improvements we've discussed will not happen without *follow-through*. Follow-through is where accountability has a starring role. In Chapter 7, we discussed the need to develop a strong culture for everyone to embrace. A vital piece of that culture for all leaders to develop and nurture is following through on commitments. And as we all know, this can be a real challenge.

While thinking about how to create a culture of accountability, I know how many people claim to love accountability until it involves their own actions. If you want a culture of accountability, it must start with you. I often find that leaders who are frustrated with their team's lack of follow-through need to look in their mirrors. They blame their own lack of follow-through on their seniority and all the things they need to do because of it. They do not realize their behavior sets the tone for everyone else. If you want others to be accountable, you must be responsible for completing your own commitments.

What Is Accountability?

According to Merriam-Webster.com, *accountability* is "an obligation or willingness to accept responsibility or to account for one's actions." It is a performance character trait that requires not just a particular mindset but also processes and tools that support that mindset. Many leaders invest in the processes and tools but fail to demonstrate the necessary mindset. It takes all three to be successful, but the mindset is the most crucial factor.

Let's begin by discussing the mindset required for accountability. Very often, organizations set goals and priorities that are decisions but not commitments.

Think about the difference between a *decision* and a *commitment*. We make decisions all the time, but many of them are like New Year's resolutions. You tell yourself you intend to act on certain matters. Our good intentions do not translate into a willingness to do whatever it takes to make them happen. Commitment takes your decision to the next level—it provides dedication to turning the decision into reality. When we make commitments, our level of effort, focus, and attention change. You can make decisions such as "I am going to lose 20 pounds" or "I am going to become a millionaire." The real question is, how committed are you to losing the 20 pounds or becoming a millionaire? With commitment, you intensify your level of energy, focus, and determination to succeed at achieving that end.

We want to challenge everyone in an organization to have a *commitment mindset* for crucial decisions, priorities set, and established goals. This mindset should start from the day you begin at a company. It is a cultural mindset. How do you describe the performance mindset of your company to a new employee? For my companies, we make it clear from day one that we work hard and play hard. We care about our employees, and we expect high performance. The mindset needs to be clearly communicated and unwavering. In the organizations that I own, we inform all who come aboard that when we establish goals and priorities, they are commitments!

We need processes and tools to support our commitment to accountability. That is where the work in the previous chapters was so important. As stewards, we clarified our purpose and core values in Chapters 6 and 7, respectively. *Stewardship* allows employees to understand how to make a difference in their roles and expected behaviors. Without such clarity, an organization would contain an assortment of subcultures and unacceptable performance levels. Each one—from the Audacious Goal to three-year, one-year, and quarterly plans—should help every employee understand what needs to get done using the tools and processes in Chapters 13 through 16. Lastly, we support our employees down the path of accountability by more clearly communicating exactly how they must perform, and we create a feedback loop should anybody fall off course.

Accountability Requires Management

In business parlance, accountability refers to the one person in the organization who tracks progress for each function, team, division, process, customer, or project. When issues arise, this person is responsible for reporting them to the management team, so that obstacles can be addressed. While this person may not have any authority and may not be a leader, they account for what is going on. If you designate more than one person to be accountable for a particular thing, then some issues will fall through the cracks. You open the opportunity for confusion and finger-pointing.

For accountability to occur, I have found that we need *active management*. Too many people in management positions don't want to manage others. They like being leaders, visionaries, thinkers, and subject matter experts. They enjoy wielding power, attending important meetings, making decisions for others to carry out, and making more money. Unfortunately, they don't like being managers. If they did, they would relish the challenges and fight to spend more of their time performing management activities.

Management activities involve clarifying what is expected of a person, monitoring those expectations, providing a feedback loop, developing people, recruiting new people, and providing for succession. When I ask leaders that I have coached to track their time, I find that very little of it has gone toward any of those activities. In other words, these leaders, who typically have eight to ten direct reports, spend less than ten hours per week performing management activities. They also spend an excessive amount of time being frustrated and disappointed in the performance of those same people. There is a direct correlation.

Accountability Requires Conflict

While I am all for harmonious cultures, my experience is that the most accountable cultures have a healthy dose of constructive conflict. One of the things I learned from Patrick Lencioni's *The Five Dysfunctions of a Team* is that there is a pyramid that builds up to results. Organizations are made up of many teams. You have a leadership team and functional teams, and we all participate in a number of those teams. Pat uses a version of Maslow's hierarchy pyramid to describe the critical needs of a team. The foundation of the pyramid is trust. Once you have strong trust among team members, the next level of the pyramid is conflict. *Constructive conflict* occurs when your team is capable of engaging in an unfiltered and passionate debate of ideas. You avoid making issues personal as well as resorting to shielded discussions and guarded comments. This critical component of a functional team is only possible when team members trust one another to the point where they are comfortable expressing differences of opinion without fear of ridicule or retribution. One thing Pat pointed out in his book was that you will not gain commitment from a team member without proper conflict.[1]

People are unlikely to commit to a priority or goal if they do not feel that they contributed to its development, don't understand it, or don't believe in it. Allowing yourself to have dialogues with direct reports provides a forum for them to express their thoughts on a goal or priority. Such conversations have two advantages: First, by allowing people to express their views, you gain insight into what they may see as challenges or obstacles to achieving the goal or priority and into how subordinates think. It provides a forum in which to discuss, challenge, and possibly modify views. Second, sometimes, people need to be heard before they consider offering their acceptance to your ideas. Knowledge workers, in particular, don't like to be told what to do. However, hearing the other leaders and employees out should not be an attempt to create consensus, though it might be viewed as a ploy to defuse resistance. The more challenging a decision, the less likely you are to have an immediate agreement. Instead, you provide the arena for soliciting input, allowing employees to feel their concerns are understood and to understand the significance of and reasons for decisions. This last part frustrates leaders when their egos get in the way. They don't know why they must explain themselves. If you see yourself as a manager, someone who is there to grow your subordinates and prepare for your succession, it should be a welcome opportunity.

How you deal with failure to perform is another area where constructive conflict and accountability (or the lack of it) are most common. Are you one of those leaders who deal with holding people accountable by "babysitting"? Are you frustrated that you need to measure performance and verify that people did what you asked of them? Both are necessary activities for an active manager.

If you were to look in the mirror, are there many things you said you were going to do but failed to do? How many days did you say you would go to the gym last week; how many times did you go? You said you would call a problematic customer and did not. You said you would help one of your subordinates with a project, but you never made time to do so. You said you were going to talk to the employee who wasn't performing and didn't get around to it. There are lots of things you said you were going to do and didn't.

We all have done these things! Accountability always starts with you. Be careful not to hold subordinates accountable to impossible standards. At the same time, make sure to challenge them to reach their full potential.

The *accountability feedback loop* is the mechanism to use in your company to help employees identify whether they are performing to expectations. It is both uncomfortable and necessary. For example, in weekly meetings, our clients review the status of top priorities and goals and address any person that is falling behind on their assigned goal or priority. It is the primary method of driving peak performance and helping people grow and develop to their full potential. The reason we set goals and create priorities is that there was something that needed to get done that required hard work. The goals and priorities are particularly useful for people on your team who perform better with extra pressure.

For example, I have been a weightlifter and have exercised since I was 13 years old. I even have a gym in my house. However, I perform best when pushed by my trainer or when I am on the Peloton. It is human nature. Some people are natural procrastinators and need that extra push. Others need a coach to keep them at peak performance and help them see their blind spots and identify when they need more resources. If you are unable to give the people who report to you the feedback they need to perform correctly and grow, then you are a nonperforming manager. Accountability is necessary if you want peak performance, and constructive conflict is your signal that you are challenging team members to their full potential.

Accountability Requires Consistency

On the surface, it may seem evident that accountability requires *consistency*. For those of you who work with me and my team, you know that we bring stuffed animals to our meetings. One of those stuffed animals is a squirrel. The squirrel is there because of my dog, Kramer. Whenever we went for a walk, Kramer was attentive and a well-behaved dog, right at my heel—until a squirrel came along. As soon as a squirrel appeared, his brain shut off, and he was off to the races. There was no command, no signal, and no tone of voice that he would respond to. All he could see or hear was the squirrel. Unfortunately, this also describes what happens to typical entrepreneurs. They create grand plans, communicate those plans, and then a shiny new squirrel pops up. We love squirrels.

It takes discipline to ignore them. I must admit that I suffer from such distractions. Unfortunately, these squirrels create confusion for teams. Our teams were comfortable with the plan, ready to implement the plan, and as soon as they started making progress on the plan, the CEO bursts into our office with this great idea that has little or nothing to do with the plan. As leaders, it always seems simple: "Let's add one more thing to the plan." This is the classic example of a leader not being accountable for committing to established priorities.

Many of you are thinking, "But we need to be nimble and can't be so rigid. This is what makes our company better than those big corporations." When you're a small company with just a few employees, you might get away with this kind of maneuver. It doesn't take much energy or effort to change priorities. A lot of things get done on the fly. However, the more employees you have, the more critical it is for you to have and maintain consistency in your organization in terms of roles, processes, and priorities. The less consistency there is, the more drama and chaos that will ensue. Lack of consistency becomes costly and makes it more certain that you will not achieve the goals and priorities that you set out at the beginning of the quarter. It destroys motivation and employee engagement. The more you deviate from your main priorities on a daily basis because you have a reactive organization, the more likely it is that accountability will dissipate. After a while, your team members will not respect your initiatives. They will wait to start projects to confirm that you're serious and will not suddenly change course. You're creating a lack of trust that will then cost time and money.

Accountability Requires Transparency

Motivation decreases if employees cannot see whether they have had a good day or a good week. *Transparency* is critical to the feedback loop. When I use this term, I consider it from two perspectives. First, can people easily understand what you are trying to convey? Second, how vividly is the picture portrayed? Would anyone receiving your vision, goals, and expectations have the same understanding of where you are headed and what is expected? Imagine going to watch your favorite sporting event and finding there is no scoreboard. There are no measures. The event becomes a bunch of people running around, passing a ball, knocking each other over, with spectators having no way of knowing whether their team is winning or losing. Both teams may be very talented, but how long do you think you would sit there and watch? You would not be as engaged as you would if you could see the lead change, if you knew the status of your favorite player, or if you knew your team was down but catching up.

Your employees must be inspired by your success, and know-how the company is doing, so they can celebrate when you're winning. Because when you're winning, everyone is winning. You can even use poor performance in your financial statements to rally the troops to turn your company around. Too often, leaders want their employees to feel as invested as they are, but they're not willing to share all the information that they have. Transparency is the key.

In summary, we have found far greater performance in organizations where cultures are infused with accountability. Employees prefer to be challenged and feel motivated by knowing they have done their jobs well! Accountability starts at the top of any organization. It requires management to be clear about what is expected. They must demonstrate that when decisions are made, they are committed to them. Once committed, they need to show commitment by consistently reviewing progress with everyone. If you do not constructively communicate concern for lack of performance, then people will no longer pay attention to your goals, priorities, and directions. The assumption will be that these are decisions and not commitments.

CREATE A CULTURE OF ACCOUNTABILITY

- As leaders, we need to create a culture where our people follow through on their commitments.
- If you want others to be accountable, you must first be responsible for fulfilling your commitments.
- Being *accountable* is an obligation or willingness to accept responsibility for one's actions.
- *Accountability* is a performance character trait that requires a particular mindset to be present and employs processes and tools to support that mindset.
- With *commitment*, you intensify your level of energy, focus, and determination toward achieving your end.
- I recommend that you communicate with all employees that when we establish goals and priorities, we are committing to achieve them!
- For accountability to occur, I have found that we need *active management.*
- *Management activities* involve clarifying what is expected of a person, monitoring those expectations, providing a feedback loop, developing people, recruiting new people, and providing for succession.
- Constructive conflict occurs when your team is capable of engaging in an unfiltered and passionate exchange of ideas. You avoid making issues personal and resorting to shielded discussions and guarded comments.
- Constructive conflict is a critical component of a functional team.

- Be careful not to hold a subordinate accountable to an impossible standard!
- *The accountability feedback loop* is the mechanism you use in your company to help employees identify whether they are performing to expectations.
- The accountability feedback loop is uncomfortable and absolutely necessary. It is the primary method of driving peak performance and helping people grow and develop to their full potential.
- Accountability is necessary if you want peak performance, and constructive conflict is your signal that you are challenging team members to reach their full potential.

CHAPTER 21
Growth Accelerator #18:
EVERYBODY **KNOWS** THEIR NUMBERS

I hope I have inspired you to want a culture of accountability. A key component to achieving this is everyone knowing their business metrics—their numbers. Of course, that is easier said than done. If you're like the average leader, you may not know what your numbers are, or which ones are critical. I have also found that a fair amount of the anxiety that CEOs, business owners, and leaders experience from their businesses stems from this issue.

Clarity about your numbers gives you power! Your organization must have an excellent financial team that provides timely and accurate information. What is *imperative* is that the entire leadership team has a firm grasp of what that information means and how it should influence the company's activities. As has been said many times, "What gets measured gets done." Once the leadership team knows and understands the numbers, its responsibility is to educate, align, and influence the rest of the organization to perform the right behaviors to improve those numbers.

In my very first business, just out of high school, I failed in that area for a long time. My company was growing, looked profitable, and had a strong team. I thought that's all you needed to know to have a successful business. I believed that if my sales were higher than my expenses, I was home free. However, when payday rolled around, there was never any money around left to pay *my* salary. I didn't understand the numbers. Luckily, I had a great accountant, Mike, who helped me understand cash flow. He explained something very simple to me. Although my profit margin was 50 percent, cash was going out faster than it was coming in. My cost structure was predominantly payroll that was paid bi-weekly, cash out. My clients were not paying me for 90 days, cash in. This was further exacerbated by the business growing 100 percent each quarter. Mike helped me see that cash was going out far faster than it was coming in, and if that continued, I would go bankrupt. I found it embarrassing that as an owner of a company, I did not already know this. It did not matter that I was just 19; I was still the owner. In hindsight, I now realize how many leaders are out there who know as little now as I did then.

I cannot possibly teach you everything I've learned about finance and accounting since that time. I sold that first business and had a successful exit at age 21. I decided to go to college and study accounting, inspired by Mike. While I've never been wired to be an accountant, I did become a CPA, and the knowledge I gained has served me well. The most important thing I've learned is that everyone should and can determine what they need to know about financial statements, how they influence what your business should or should not be doing, and then take actions to improve its results.

Fear of Sharing

The first hurdle we often encounter when working with new clients is getting them over the fear of sharing financial data. This fear may stem from several causes. I want to address each of these here, because your team must always know whether you are winning or losing. I believe this is one reason why people enjoy video games so much—the immediate feedback. They do something, and then get feedback on whether it's right or wrong, win or lose. Somebody can work a 50-hour week—10 hours unpaid overtime—only to have their boss come to them and say they did a poor job. In their minds, they felt like they gave 125 percent. There was a disconnect between the results the company needed and that employee's definition of doing a good job. We need to connect the dots. Sharing your financial data is a crucial component of motivating desired results.

The first reason many CEOs do not want to share their numbers is that they are not comfortable or do not feel they understand their numbers well enough. If this is not their area of strength, they do not want to expose themselves to the rest of the team. This issue has two components. First, it is okay that this is not your strong suit. If this is the case, there must be other team members who are the functional experts. You need to have someone, either internal or external, who can help you and your team understand that information clearly. If that is not happening, you need to strengthen your advisors. We have walked into some dire situations where leaders were blindsided when they chose to be uninformed because of their discomfort. The second component is an ego issue. You may rest assured that the rest of your colleagues already know you are not the All-Powerful Wizard of Oz, even if that's what you want them to think. Recognize that even though you are not a functional expert in finance and accounting, with enough practice, you will find yourself asking some outstanding and important questions about your numbers. This cannot be overstressed.

The second reason many CEOs do not want to share their numbers relates to how they keep their books. You may be doing some things for tax purposes or running personal expenses through the business account, things that skew your numbers and affect performance on an operating basis. You can easily adjust what you present to your team to accurately depict true performance. So long as what is shown is an accurate representation of performance, there is no reason why the team needs to see the other numbers.

A third reason many CEOs do not want to share their numbers is related to trust. They're concerned about what people will do with the information. You may worry about employees figuring out what you earn and wanting raises. In most cases, they are guessing and usually think you make far more than you do. Even if you make more than they think, so what? That is your business. If you pay a fair wage at all levels, that is all you need to worry about. There are always factors to be aware of and concerned about, but this one comes back to core values. You should not have people in your organization that you cannot trust. Confidence in your team allows you to run your organization correctly. The benefits of sharing information have always far outweighed the cost of those few outliers who you could not trust. Companies that share their information far outperform the ones that don't.

Aligning Everyone

To *align everyone* means that every person in the organization understands how they affect results. Every employee in the organization is an investment you made that produces a result. Some have a more direct impact and others less. The more we help everyone understand their roles—how they influence the purpose of the organization, contribute to your product and service, help sales grow, and help the business be more profitable—the more *aligned* they are.

It is our job as leaders to connect the dots, which is a complicated job. The more processes, products and services, employees, functions, and roles, the harder it is to connect the dots. The clearer we can make the picture, the more defined and measurable, the more engaged your employees will be—and the better your results.

Leading versus Lagging Indicators

For most leaders, the primary metrics used to set goals and manage the business come from their income statement and balance sheet. The numbers most often discussed are sales, cost of goods sold, gross margin, overhead, labor costs, profit, receivables, inventory, work-in-process, payables, and cash. While you do need to monitor these measures, they are all *lagging indicators*—results from decisions and actions taken in the past. They comprise the scorecard used to measure the success of those actions and decisions. The problem with trying to use these measures to manage your business is that they come after the fact. While there is some benefit to using lagging indicators, they do not tell you why your results turned out the way they did. It is also too late to change the outcome. It is the equivalent of trying to drive your car forward by looking in your rearview mirror.

Instead, leaders should focus on primary key performance indicators, the *leading measures* that influence lagging results the most. By choosing the right leading indicators, you can help your team improve the lagging indicators. For example, let's revisit a human resource example from earlier in the book. Assume you want to hire a new salesperson. Your historical statistics tell you it takes 30 candidates to arrive at the right final candidate. You want to fill the position within 30 days. If the person you're going to hire is already employed, and we assume that person will want to give two weeks' notice to their current employer, you have only two weeks to choose that person. Taking this even further, you need one week to go through all the interviewing processes. That leaves just one week to find and assess 30 candidates. In this situation, the leading indicator that is most important for human resources is five applicants per day (six per day if you have a five-day workweek) to consider 30 candidates by the end of one week. If human resources do not meet that leading indicator, you can forget about properly filling that job in 30 days.

Clear Expectations

Can every employee in your organization clearly and correctly answer the question, "What is expected of me?" The chances are their answers will be different from yours. There is also a good chance that your and their answers change by the week. This variation shows the lack of clear expectations that is a problem for many companies. It may occur in some positions and not in others. It may also lead you to discover that the expectations outlined in your job descriptions and employee scorecards are not be aligned with your quarterly plans.

Aligning personal scorecards to company priorities is an excellent opportunity to increase velocity in most companies. One of my colleagues, Dave Baney, wrote a book called, *The 3 x 5 Coach: A Practical Guide to Coaching Your Team*. In the book, he introduces the concept of providing every employee a 3 x 5 card that clarifies for them and you why they get paid. It is a simple but profound method on how to address this critically important subject.[1]

On the front of the card, you name the employee, specify his or her role, and write the mission of the position. On the back of the card, list no more than five accountabilities and how you measure success for each one. It all must fit on the 3 x 5 card.[2]

Here is an example of the front of the card:

Jane Smith

- **Role:** General Manager
- **Mission:** Drive the ideology of the organization, build a high-functioning leadership team, hire the right people, build an organization that grows and develops those people, and optimize labor in a manner that achieves the company's lofty standards for growth and profit.

Here is an example of the back of the card:

- High-Performing Leadership Team – x percent of Performing Leaders, x percent Achievement of Quarterly Initiatives
- Employee Engagement – Employee Net Promoter Score, x percent of Improvement Generated from Not Leaders
- Customer Satisfaction – Customer Net Promoter Score, Ratio of Positive to Negative Feedback
- Achieve Budget – Revenue Budget, Profit Budget[3]

The power of creating one of these cards is extraordinary. It helps make sure you are not creating ambiguity in expectations. Having little space on the card compels you to keep it simple. The process also forces you and the employee to sit down and have a conversation about what is expected. It affords both of you the opportunity to have a dialogue later should the outcomes not be aligned with the card.

The only complaint I've gotten about this card from leaders is that they don't want to commit to its limits—the same problem the cards are trying to solve. They think that by clearly defining someone's role, it means an employee will never have someone else's back or can never be asked to do something *not* on their list. That is not the intent of clarifying expectations. Your company's core values should define how people need to behave when a colleague needs help. However, as managers, it is our job to help our employees make *our* main things *their* main things. If employees do not perform well in their primary jobs, why would you ask them to do anything else? If you are causing them to spend too much time on performing duties outside of their primary responsibilities, then you are demonstrating poor prioritization. They are not the problem; you are!

Be careful not to be one of those leaders who set people up for failure. Such leaders create a very hard-to-achieve 3 x 5 card, add to it some lofty company initiatives, and then daily pull those people away from doing what they thought was expected. I regularly encounter this behavior. Leaders who engage in this kind of sabotage tend to be disorganized and unable to prioritize. They try to make their fluctuating priorities everyone else's. They cause real priorities to cease, and then get upset when other leaders fail to achieve what was expected.

Let me share a silly example of how someone created a mixed message for their team. I was in a coaching session with a CEO who was the sales leader in his company at the time. We were discussing a nonperformer on the sales team and an accountability discussion he had with that person. He mentioned that he requires the COO to sit in on all sales meetings and accountability meetings with the salespeople. I knew that the COO regularly worked 75 to 80 hours a week. I asked, "Does the COO have any responsibility on her 3 x 5 card for sales?" His answer: "No." Then I asked, "Why do you insist that she go to these meetings?" The short version of his long answer was that it made him feel better. He was using two of the most productive people in the company to deal with the poor performance of someone in sales—someone who probably should have been fired two months ago. Thus, all three people were unproductive.

Finding the Right Numbers

Just as some leaders fear to share their numbers, so do people fear developing key performance indicators (KPIs). After all, this is another area that's not a core competency for people without a financial background. But finding the right KPIs is not as difficult as one might imagine. We know that every person in your company is involved in one or more processes. The key to finding the right numbers is first to identify the main processes driving your business. For each process, identify all the steps it involves. Notice that each step has measurements that indicate whether the process is healthy or not. We look for places in these processes that exhibit wide variability in outcomes. Those typically make great KPIs. The next task is to identify people who are most able to influence that variability and have them help work on reducing unwanted outcomes.

Steps within a process that have little or no variability may or may not be good KPIs. Even a step with no variability could still be a problematic KPI. For example, you may have the same number of errors happening in a step every day. While it may not be changing very much, it may be making customers unhappy and costing you a lot of money. There may be a KPI that indicates a high cost for you, and the reduction could be worth your effort.

Good KPIs are not only process steps. They could be ratios, such as the number of days in inventory or the number of days it takes to collect receivables. The point is, *you want to find the numbers in your business that represent constraints.* The idea is to focus people on those constraints until they are brought to an acceptable level. You then move the focus to a new constraint that is not at an adequate level. These are the numbers you need to use for critical numbers, 3 x 5 cards, department plans, and quarterly company plans. When you improve the right leading key performance indicators, you're more in control of producing much better income statements and balance sheets—your lagging indicators.

It is vital for every person in your company to know the numbers. You want employees to feel part of something bigger than themselves—to be part of the team. To accomplish this, they must know how the company is performing and what their contribution is to that performance. This is essential for proper motivation and clarity. You cannot expect people to perform, provide the right contributions, and to feel connected if they cannot see the effects of their actions. Identifying the right key performance indicators for each employee, tracking those indicators, and publishing them are essential to your peak performance.

EVERYBODY KNOWS THEIR NUMBERS

- A key component to achieving a culture of accountability is everyone knowing their numbers.
- *Clarity* around your numbers is power.
- It is imperative that the entire leadership team has a firm grasp of what these numbers mean and how they should influence company activities.
- Sharing your financial data is a crucial component of motivation.
- The importance of understanding your numbers cannot be overemphasized.
- Recognize that even though you are not a functional expert in finance and accounting, with enough practice, you will find yourself asking some outstanding and essential questions about the numbers.
- The more we can help everyone understand how they influence the purpose of the organization, contribute to its product(s) and service(s), help sales grow, and can help the company be more profitable, the more *aligned* they are.
- Focus your primary key performance indicators (KPIs) on the leading measures that influence your lagging results the most.
- Can every employee clearly and correctly answer the question, "What is expected of me?"
- Aligning personal scorecards to the company priorities is an excellent opportunity to increase velocity in most companies.
- Create a 3 x 5 card for every employee in the company, including yourself.

CHAPTER 22
Growth Accelerator #19:
STRENGTHEN
COMMUNICATIONS

We are in the home stretch—only one more growth accelerator to discuss! It is the last, but no less important than the
other 18. There are so many topics to cover on the subject
of communication. To make the issue even more challenging, we now
have technology that was designed to make communication better, but
often makes it worse.

Although many leaders among my clients were happy to say how great
they are at communicating, the number one complaint in their organizations was lack of communication. When I brought that complaint to
the attention of those leaders, they promptly told me that everyone else
must be causing that problem.

In Chapter 18 of *Your Business is a Leaky Bucket,* I covered the topic
of holding better meetings, which should be a primary communication tool for all organizations. For those who have read that book, I do
not want to be repetitive. You can download those best practices and
agendas at www.howardmshore.com/tools. In this chapter, we'll discuss

some common communication issues within companies—those that affect their ability to implement the other growth accelerators—and the methods for correcting them.[1]

Keep It Simple

As CEO, leader, and coach, I have experienced and witnessed this common problem in businesses: We make things complicated! A primary contributor to this complexity occurs when we add layers to what we express to others because we're not sure they're getting our message. In some cases, unconscious societal factors place value on complexity. Think about the times when you've seen people get compliments and beam with pride when someone has said, "You are so intelligent, shrewd, and innovative!" Leaders take pride in telling people about the sophistication of their products, strategy, and plans. These are just different ways of saying, "Let me tell you how complicated I am." It all boils down to one thing. *We need to put more thought into what we say and how we say it.* We know and preach that we want to keep things simple, and then we do the opposite. (I know I am guilty of this behavior. Friends and colleagues who are reading this are probably laughing right now!)

Complexity has several drawbacks. In some cases, it causes a few people—the workhorses—to carry more than their share of the weight, all while complaining that everyone else should be doing more. Usually, it is a communication problem on the part of the workhorse, not others' unwillingness to cooperate, inability to do what is needed, laziness, or stupidity. Workhorses are rarely forced to take on tasks that others could and should. While workhorses claim they need to make up for others' lack of knowledge and awareness, that's not necessarily the case.

I am sure you have found yourself doing something because you felt that getting others up to speed would take too long, that they could not see what you see, or that they aren't sharp enough. But is the task really so complex that it could not be explained? If your people do not understand the total picture, is it because their leader failed to disclose enough information, simply, so they could? When you do not fully access your team's contributions in terms of creativity and thought, you are treating them as automatons instead of colleagues and knowledge workers. You leave tremendous potential value—and actual money—on the table. After all, you hired and are paying these people for abilities you're not using.

Our job as leaders is to make everything easier for everyone: clients, vendors, and employees. The more comfortable we make it, the faster we will grow. Making life easier starts with communication. Anyone that finds themselves telling someone, "it's complicated," may not understand the concepts well enough or has not spent enough time distilling how to communicate the ideas. Many times, it is the latter. (I have had to face that situation my entire life.) You may understand what you want to say or do, but if others don't, you need to spend the necessary time to learn how to express your thoughts, brand, strategy, process, or any other concept in a way that a young child can understand it.

Conditions Matter

You need to consider that conditions affect performance. Imagine driving your car when it's dark, foggy, and raining. How is your driving affected? I find that I slow down and am more cautious. Depending on how adverse conditions are, I may choose to pull over or not drive at all. Compare the first scenario to driving on an open road on a sunny day with no other cars on the road. Driving is so much easier! You feel free to relax and enjoy the trip. In such conditions, we speed up, even take a little risk (which we do not see as a risk at all), for which some of us have earned a few tickets. When conditions are bright, there is nothing to deter you from getting to your destination as quickly as possible. The same goes for business. Conditions matter.

Unfortunately, many leaders believe they have created that bright, sunny day. In fact, their employees feel more like they're in the dark, foggy, and raining conditions. You must consider the conditions for every employee. If one person's condition becomes murky, it may affect that of someone else. Conditions may be different depending on your role, function, and leadership seniority. If you want to unlock the full potential of your company, you need to create excellent conditions for everyone.

I see two key factors critical to creating optimal conditions for employees. The first is *clarity*. Fortunately, I've been sharing with you the fundamental principles and components of clarity throughout this book. *Clarity* requires:

- Company purpose
- Core values
- Company goals
- Company priorities
- The mission of a person's role
- Key accountabilities expected of a person
- Key performance indicators that show the person performed those expectations
- Key priorities for the person

If any of the above information is unavailable or ambiguous, then you are not providing ideal conditions for an employee. If an employee performs in a manner inconsistent with established expectations for an extended period, your allowance of that lack of performance sends mixed messages.

The second factor relates to *how* we communicate. Many leaders were taught to believe that the only ways to motivate people are by using carrots and sticks. The challenge with this approach is that the positive impact tends to be short-lived. The sticks, in many cases, result in long-term negative consequences because you wind up with employees who resent the managers who use them. Similarly, carrots tend to make employees perform well only when a carrot is present. They send the message that their regular wages do not require reasonably high performance. Instead of holding people accountable to do their jobs well, we bribe them.[2]

I am not an *always* and *never* person. There are times to use carrots and sticks, but there are diminishing returns when used as regular courses of business. I would recommend using them sparingly and in specific circumstances rather than as a rule. If you need data to support this concept, I suggest that you read *Drive* by Daniel Pink. He has long researched this subject and provides a lot of data to support the diminished return theories. My observations corroborate his research.

Another critical factor for creating the right conditions is safety. When we feel safe, we can be the most creative and do our best work. When employees feel their jobs are unsafe, their performances will drop. Unfortunately, too many employees (and leaders, for that matter) do not feel safe enough in their current roles. Don't get me wrong; we need people to be subject to company policy, to be accountable for performing. But they should also be in an environment where they feel inwardly compelled and responsible for doing so.

I have observed (and been guilty of creating) situations that foster an environment that is not conducive to safety. When people are talked to harshly, micromanaged, subjected to too much bureaucracy, or hear things that threaten their self-esteem or provoke anger, their performance will drop. All of this is *communication*. Think about what happens when someone speaks to you harshly, challenges your integrity, or calls you out in front of your peers. What happens to your productivity? Think about what happens to people who are told too frequently to follow the script, that our procedures and policies are the holy grail, that they have no authority to make any decisions. How can that organization possibly unlock that person's full value and potential? We must help employees feel that there is a balance, that policies and procedures are not arbitrary, that we follow best practices, and that they are in a safe environment to make a full contribution. Obviously, the more we do those things, the more we are creating the conditions to help our company achieve its true potential.

Effective Communication Results in the Right Behaviors

One of my first coaches helped with my approach to communication by asking me two questions that have stuck with me for over a decade: "What is communication?" and "How do you know if it was effective?" These two simple questions have had a profound impact on how I communicate today and continue to challenge me to improve communications. Earlier in my life, I would have told you I'm a great communicator. As I reach my mid-fifties, and am now more aware than ever that I'm not perfect, I realize I'm lucky that anybody understands me and feel fortunate to still have any friends. For those who have received some of my horrible text messages and emails, thank you for not abandoning me! For the rest of you, let me apologize in advance for missteps I may make as I continue to try to master communication.

My coach and I settled on a definition of *communication* as "the process of sending and receiving information to cause action and a result." I was proud of that definition until we started talking about how to measure success. For those who know me, I am a national speaker, author of a best-selling business book, and leader of several companies. I thought I had the gift of gab and could compete with the best. However, some of my communications should never have been sent at all. For example, have you ever sent a communication and realized later, after you cleaned up the mess it caused, that the real purpose of the communication was to make yourself feel better? Those were killers because all they did was create more problems and make more trouble.

Then there were the many instances when the communication I sent was not received in the way I thought it would be. Receiving is a two-sided problem. First, as the sender, had I correctly understood the communication I was responding to and was I addressing the right person or people? Second, too often, reactions that followed did not match my intentions. As the communicator, that meant my communication failed. This is not an all-the-time occurrence, but it was and still is something that happens often enough to render me a work in progress.

I challenge you to consider how effective your communication is. My need to improve myself sent me on a search to learn why so many communications fail. Part of it starts with understanding the components of communication, which can get lost when you use technology.

One thing I've learned over time is that there are three components to face-to-face communication: body language, tone, and the actual words we use. I've seen different percentages on the importance of each element, but the most common conclusion is that body language comprises 55 percent, tone 38 percent, and the words we use only 7 percent of the interaction. I have learned that the use of these percentages can be a misunderstanding of findings published in 1971 by Albert Mehrabian in his book *Silent Message*. However, the importance of non-verbal communication is still an essential concept. You must consider the nonverbals to listen actively. Failure to do so leads one to miss important cues in the communication process.[3]

Too often, senders of information do not investigate what body language means. They are pleased with the fact that they have sent information but do not recognize that the other person has not received it in the way it was intended. For example, you might be talking to someone and notice a blank look on their face after you speak. That is body language. If you are a student of communication, you know you need to investigate that blank look. Is the person you are talking to not paying attention, not comprehending, or was it something else? You need to ask! Sometimes, you may recognize the body language but choose to ignore it because you do not like conflict, or you have other more pressing matters. In either case, these examples of poor communication result in lower business productivity and cost you in the long run.

Tone works in the same way. If you use the wrong tone when delivering your message, the listener may not understand the information you're sending but not feel comfortable asking questions. That occurs quite often.

Here are some of the things I informally measure about my face-to-face communications:

- Did the person do what I expected?
- If it was a group, what percentage acted as expected or desired?
- How many times did I have to cover the same ground because I did not communicate the first time effectively?
- What did the other person's body language look like before and after our communication?
- How often do other people make comments about my communication style and approach, and what can be gleaned from their critique?
- Did any communications go poorly today, and what could I have done differently?

I suggest you review this list of questions at the end of each day as you consider how your day went. After all, communication is one of the most essential skills leaders are supposed to have and use continually.

The Right Method of Communication

Are you using the right method of communication for each situation? I find that people hide behind instant messaging, text messaging, and email for various reasons, some of them counterproductive. I'm thankful that we have these modes of communication. They save time and allow us to communicate more information faster. However, as I mentioned earlier, do they communicate body language and tone, or just words?

Obviously, like the other facets of businesses, there is no exact formula for everyone's use of the modes of communication. I prefer email for sending information that needs to be consumed or can be quickly replied to. For example, "What would you like for lunch from the attached menu?" If it takes more than three minutes to compose an email, I consider stopping and calling the person. If I think the other person may take issue with the email, I stop and call the other person. The challenge is to slow down and recognize the situation. I use instant messaging and text messaging only for more urgent issues that can be communicated in just a few sentences, mainly if I need an immediate answer or quick action when voice communication is not possible. For everything else, I use video conferencing, the phone, or a face-to-face meeting. Whenever I violate these rules of thumb, it takes far longer to communicate, tends to create more frustration for all parties, and leads to a lot more miscommunication. Putting aside your convenience, challenge yourself on the effectiveness of your methods and consider how those methods are used as it will affect the outcomes.

As I close out this chapter, I must acknowledge that this is the most challenging accelerator in the whole book to master. I must be vulnerable to you and admit that my team wishes I would do a better job in this area. I agree. I have great intentions, know what must be done, and am inconsistent, at best. Effective communication takes attention, focus, and discipline to get right. And we will not get it right every time. With that said, communication is the accelerator for all the other chapters. It must get the attention it deserves.

STRENGTHEN COMMUNICATIONS

- In Chapter 18 of *Your Business is a Leaky Bucket*, I covered the topic of better meetings. Go to www.howardmshore.com/tools to download best practices and agendas for the meeting rhythms recommended in my last book.
- The primary contributors to complexity are the facts that we can't see what we overcomplicate in what we express to others, that there are unconscious societal factors that place value on complexity, and that we need to put more thought into our communications.
- Complexity causes a few people to carry more weight on their shoulders than they should.
- I challenge you to learn to understand why another person's lack of knowledge and awareness may equate to your failure to explain the subject adequately.
- Examples of creating unnecessary complexity: you are doing something because you believe that getting others up to speed would take too long, that they could not see what you see, or that they aren't sharp enough.
- Our job as leaders is to make everything easier for everyone: our clients, vendors, and employees.
- You need to consider that conditions affect performance.
- The two key factors critical to creating optimal conditions are *clarity* and *communication*.
- A critical factor in creating optimal conditions is safety.
- When people are spoken to in harsh ways, micromanaged, subjected to too much bureaucracy, hear things that threaten

their self-esteem, or cause them to be angry, their performance will drop.

- The more we can help our employees feel they are in a safe environment to make a full contribution, the more we are creating the conditions to help our company achieve its true potential.
- The definition of *communication*: "The process of sending and receiving information to cause action and a result."
- Determine the right method of communication for each type of situation.
- Putting aside your convenience, challenge yourself on the effectiveness of your communications, and consider how the methods you use affect outcomes.

BUSINESS ACCELERATION CALCULATOR™

There is no specific exercise to complete in the *Calculator* for this chapter. Strengthening communications is a component of accountability and is about making sure that what has been decided gets done. You must implement this chapter to yield the results you are aiming for from the other chapters.

Contact Me

As you apply the concepts and see the differences they make, please email me at howard@howardmshore.com to let me know what you did and how it worked. I wrote this book to have an impact, and it will make my day to see that I have done so.

YOUR PATH TO
FREEDOM

Congratulations. You have reached the starting line on your path to freedom. We've been talking about acceleration, but once your business takes off like a rocket, you will enjoy the freedom that gives you.

I'm sure you recognize that the best practices provided in this book make sense. If you have done an honest inventory, you're now aware of all the work it takes to unlock the true potential within your organization. All organizations have a lot of work to do; the bigger the organization, the more work there is. The good news is that it all starts with those one percent moves that have huge impacts. A combination of those moves will cause a massive shift in your results. Each effort will pay huge dividends.

At this point, you should feel better equipped to create an environment that will make your business accelerate. Please don't feel overwhelmed. Instead, be inspired and stay aware of how to continually increase mastery of the "five plates": stewardship, human capital management, strategy, planning, and accountability. Remember that each one percent move acts as a multiplier rather than an additive.

Working on all five plates rather than one or a few of them represents clock-building instead of time-telling. Throughout this book, we have examined 19 specific areas that provide you opportunities for significant improvement in building your clock.

What to Do Now?

I wrote this book because I wanted to have an impact on as many businesses as possible and because I know that some organizations and leaders prefer to self-implement. Another way to extract full value from this book is to hire a coach who can simplify and help you achieve the changes you want to make.

To begin the transformation process, improve your meetings by implementing the suggestions in the Meeting Rhythms Summary you downloaded in Chapter 22. Then, consider the five plates with your team and determine on a scale of one to five (one being "Not a Problem" and five "A Severe Problem") which plate needs the most attention. After you have made significant progress on the first plate, redo this exercise. All the plates are essential, but there is always one plate that needs more attention than the others. Also, remember that you can only implement a certain amount of change at any given time. Recognize that as you apply these concepts, they're all changes from "the way we've always done it here." They may meet some resistance.

Self-implementation is time-consuming and requires extraordinary self-discipline. It can also create friction among leaders. For most organizations, hiring a coach is a better way to go. Before I get into the details, I need to explain the differences between a *coach* and a *consultant*.

Why Hire a Coach?

This section may seem a little self-serving, yet I feel compelled to say that without a coach, I am confident that your organization will reach success but never its true potential. I have seen this firsthand. There is a reason why our profession has grown exponentially.

I have hired several coaches over the years, which has been transformational for me. I am a coach who continues to hire a coach for myself. People who have worked with the right coach will tell you that they and their organizations are better as a result. My wife will tell you that, thanks to this profession, I am a far better version of myself.

You might believe that hiring a coach implies that something's wrong. To the contrary, hiring a coach is an indication that you want you and your organization to operate at peak performance all the time. We all need a coach. I find the people who say that using coaches is a waste of time and money are indulging their egos more than exercising common sense.

The best analogy I can share relates to exercise. As I mentioned earlier, I have been weightlifting since I was 13. Then, I had the discipline to walk up to two miles to get to the gym and to pay for the membership using the money I earned working for my dad's company. As a young adult, I bench-pressed more than 400 pounds, won a strongman competition for my weight group, and was always a person other people came to when they wanted to learn about lifting weights. With all that experience, I still use a professional trainer. Why? My trainer challenges me to do things that I would never do myself. For example, when I start feeling tired, I might skip those extra repetitions, not run stairs, and God knows, I would never subject myself to burpees. My trainer always challenges me to do more, and I follow his instructions. He reminds me to do the things I know I'm supposed to do but sometimes forget. I'm in better shape because of it. You can expect similar experiences when working with business and executive coaches.

Here are the types of comments we hear from clients describing the benefits they've received from coaching:

- **Challenge and Support** – They got the extra push they needed. At times, they did not realize they needed it.
- **Exit Strategy** – Valuations more than doubled, and companies were prepared for the sale.
- **Improved Performance** – Created better and more sustainable business models.
- **More Clarity** – Everyone in the company, including the leadership team, was more aligned on how to win.
- **Better Ideas and Decisions** – Their ideas and decisions showed more innovation and scope.
- **Stronger Leaders** – Heightened ability to influence others, increased self-confidence, and increased self-awareness.
- **Employee Engagement** – More employees were willing to give their all.
- **Fun** – Some leaders learned how to have fun again in their businesses.

The main reason for engaging a coach is well documented in Allen Gannett's *Fast Company* article, "Dismantling the Myth of the Self-Reliant CEO." In the article, he describes how leaders obtain and choose their professional support systems.[1]

Gannett found that more and more CEOs are joining support groups like YPO, Vistage, and Entrepreneurs' Organization for peer mentoring. In fact, they are more likely to get a coach as their company scales. They are not the bulletproof superheroes they appear to be from the outside. Interestingly, serial CEOs and growing companies are the ones who most often seek help. You would think it would be the opposite, but the best leaders are always the ones seeking the most support. According to the data, 60 percent of growth-stage CEOs found help from executive coaches, while only 32 percent of early-stage CEOs did the same.

Executive coaching employs methods such as asking crucial questions to gain insight from your assumptions. It is a delicate process that provides a more direct and personal angle to arrive at a self-initiated meaningful action and outcome.[2]

The process of business coaching addresses long-term questions and possible results—to help you understand how your decisions contribute to the current standing of your business. An executive coach understands the urgency and demands of the modern business landscape. A coach is not there to be your best buddy. A coach's job is to ask those difficult and challenging questions that others may not ask. They make it a point to provide you with a broader take on identifying and tackling problems, working them out strategically, and applying the right kind of solutions. You can expect that after all the plans are laid out, you can review them and carefully consider the best course of action—because you're always the best person to make the call.

A coach functions as an external consultation partner and is not part of the company. Their job is to guide you through the process of generating a new outlook toward the business so you can think clearly, make the tough decisions, and avoid repeating harmful patterns. Coaches are usually professionals who are experts in the field of business acceleration and improvisation. Throughout your relationship with a coach, expect full transparency, encouragement, and constructive conflict.

Executive coaching helps you develop and hone your skills in real time, within the context of the issues and challenges you want to address. While all forms of self-development and improvement are advantageous, executive coaching is more practical and useful than books, seminars, and improvement programs because it integrates teaching and insights into your life.

Rather than starting and stopping (like reading self-improvement books) or trying to cram all your self-improvement into one small time-frame outside your normal life (like attending a seminar), the benefits of executive coaching become an integral part of your life—the life you envisioned—as your dreams begin to become a reality. Your self-esteem and confidence will start to soar as you begin to realize more of your potential than you thought possible!

An executive coach can help you understand your circumstances from various perspectives, learn new approaches, break bad habits, and challenge you to develop better strategies. Your coach can help you see how to move your skills forward, find blind spots, and learn how to become a more effective leader.

Differences between a Coach and a Consultant

A difficult decision for a CEO, owner, or other senior executive is what kind of outside assistance to retain to best help strengthen themselves and their businesses. Different types of advisors can assist you. Do not assume they all do the same thing! There are similarities among the choices, but don't be fooled. There are significant differences between coaching and consulting and between business and executive coaching. You must choose the right type of advisor for your situation.

The following table helps explain the differences between a consultant and a coach.

As you can see, both consultants and coaches can be valuable. However, they are very different business catalysts. You may not need a consultant because you have a deep team with many years of industry and business experience, up-to-date skills, and the understanding required to accomplish your goals. Your team may not lack ideas or know-how. In these cases, you can recognize that the coach is the right catalyst for you.

CONSULTANT	COACH
Often works with more than one person in a department, function, or team.	Works on a one-to-one basis or with a team.
Is an expert who is hired to solve a specific problem. They fill a void in technical expertise in terms of knowledge, process, and experience your internal team does not possess.	The coach is an enabler who provides a process that helps empower you and holds you accountable to solve problems and create more ideal outcomes.
Structures projects for specific deliverables or results. They may work directly with your internal team. The consultant is accountable and responsible for the outcomes.	The coach challenges you to think and act in new ways, to find your blind spots. You are accountable and responsible for the outcomes.
Closes the gap for your team's weaknesses.	Builds on and unlocks the team and individual strengths.
Most consultants generally don't get involved in behavior change.	A primary focus is on individual and interpersonal dynamics **designed to cause behavior change.**
Gathers data and reports on what needs to be done.	You gather the data and reports. Your **coach facilitates** the meetings and process.
Engagement is time-limited; generally short-term and project-oriented results.	Occurs over a period that many times involve renewable contracts; focused on long-term results.
Transactional	Self-discovery leads to behavioral and mind shifts and can be transformational.
Requires **limited commitment from you** to implement.	Requires your participation and commitment to implement solutions.

Choosing the Right Coach

Getting the right coach for your business is more complicated than it used to be. When I first became a coach in 2004, not many people knew what executive coaches and business coaches were. Frankly, there were not many of us out there. Fast forward to 2019, and coaches appear to be as numerous as cockroaches. They are multiplying and seem to show up everywhere. It is an unregulated field, so there is no barrier to entry. Your age can be 22 or over 70. Backgrounds and genders are varied, and none of those factors predict success. Some use proven processes and methods, and others don't. As the industry grew, many decided to turn it into a specialization fest. You now have life coaches, etiquette coaches, speaking coaches, executive coaches, business coaches, team coaches, behavioral coaches, and so on. A coach can cost you anywhere from $75 per hour to $25,000 or more per day.

As with any business where there is complexity, I see opportunity. I was inspired to turn my coaching practice into the growing firm I lead today. I decided to become a clock-builder instead of a time-teller. Clients deserve a product and service they can trust. Similarly, coaches need an industry that can support them better.

I have been and still am affiliated with several organizations that developed excellent tools and methods for coaches. I was able to see how coaches using those same tools were getting very different outcomes. I also saw a lot of malpractice and too many people who should not be coaches jumping into the field. There was no one policing these coaches and protecting clients. There was high turnover, and some who dropped out had the potential to be great coaches but did not get the right support. Concurrently, some licensors of the tools and methods became more concerned with getting those methods into as many hands as possible rather than whether those tools and techniques were appropriately used. They were playing a numbers game, and I wanted to change that game.

Results Matter

Results matter—so much so that my firm guarantees them. In the past year, several of our clients doubled their values, doubled their revenues, and benefited from personal transformations. It is essential to have clarity on what results you expect to achieve with your coach and that the coach has a precise measurement system to show you those results. When I hear from CEOs that they do not know what outcomes they got from working with a coach, it upsets me. Those coaches give my profession a black eye. When you speak to a prospective coach, listen carefully. Are they focused on your results or their methods? Coaches who are too excited about their methods and being a coach tend to forget why you hired them and often are not prepared to help you attain the kinds of results you want.

The following is an example of how we track results for one of our clients:

- **Business Acceleration Calculator™** – A vital tool for finding the right priorities and placing value on the ones selected in our meetings.
- **Cash-Flow Story** – We educate nonfinancial people about how to improve the cash-flow story and get them to commit to quarterly improvements and measure success or failure.
- **Business Acceleration Checklist** – Our proprietary checklist of 60 best practices measures progress on implementing habits that are necessary to scale your business and increase employee engagement.
- **Five Dysfunctions of a Team Survey** – This tool is used to enhance and improve the functioning of the executive team.
- **Culture Survey** – This tool helps to identify and drive necessary improvements in employee engagement.

Our clients not only achieve results; they also know why!

The Process Leads to Results

To achieve exceptional results, you need the right process and tools. Most coaches use too shallow an approach. We do not believe in one-size-fits-all solutions. If the coach you hire is not rigid about your following the approach you've agreed on, beware! You should be asking the coach to prescribe how to drive the best outcomes, not the other way around. If your doctor wrote prescriptions knowing they were not the right treatment for your ailment, it would be considered malpractice. One would question the value of the doctor and whether the patient respected the doctor's expertise.

The first element of a coaching relationship is to understand how much interaction there will be. In my experience, many engagements fail because there is too little interaction. This occurs either because clients do not make themselves available or their budgets are too small. Our most successful engagements involve a combination of one-on-one and team coaching. We provide fixed-fee engagements that offer unlimited access to our coaches for the leadership. This allows for maximum impact. These interactions involve off-site quarterly strategic meetings; on-site meetings; video conference calls; and phone, text, and direct messaging. We do our best to make each client feel as if they are our only client.

The second element to a coaching relationship is the content. What is the track record of the system the coach is using? Is it made up, or has it been proven over time? How precise is the content, and will it be broad enough to raise the bar in your organization? One of our customer promises is that they will never stop learning. Our content is broad and deep enough to keep our clients learning for years and to fully cover all five of the plates required to scale your business. As you can see from this book, we pull from the works of many masters. Each time we meet, you can expect at least one "aha" moment and something practical that you will want to apply as soon as you return to your office.

Coach Qualifications

The qualifications to become a coach are not regulated, and certifications are easy to obtain compared to those required for a doctor, lawyer, accountant, and other professionals. I have the CPA designation, which is something to be proud of. While I am proud of my coaching certifications, they do not deserve the same level of accolades as the professional designation. When I took the CPA exam, less than 10 percent of the candidates passed the entire exam the first time. The exam had four parts, and many never passed all four. From what I have seen, nearly everyone who aspires to be a coach will get certified in the coaching world, which is not exactly what the client wants to hear.

A coach does not need to have experience in your industry, or have been a CEO. However, to help your organization, we know that a coach's capabilities, executive presence, and a proven track record are necessary. At our firm, we have an "identify the success" formula. A typical coach is a solo practitioner—no firm to join, no deep bench to draw from. In our firm, it takes 100 candidates or more for us to add one coach with the breadth of knowledge and track record we're after. We are one of the most selective in the industry. Our coaches will tell you it was a badge of honor to be chosen to join our team.

Coach Development

I believe that to unlock a client's potential, we must first unlock the potential of our coaches. We work from the inside out. In our firm, when you become a new coach, there is a continuous process of growth. When a coach starts with Activate Group, they go through a six-month onboarding process. Our coaches will tell you they go through some of the most in-depth training and learning they have ever experienced in their careers. In addition to our "core curriculum," we read a new book at a minimum of every two weeks. Coaches are peer-reviewed while they are delivering to clients, receive their one-on-one coaching, participate in mastermind groups, and have a weekly coach's call to work on skills and knowledge. We expect our coaches to be certified and participate in at least 60 hours of continuing education each year. We not only hire sharp people; we keep them sharp.

Are You Buying a Team or a Person?

The weakness of most coaches is they are a one-person band. At Activate Group, our clients get a team instead of just one person. They get our whole team for one price. This team includes your head coach and then access to all the other coaches on the team, including me. We also have a strong support team that helps drive engagement. This team continues to evaluate client circumstances to help deliver maximum results. We work on achieving outcomes rather than holding meetings and handing out tools and materials. We consider ourselves an extension of your management team, tasked with helping you drive toward your Audacious Goals and helping all your leaders find freedom from being slaves to the business.

Finding a Coach

I am frequently asked, "Do you have a coach in my local area?" The answer is, "Possibly," but that does not matter. We are growing our team across the country. Locality is less critical than finding the right coach. Sometimes, we do not assign the coach that is in your backyard because the chemistry would not be a good fit or the backgrounds are not a good match. Given how coaches and meetings are structured, locale never matters. Travel costs are always negligible, and after we have done our job, we typically provide at least five times return on investment or more. As one of my clients told one of his colleagues, there is no cost.

You invest money to make money and, in the end, you always make a lot more than you spent.

"Just Do It!"

I hope you're as excited as I am that you have read this far. It means this book is valuable to you and you are likely to act. Now it's time to make like Nike and "just do it!" I want to see that happen, and as I've mentioned, as you see results, please contact me at howard@howardmshore.com and tell me about them.

Don't put off traveling the road to acceleration. By reading this book, you've already started that journey. You either are or are not going to practice these habits. You may be implementing a new system right now, or focused on some other major project, and see this as something to do afterward. In a way, you're correct and incorrect. If you meet regularly with your leadership team, if you're setting priorities, if you're making people decisions, and if you are addressing culture, then you're already dealing with the issues in this book. How long do you want to wait to do those things better?

I want to thank you for taking the time to read my book because I know I'm now part of your success journey. If you think it would be valuable to have a coach help you implement the concepts in this book, please visit our website at www.activategroupinc.com or call us at 305-722-7213 to schedule your free consultation.

ACKNOWLEDGMENTS

I want to thank the many CEOs and executives who have given me the honor of being part of their success journeys. As I have always said, we gain wisdom together! It is through our experiences together that I was able to accumulate the knowledge, experience, and insight that I now share in this book. Through our obstacles and challenges, I have been able to distill a wealth of information I could not wait to share with you and others.

Key Contributors

Several people went above and beyond the call of duty to help me improve the book. I must start with thanking my mom, Sheryl Shore, who did significant editing and has been a considerable influence in helping shape who I am. My wife Sylvia Medina-Shore, a great leader in her own right, made very important contributions to this book. I also want to thank the members of my team who also made crucial contributions: Andrea Brooks, Theresa Pidcock, and Larry Rutkowski.

Thought Leaders

I am so thankful for the many thought leaders who have helped influence and shape my ideas. Just like running a company, it takes the knowledge and experience of many to get the best results.

While I cite some of their works at the end of this book, I want to recognize a few of the critical gurus that who have really influenced our toolkit and this book: Marcus Buckingham, Jim Collins, Greg Crabtree, Stephen Covey, Verne Harnish, Patrick Lencioni, W. Chan Kim, Renée Mauborgne, Alexander Osterwalder, Yves Pigneur, Bradford D. Smart, Shannon Susko, and Jack Stack.

ABOUT THE AUTHOR

S peaker, author, serial entrepreneur, and master business coach Howard M. Shore inspires leaders to maximize their growth and profit potential. He is passionate about helping other entrepreneurs achieve their most audacious goals personally and professionally.

Howard has become a sought-after business mentor, executive coach, and keynote speaker who covers employee empowerment, cash flow enhancement, human capital management, entrepreneurial freedom, and business growth.

As the founder and president of Activate Group, Inc., Howard has helped thousands of executives and teams improve and systemize their productivity, profit, and scalability. Howard's 20-year track record with start-up, Fortune 500, and multinational public and private companies, including Ryder Systems, AutoNation, and KPMG, has earned him a reputation of excellence. His clients range from $1 million in revenue to over $1 billion, spanning most industries.

He guarantees any organization with 10 employees or more that he can help them uncover as much as $2 million to their bottom line using his proprietary Business Acceleration System™.

Howard earned his bachelor's degree and MBA from Florida International University and completed advanced executive programs at Harvard Law School and the University of Chicago. Additionally, he is a Certified Gazelles Coach, 3HAG Coach, Certified Executive Coach, and Certified Public Accountant.

REFERENCES

Part 1: Introduction

1   "Confucius Quotes," as of 3/13/2019, https://www.brainyquote.com/quotes/confucius_119275.

Chapter 1: Launching Your Rocket

1   Howard Shore, *Your Business is a Leaky Bucket,* (Morgan James, 2018), 27-32.

2   Jim Collins, *Good to Great,* (HarperCollins Publishers, 2001), 41-64.

3   Alina Dizik, "Career Advice from Iconic Leaders," April 4, 2011, CNN Website Living Section, http://www.cnn.com/2011/LIVING/04/04/cb.world.leader.career.tips/.

Chapter 2: Leadership Mindsets for Rocket Launchers

1   Amazon.com, Inc., Form 10K for the fiscal year ended December 31, 2018, 17.

2   Ibid, 23-24.

3   Merrick Rosenberg and Daniel Silvert, *Taking Flight!: Master the DISC Styles to Transform Your Career, Your Relationships...Your Life,* (Pearson Education, Inc. publishing as FT Press, 2015).

Chapter 3: Modern-Day Growth Accelerators

1   Jim Collins and Jerry I. Porras, *Built to Last,* (Harper Business Essentials 2002), 94-97.
2   Verne Harnish, *Scaling Up: How a Few Companies Make It...and Why the Rest Don't,* (Gazelles, Inc., 2014), 15-17.

Part II: Stewardship

1   "The 25 Smartest Things Warren Buffett Ever Said," *The Motley Fool,* February 26, 2012, http://www.fool.com.au/2012/02/26/the-25-smartest-things-warren-buffett-ever-said/.

Chapter 4: Replace Poor Managers

1   Bob Hill, "Apple CEO Steve Jobs' '12 Rules of Success'," BusinessBrief.com, September 9, 2009, http://www.businessbrief.com/apple-ceo-steve-jobs-12-rules-of-success/.
2   Gallup, Inc. (2017) *State of the American Workplace,* (3rd ed.), Gallup®, 1.
3   Ibid, 2.
4   Ibid, 2-61.
5   Ibid, 72-103.
6   Ibid, 82.
7   Ibid, 18.
8   Ibid, 19-70.
9   Ibid, 73.
10   Bradford D. Smart PhD, *Topgrading, 3rd Edition: The Proven Hiring and Promoting Method That Turbocharges Company Performance,* (Penguin, 2012), 74.

Chapter 5: Address Team Dysfunction

1   Patrick Lencioni, *Five Dysfunctions of a Team,* (Jossey-Bass, 2002), 187-190.
2   Patrick Lencioni, *The Ideal Team Player,* (Jossey-Bass, 2016), 167.
3   Ibid, 192.

4   Ibid.

5   Process Excellence Network, Tristan Boutros, as of May 17, 2015, http://www.processexcellencenetwork.com/organizational-change/articles/the-ego-the-biggest-barrier-to-success-leadership.

6   Ibid.

7   Patrick Lencioni, *The Ideal Team Player,* (Jossey-Bass, 2016), 160.

Chapter 6: Establish a Clear and Compelling Purpose

1   Howard Shore, *Your Business is a Leaky Bucket*, (Morgan James, 2018), 19.

2   Ibid, 91-92.

3   Ibid, 92.

4   Ibid.

5   Ibid, 92-93.

6   Ibid, 93.

7   Ibid.

8   Ibid, 94.

9   Ibid.

10 "How to Act from Purpose: Ask and Listen," *Huffington Post*, February 11, 2014, http://www.huffingtonpost.com/cortney-mcdermott/how-to-act-from-purpose-a_b_4428355.html.

11 Howard Shore, *Your Business is a Leaky Bucket*, (Morgan James, 2018), 94.

12 Ibid, 94-95.

13 "10 Companies that are Changing the World," *Fortune,* August 22, 2016, http://time.com/4461874/change-the-world-companies-fortune/.

14 Howard Shore, *Your Business is a Leaky Bucket*, (Morgan James, 2018), 94-96.

15 Ibid, 96.

16 Ibid, 97.

17 Ibid, 98.

Chapter 7: Develop a Strong Culture

1   Cindy Kirschner Goodman, "Culture Change: Just Do It," *Miami Herald*, 10/6/2010.

2   Ibid.

3   "Building a Company with Heart," Salesforce.com website, https://
     www.salesforce.com/company/ventures/pledge1/.

4   Salesforce.com website, https://www.salesforce.org/pledge-1/, April 6,
     2019.

5   Bradford D. Smart PhD, *Topgrading, 3rd Edition: The Proven Hiring and
     Promoting Method That Turbocharges Company Performance,* (Penguin,
     2012), 74.

Chapter 8: Optimize Your Return on Human Assets

1   Greg Crabtree and Beverly Blair Harzog, *Simple Numbers, Straight Talk,
     Big Profits,* (Texas, Greenleaf Book Group Press, 2011).

2   Ibid, 66.

3   Ibid.

4   Ibid.

Chapter 9: Increase the Percentage of Performing Talent

1   General Stanley McChrystal et al, *Team of Teams: New Rules of
     Engagement for a Complex World,* (Penguin 2015), 220-226.

2   Bradford D. Smart PhD, *Topgrading, 3rd Edition: The Proven Hiring and
     Promoting Method That Turbocharges Company Performance,* (Penguin,
     2012), 24-52.

3   Kip Tindell, "Uncontainable" (presentation about his new book regard
     the keys to his organization's success from start-up to present, Fortune
     Growth Summit, Dallas, Texas, October 20, 2015).

Chapter 11: Increase Hiring Success

1   Ibid.

2   Bradford D. Smart PhD, *Topgrading, 3rd Edition: The Proven Hiring and
     Promoting Method That Turbocharges Company Performance,* (Penguin,
     2012), 53-179.

3   Adam Vaccaro, "Why Employees Quit Jobs Right after They've Started,"
     Inc., April 17, 2014, http://www.inc.com/adam-vaccaro/voluntary-
     turnover-six-months.html.

4   Patrick Mieritz, "State of the American Workplace," July 16, 2018, PowerPoint Presentation to the NC Government Finance Officers Association.

Part IV: Strategy

1   https://winstonchurchill.org/resources/quotes/quotes-falsely-attributed/

Chapter 12: Design a Profitable and Scalable Business Model

1   Alexander Osterwalder & Yves Pigneur, *Business Model Generation*, (Wiley 2010), 17.
2   Ibid, 20-21.
3   Ibid, 22-23.
4   "The Global Unicorn Club," *CBInsights*, July 21, 2019, https://www.cbinsights.com/research-unicorn-companies.
5   Alexander Osterwalder & Yves Pigneur, *Business Model Generation*, (Wiley 2010), 26-27.
6   Ibid, 36-37.
7   Ibid, 28-29.
8   Ibid, 30-31.
9   Ibid, 34-35.
10   Ibid, 38-39.
11   Ibid, 40-41.

Chapter 13: Narrow Your Target Market

1   Marcia Heroux Pounds, "Sale of Plantation-based e-Builder creates 10 employee-millionaires" *Sun Sentinel*, February 12, 2018, https://www.sun-sentinel.com/business/fl-bz-ebuilder-millionaires-20180208-story.html.
2   Matthew Michaels, "The 20 companies that create the most profit per employee," December 18, 2017, https://www.businessinsider.com/apple-facebook-alphabet-most-profitable-companies-per-employee-2017-12.

3   *CSI Market*, February 16, 2019, https://csimarket.com/Industry/industry_Efficiency.php?sp.

Chapter 14: Differentiate Properly

1   "Trader Joe's," Wikipedia, https://en.wikipedia.org/wiki/Trader_Joe%27s, As of February 23, 2019.
2   Stephen J. Dubner, Freakonomics Radio, http://freakonomics.com/podcast/trader-joes/, November 28, 2018 @ 11:00 pm.
3   Ibid.
4   Ibid.
5   Ibid.
6   Ibid.
7   "Trader Joe's," Wikipedia, https://en.wikipedia.org/wiki/Trader_Joe%27s, As of February 23, 2019.
8   Sharon Terlep, "Unilever Buys Dollar Shave Club: European Giant to Pay $1 Billion for Startup in Challenge to P&G," July 20, 2016, http://www.wsj.com/articles/unilever-buys-dollar-shave-club-1468987836.
9   Howard Shore, *Your Business is a Leaky Bucket*, (Morgan James, 2018), 103-105.
10   Ibid, 106.

Chapter 15: Lay the Foundation for Continuous Growth

1   Jim Collins, *Good to Great,* (HarperCollins Publishers, 2001), 41-64.
2   Ibid.
3   Jim Collins and Jerry I. Porras, *Built to Last,* (Harper Business Essentials, 2002), 21-25.
4   Randy McDaniel, Google Street View, https://kxrb.com/whatever-happened-to-tcby/, 3/9/19.
5   Todd Spangler, "Apple Sets $1 Billion Budget for Original TV Shows, Movies," (*Variety*, August 16, 2017), https://variety.com/2017/digital/news/apple-1-billion-original-tv-shows-movies-budget-1202529421/.

Part V: Planning

1   Benjamin Franklin Quotes, *Goodreads*, as of 2/24/2019, https://www.
    goodreads.com/quotes/460142-if-you-fail-to-plan-you-are-planning-to-
    fail.

Chapter 16: Commit to an Audacious Goal

1   Jim Collins and Jerry I. Porras, *Built to Last,* (Harper Business
    Essentials, 2002), 93-95.
2   Ibid.
3   Ibid.
4   Ibid.
5   Ibid.
6   Ibid, 93-114.
7   Ibid, 93-95.
8   Ibid.

Chapter 17: Establish a Long-Term Plan

1   Shannon Byrne Susko, *3HAG Way,* (Amazon Digital Services LLC,
    2018).
2   Jim Collins, "How Does Your Flywheel Turn?: 'A Good to Great'
    Strategic Tool," whitepaper, 2017.
3   Ibid.
4   Ibid.

Part VI: Accountability

1   Stephen Covey, as of 3/10/2019, "BrainyQuote," https://www.
    brainyquote.com/topics/accountability

Chapter 20: Create a Culture of Accountability

1   Patrick Lencioni, *Five Dysfunctions of a Team,* (Jossey-Bass, 2002), 187-
    220.

Chapter 21: Everybody Knows Their Numbers

1 Dave Baney, *3 x 5 Coach,* (CreateSpace Independent Publishing Platform, 2017), 5-8.
2 Ibid.
3 Ibid.

Chapter 22: Strengthen Communications

1 Howard Shore, *Your Business is a Leaky Bucket,* (Morgan James, 2018), 163-174.
2 Daniel Pink, *Drive* (New York: Riverhead Books, 2009), 17-21.
3 Philip Yaffe, "The 7% Rule: Fact, Fiction, or Misunderstanding," Ubiquity, October 2011, https://ubiquity.acm.org/article.cfm?id=2043156.

Conclusion: Your Path to Freedom

1 Allen Gannett, "Dismantling The Myth Of The Self-Reliant CEO," *Fast Company*, May 26, 2016, https://www.fastcompany.com/3060235/dismantling-the-myth-of-the-self-reliant-ceo.
2 Ibid.